THE PICNIC GOURMET

Joan Hemingway
and Connie Maricich

With an Introduction
by John Hemingway

Drawings by Dennis Abbe

Vintage Books
A Division of Random House, New York

VINTAGE BOOKS EDITION, June 1978

Copyright © 1975, 1977 by Joan Hemingway and Connie Maricich
All rights reserved under International and Pan-American Copyright
Conventions. Published in the United States by Random House, Inc.,
New York, and simultaneously in Canada by Random House of Canada
Limited, Toronto. Originally published by Random House, Inc., in June 1977.

Library of Congress Cataloging in Publication Data

Hemingway, Joan.
    The picnic gourmet.

    1. Outdoor cookery. 2. Picnicking. I. Maricich,
Connie, joint author. II. Title.
[TX823.H42   1978]   641.5'78   77–12487
ISBN 0–394–72164–0

Manufactured in the United States of America

Design by Clint Anglin

ACKNOWLEDGMENTS

We would like to give special thanks to our mothers and grandmothers, who have shared their culinary secrets and some treasured family recipes. We want to dedicate this book to all our friends whose enthusiastic picnicking spirit inspired it, especially Milli Wiggins, Karin and John Davies, Jim Belson, Polly Read, Sherry Fowler, Allison Evans, Fayre and Nancy Shillington, Kathy Troutner, Jack and Carol Gelber, Laurie Lazar, Darcie Dupont, Jan McFarland and Bettye Robinson.

A special thanks to all the inspired cooks who contributed recipes. Penelope Bonnecarrere, Clarice Blechmann, Mrs. Roundy, Bessie Bentley, Harriet Barnett, Hildegard Raeber, Ross Pullen, Margie Best and Bruce LeFavour. We appreciate the recipes from La Goulue Restaurant, Joseph and Jean-Claude of New York's Plaza Hotel.

Introduction

Picnics play an important part in many of our family's most pleasant memories. Though she was far too young to remember them, my daughter Joan's first picnics were on the shores of pine-scented trout streams in the Black Forest, where I was stationed as liaison officer with the French occupation forces in the early fifties. She would sleep in the cool of the pine shade in a jerry-rigged hammock while my wife Puck and I rested from the trout fishing and washed down culinary delights with fine and simple dry young wines from the Rhine plain. A few years later, when we lived and worked in Havana, there were the rich picnics with Joan's grandfather Ernest and his wife Miss Mary on the edge of the lush spring-fed river that winds down steeply from the high plateau at Güines to the north Cuban coast at the ancient colonial city of Matanzas. Someone would drive into the old port and fetch freshly boiled shrimp, prawns or freshwater crayfish to add to Mary's already sumptuous and always delightful picnic fare. The chilled red Spanish wine would make the older generation sleepy and we'd nap in the shade of a ceiba tree while the girls, Muffet—that's what we call Joan—and Margot, played in the shallows of the sun-bathed stream.

More recently our Fourth of July picnics have taken place on the foot trail below Steamboat on the North Umpqua River in the Oregon Cascades, under the cool shade of the big Douglas firs with vine maple and five-fingered ferns all about us. Out in Idaho there are our Silver Creek picnics down by our friend Dottie Teren's lower place. Before World War II the Stutter Man used to live there in his shack and challenge all trespassers imagined or real with a loud "GGGGET OFF MMMMMY PPPPPLACE! GGGGOD DDDDAMIT!" It's quiet there now. The shack is gone, and it's a fine place for a picnic. It's now a favorite site, along with many other beautiful locations in the mountains, perfect for both summer and sunny winter days. All these picnics and many more were leading their inexorable way to the preparation of this book.

Co-author Connie Maricich is both a dedicated picnicker and a sensitive and creative cook. She feels picnicking is the highest form of human entertainment, and I believe that when you've tried some of her and Muffet's unusual picnic menus you'll agree completely. It's been Puck's and my good luck to sample many of the recipes. We know they work.

The right friends with whom to share your picnics and the selection of site and season are up to you. Here you will find all the rest. Enjoy your picnics, and don't forget to leave your picnic spots as pristine as you found them.

—*John H. Hemingway*

Contents

Preface

A picnic is a ritual, a ceremony in sharing food with friends. Dining out-doors makes the experience distinctive and exhilarating. Our senses are heightened, and we are especially receptive to the pleasures of eating. A certain ambience is created which puts everyone in the best of spirits . . . the picnic spirit. A picnic is a special affair, an experience to be remembered.

The idea for this book evolved naturally from our hiking experiences in the mountains. Our picnics began simply. We hiked in summer with a small group of friends, and our lunch was usually salami, French bread, fruit, cheese, and *vin ordinaire*. Dessert was nothing more than chocolate bars or gorp. (Gorp is a backpackers' concoction of raisins, nuts, chocolate bits and dried fruits all mixed together in a plastic bag. Called gorp because of the texture it assumes on a warm day, it doubles as a high-energy trail snack and a great dessert with fruit.)

Everyone began to anticipate these mountain lunches. As our culinary interests developed and our palates became more refined, we began to prepare more varied and interesting dishes. Lunch became a picnic, a special event to prepare for. Instead of buying food at the delicatessen, we made more sophisticated picnic fare. A particular menu developed, so nicely balanced that it became a favorite for some time. Except for the wine and cheese, the menu remained constant. It was:

> *Cold Strawberry Soup*
> *Eggs Stuffed with Caviar and Sour Cream*
> *Chicken Shangri-la*
> *Grapes, Apples or Pears*
> *Cheese and French Bread*
> *California Wine, Red or White*

We now enjoy hiking or skiing picnics through all the seasons. The magnificent mountains of the Pioneer, Sawtooth and White Cloud ranges which surround the resort area of Sun Valley and Ketchum offer a constant stimulus for being outdoors.

Each season has its own appeal. In fall, ripening fruits of all sorts fill the flowering branches of August. We stop to pick red, orange and black cur-rants, huckleberries, rose hips, Oregon grapes and juniper berries to take home for making jam.

We always try to match our menus to the mood of the season. For instance, a fall menu might include something pungent and filling, like game birds served with chutney, and curried eggs. The chill in the air stimulates the appetite, and dessert—always welcome on these days—might be a small loaf of apple spice cake along with some of the wild berries picked the same day, served with dark hot tea laced with rum and honey.

In winter, we make regular ski touring trips and have our picnics in the snow, choosing a spot protected from the wind. The sun feels warm even when temperatures drop below freezing; still, it's important to plan the trip so that the picnic takes place when the sun is high in the sky.

The food for winter picnics is rich, substantial fare. Hot soup from a thermos is always seved first to warm us, then perhaps a savory meat dish such as Cornish pasties or a rolled meatloaf stuffed with herbs and cheese. A hearty red wine accompanies the meal. In winter, too, we maintain all the accoutrements of gourmet picnicking— a colorful cloth, cotton napkins and pretty serving things.

When spring comes, we hike on the surface of the remaining snowfields and on the wet earth where the snow has melted, trying to follow familiar trails that lead to our favorite alpine lakes. If we're lucky we hold the picnic at the edge of a lake, which is perhaps just beginning to thaw. The sun, reflected on the snow and ice, can be intensely warm. Only when it's very cold or cloudy do we build a fire, using a place where backpackers built fires the summer before.

Spring menus include dishes made with fresh fruits and vegetables. In May and early June, wild asparagus grows in profusion along the roadsides and in the ditches south of Sun Valley. We like to pick it for preparing picnic food, especially wild asparagus soup. Spears of wild asparagus wrapped in thin slices of ham and served with hot mustard sauce is another favorite spring recipe. Wild mushrooms also come up in spring, and last year we feasted on snow morels, a wild mushroom indigenous to the area.

The day hikes of summer set the scene for the most glorious picnics of all. The wildflowers begin to bloom as soon as the snow melts. Tiny yellow and blue violets appear first, and then the show begins, lasting throughout the summer season.

As we hike upwards, the colors of the flowers in each ascending meadow become more and more intense. Indian paintbrush turns the deepest cyclamen pink, blue gentian becomes the richest purple-blue imaginable, and buttercups are vividly golden. The highest meadows, where we have our picnic, are completely carpeted in these colors.

The streams along the trails and the lakes themselves are icy cold. In the middle of some alpine lakes float enormous pieces of ice that have broken off from adjacent snowfields. Some remain the entire summer. The lake waters are clear and toned with different shades of blue, green and turquoise. We explore the shores to choose the most appealing spot at which to eat—usually a meadow surrounded by magnificent snowcapped peaks. The colors and the flowers complement the "table" beautifully as we chill the wine in a snowfield or an icy stream. The large, smooth rocks near the lake edge are perfect for reclining upon after a quick dip before lunch. The intensity of the sun's rays contrasts sharply with the cold water and the thin pure air. It's not difficult to imagine how marvelously good the food will taste in this setting.

Summer menus begin with a flavorful soup, perhaps cream of watercress or chilled borscht; the main course might be an arrangement of cold sliced chicken covered with a rich purée of walnut sauce and accompanied by slices of melons and bunches of grapes, French bread, a mild soft Brie and a dry white Bordeaux, with a sweet orange tart to complete the menu.

We now picnic not only in all climates, but also in all places. One Sunday afternoon we picnicked in a London flat on a beautiful mirrored table. Our picnic had been planned for Kensington Gardens. The weather was warm and sunny that morning, and our hostess had cooked enthusiastically for the occasion. By noon the sky was dark and it was pouring rain. We had our picnic indoors, placing everything on the dining table just as we would have on the grass. We enjoyed hard-boiled eggs, stuffed cucumbers, and exotic little spicy meatballs, and had champagne to raise our spirits to picnic proportions.

Preparing food for a picnic is a specialized aspect of the art of cooking, one calling for patience and inventiveness. A cook can aspire to the highest level of the culinary arts for a picnic just as much as for an elegant dinner party. Finding ways to prepare and pack a meal that must be transported is an amusing challenge. With a little effort a picnic can become an artful creation. Besides, it's fun to cook for a picnic, and the anticipation of the outing minimizes the work involved.

On our regular hiking picnics, we rarely have a set menu. We arrange for each person to contribute a dish with the accompanying serving items and a bottle of wine. Most of our friends have gotten into the habit of preparing picnic food in the course of cooking weekly meals. For example, some boiled new potatoes in the refrigerator can inspire a *salade Niçoise* or a *pommes à l'huile*. (Easy concoctions, the first made with tuna fish and fresh green beans, the other being literally "potatoes with oil" or vinaigrette sauce). A package of cream cheese blended with a little wine and lots of freshly minced herbs and *voilà*: homemade herbed cheese, as good as Boursin, in a matter of minutes. (That same herb mixture can also be the filling for the cold and delicious picnic omelettes on page 149.) Then there are the fulfilling times when one can set aside several hours to create a truly wonderful *pâté en croûte,* a perfectly roasted chicken, or a stuffed veal roll worthy of an elegant picnic.

The idea of gourmet picnic food should intimidate neither the beginning cook nor one dedicated to natural foods. There are many simple recipes included here as well as suggestions for choosing things at your local delicatessen. And conversely, the idea of picnicking should not intimidate the gourmet cook. We often take the most unlikely and elaborate dishes—such as pheasant mousse, cold poached salmon with green mayonnaise and even open-faced fruit tarts—up the mountains in our packs. There is hardly any dish which cannot be carried in a backpack if it is thoughtfully arranged. (Each recipe has its own specific instructions for transporting and serving.)

There are two sections to the cookbook. The first, a series of suggested picnic menus, comes from our own experiences. The other part is a reference section for making up your own picnic menus. This section is further divided into categories of soup, main dishes, salads, bread, side dishes and condiments, and desserts. You'll find that the recipes in this book will serve more people than those in conventional cookbooks. Because a picnic is nearly always a potluck kind of affair with a variety of dishes to sample, smaller portions are adequate.

You can use the concepts presented here to create your own special picnics defined by where you are, the seasons, and available foods. One can have a picnic any place, any time. The possibilities are endless, the choice is yours.

Packing Notes

It is important to learn to organize the picnic food and supplies in your basket or pack. Many of the following recipes may seem too fragile or too elaborate to carry to a picnic, but we have experimented and know that you can carry them all with you, if you take care in packing them. For instance, last summer at a picnic served high in the mountains from backpacks we had a pear tart with a frangipane custard base and a glaze of apple jelly. It survived the trip without damage because we packed the tart, pan and all, in two larger foil pie pans, one inverted over the other, with the two held together securely with heavy masking tape. We wedged the pans containing the tart in a horizontal position in the top of the pack, and stuffed folded napkins and a tablecloth around the tart container to secure it in position.

But we have also arrived at a picnic site to find our packs soaked with vinaigrette, coated with moussaka and drenched in Chablis. We now avoid most such disasters by packing our backpacks with care. First and most important, every container must be leakproof. Some of our favorite containers, made in Holland under the brand name GraLock, are attractively designed in clear plastic with brightly colored vacuum-closing lids. Unfortunately, the lids are not always secure enough to withstand a rough hike, but the closing can be reinforced with heavy masking tape. Always tape all plastic containers, and check the top of any container to be sure it's secure before putting the jar in the pack. Use screw-on tops for liquids. Also, put anything that might leak at all in heavy-duty plastic bags—freezer bags, for example—and tie tightly with rubber bands. Foods that bruise easily or become mushy, such as peaches, grapes, tomatoes or deviled eggs, must be carried in hard-sided containers for protection.

Wrap anything breakable in the tablecloth or your sweater. The most easily broken item in a pack is usually a wine bottle, but since pouring wine into a plastic container imparts an artificial flavor, we prefer to carry the heavy bottle both to and from the picnic. Besides, uncorking a bottle of wine is a titillating way to begin the meal.

Cook your picnic food in shapes that fit easily into your pack. Breads and cakes can be cooked in small loaf pans or in cans. (A one-pound coffee can makes a nice loaf. To serve, simply open the closed end and push out.) Mousses and pâtés can also be cooked in small molds or loaf pans. And any small 6½-inch tart pan will fit nicely in a day pack. If the pan has a removable bottom, tape the bottom to the sides of the pan. Then wrap the tart, pan and all, in a plastic bag or foil. Place it into the pack in such a way that it will sit squarely, right side up, held in place by other items.

Your whole packing procedure will be easier if your pack or basket is always ready. For hiking or cross-country picnics, keep these items in your backpack*:

> *a Swiss army knife, with corkscrew*
> *a small case with personal items*
>   *such as lip gloss, suntan cream,*
>   *insect repellent and comb*
> *a small first-aid kit*
> *matches*
> *paper to start a fire (winter only)*
> *a Sierra Club–type tin cup*
>   *that hooks on the outside*
>   *of your pack*
> *a poncho or plastic groundsheet*
> *napkins of colorful, lightweight cloth*
> *paper plates*
> *a tablecloth, three to four feet square,*
>   *of colorful, lightweight cloth*
> *several small plastic glasses*
>   *(Since most plastic glasses crack,*
>   *look for sturdy ones.)*
> *a parka or sweater*
> *one pair of extra socks*

All picnic and hiking items take up very little room in a pack, but you must count on other members of the hiking group to bring more glasses, paper plates, or perhaps another tablecloth or groundsheet. Each picnic will require slightly different equipment, but you'll probably also be carrying wine—one bottle for every two hikers is our general rule—the food you're contributing to the meal, and appropriate serving and eating utensils. Much picnic food, such as bread, cheese, stuffed mushrooms, deviled eggs and chicken, can be eaten nicely with fingers, so you won't always need to bring flatwear. In those cases, you will only have to consider how you wish to present the food on the picnic table. If you've packed the food in attractive plastic containers, it can go directly from pack to "table." If the container is not particularly attractive, transfer the contents to something else —a pretty plastic or wooden bowl or a paper or plastic plate. (Don't forget to include a serving spoon or fork when necessary.)

* We recommend a pack with a rigid bottom of heavy canvas or leather and two separate compartments. Alp Sport makes a nice small pack, as well as a larger one with inner stays that is perfect when you have to carry bulkier items.

When packing drinks, bring glasses for everyone. When bringing salad, take forks or chopsticks and a nice serving dish and paper plates.

Bread on the menu calls for a bread knife and a small wooden cutting board.

You can serve cold soup in clear plastic glasses or cups. Dip up hot soups with thermos tops (insulated if possible) or metal cups.

For whole roasted birds, bring poultry shears. It's nice to present the whole bird on the picnic table, on a plate garnished with greens. Cut the bird into pieces with poultry shears to serve.

For tarts, cakes and pies, bring a knife for cutting and a spatula for serving unless you think the largest blade of the Swiss army knife will suffice (which it always will in a pinch).

Your picnic pack remains the same in winter as in summer, except it should include some newspaper to start a fire and some extra, very warm mittens and a warmer parka than you might want to wear while skiing or hiking to the site. The cups you take should hold hot beverages. Also, a waterproof groundsheet that merely keeps out the dampness of the ground in summer is essential in winter for warmth. A piece of plastic to put under the tablecloth is a good idea, too, in any season.

For city or driving picnics, keep a picnic basket stocked with basic items:

> *a tablecloth and cloth napkins*
> *a corkscrew*
> *a bread knife*
> *a small wooden board*
>   *for cutting or serving*
> *a paring knife*
> *matches*
> *insect repellent*
> *salt and pepper shakers*
> *candles or a flashlight*
> *can opener*
> *some paper towels*

Adding only the plates, glasses, and silverware you will need, and with a quick stop at a delicatessen, you can be off at a moment's notice.

Last-Minute Preparations and Serving

Picnic food is generally served at natural temperatures. Everything is cooked ahead of time and served directly from a pack or a basket. Fires are built only for warmth and are not used for cooking, except for occasional cook-out-style picnics. Our usual "refrigeration" is a cold stream or a snowfield. Sometimes we take a cooler and perhaps ice, but, like cheese and red wine, most of the food we prepare for picnics tastes best at natural, medium temperatures.

We should mention the problem of spoilage. Although we have never had anything spoil in many years of taking food for several hours on the trail, we must admit a concern about mayonnaise and any sauces or dips that use eggs. Commercial mayonnaise has so many preservatives that it takes a long time and very warm temperatures to spoil it. Though we like the homemade variety for our picnics, we don't take it in very hot weather, even to places we know will have snow or icy water nearby.

One solution is a small zip-up insulated bag. Cool it in the refrigerator until time to go, and then add a small plastic sack with a couple of ice cubes and your little container of mayonnaise, or any other food which might spoil. Whatever you do, be sure to leave anything that could spoil in the re-frigerator until it's time to pack. In the case of picnicking trips by car, be sure you have enough cooler space for anything that could spoil in warm weather.

Make last-minute preparations for serving at the site. Remember to pack everything with an idea of how you will want to present it on the picnic cloth. Such garnishes as parsley, mint and watercress—when sprinkled with water and stored in a plastic bag—are easy to tuck in on top of your pack. Sometimes we tie a bag of greens on the outside of a pack so that the greens won't be crushed. Salad dressings should also be added only at the last minute.

In winter it is important that the menu consist of dishes which can be served with very little last-minute preparation. Carving a duck is awkward with cold or gloved fingers. It's best to have most food already cut and di-vided into serving portions. You might find it even easier to serve dishes like individual turnovers. Meatloaves and meat rolls can be sliced and then re-formed into the original shape and wrapped tightly in foil.

Whatever the season, or whether your picnic is simple or fancy, just be sure that you don't let it be ruined by careless packing and transporting.

A Note on Wild Foods

This book does not purport to teach the gathering and use of wild foods. However, picnics take place out of doors, and often in places where wild plants grow abundantly. Who can walk by a patch of wild strawberries or a group of iridescent violet mushrooms? Who can ignore the pungent smell of wild spearmint? (Although first-century naturalist Pliny said "the smell of mint stirs up the mind," it has the effect of stirring up our senses.)

When we are walking in the mountains or picnicking in the valleys, we often gather wild food to take home where identification, cooking, canning or drying can be carried out. Many of the recipes in this book have evolved from this practice.

Wild plants are also very nice as garnishes for serving dishes, or as centerpieces for the picnic "tables." A word of warning here: be sure you know your plants! A meatloaf is enhanced by a bed of wild watercress or a garnish of mint leaves, but not by bitter fern fronds. Many leaves are pretty, but not all should be used when serving food, even if they are not to be eaten. You might like to decorate your "table" with mushrooms arranged artfully with an interesting piece of worn wood or mossy limb, but even if they're not eaten, no one wants to dine with deadly poison amanita mushrooms as a centerpiece.

During the spring and summer, many wild foods grow that can be eaten on the spot. Watercress is the best known and most useful, both as a garnish and as a complete vegetable in itself. It can be picked in a stream along the trail, tosed with a little vinaigrette if you happen to have some, and served immediately. Don't pick watercress growing in obviously muddy or dirty water or in a location where you know sheep or cattle are pasturing upstream. In any case, wash it well in clear stream water.

Among the first flowers of spring are tiny violets with tender leaves. Both flowers and leaves can be eaten on the spot or put into a salad for an exotic touch. According to Euell Gibbons in his field guide *Stalking the Healthful Herbs*, violets and their leaves are very high in vitamin C.

When we find wild sorrel—"miner's lettuce"—growing in rock crevices at high altitudes, we eat it as we pick, and also make a salad for our lunch. The flavor is uniquely piquant and lemony. We also always eat wild garlic and onions when we come across them. In early summer they grow profusely in grassy areas in meadows and valleys. Their flavors are wonderful, much more delicate than their domestic counterparts. We only pick the onions and garlic when in bloom. The leaves of these plants resemble "death camas" and other inedible plants, but can be easily identified by their flower.

In late summer and fall berries begin to ripen, and many of the trails we travel are lined with currants, wild raspberries, huckleberries and many other varieties of wild berries. We can't help eating these delicious wild fruits as we pick, but we serve what's left for our picnic. We have to make special berry-picking trips to gather quantities for making jams and jellies.

One final word: know your mushrooms! We often find them growing near a picnic site or along a trail, but we make quite sure of the identification before we eat any wild mushrooms, as some of the thousands of varieties are deadly poisonous and others cause digestive disturbances. For any mushroom you're unsure of, consult a mushroom guide. We usually refer to Miller's *Mushrooms of North America*, but we also use many other books on the subject, as identification can be extensive and complicated. There are several species—oyster mushrooms, most boletes (French *cèpes*) and most morels—we gather and eat without a thought. But there are some toxic species in these categories too: a "false" morel called the "brain mushroom" and a bolete called "Satan's boletus," for example. A mushroom hunter must be on his guard constantly; but mushrooms are the most seductive of wild foods, not to be ignored. Wild mushrooms should be cooked before being eaten, so carry your day's harvest home carefully to be identified and prepared, perhaps for the next picnic.

Notes on Picnic Wines

Many picnickers will include wine in their *al fresco* menu; yet most will only spend minimal time and effort when choosing that wine. Though they may have worked the entire morning to prepare the food, they dash into the market at the last minute and grab almost any white wine that the store happens to have chilled. Since a good setting and fresh air seem to increase the enjoyment of any beverage but vinegar, this method doesn't often lead to disaster. But with minimal forethought, wine can become an integral part of the picnic, rather than just something that washes down the bread and lends a hazy glow to a fine afternoon.

I don't mean to imply that the wine you choose has to be expensive; in fact, most of the really expensive wines except, rarely, champagne, are inappropriate for all but a very specialized picnic menu. The fine, aged reds are both too delicate for rough outdoor handling and often too heavy and overpowering in taste. The expensive German whites are sweet, and like French Sauterne, would smother the flavor of most foods other than desserts. Even the costly French white wines from the Puligny-Montrachet and Meursault regions and the American Pinot Chardonnays from growers like Ridge are too full, too strong to accompany the varied fare of most picnics. You could build a delicious, specialized picnic around each of these expensive and strong-flavored wines, but in general it is the straightforward and relatively inexpensive wine which seems to taste best at picnics. Identifying and sorting out the good wines, or at least the potentially good wines, then becomes the problem, but by remembering a few rules and names the task can become relatively easy.

American Wines: Since the supply of quality grapes in California exceeds demand, a large amount of good wine is available at prices that seem destined to stay reasonable for a number of years, so I'll speak mostly of these nationally distributed California wines. Some growers in Washington, Oregon, Illinois, Michigan, Ohio and, above all, New York have over the past few years started making excellent table wines. So far their best efforts are only regionally distributed and even within these areas tend to be in short supply. But you can apply the comments that follow to any wine, and you should definitely experiment with your "local" wines.

All American red, white and rosé wines fall into one of two categories: varietal or generic. Varietal wines are, as their name implies, named after the grape variety—which by U.S. law must make up at least 51 percent of the wine. Any Johannisberg Riesling wine must be made from at least 51 percent Johannisberg Riesling grape juice and, further, any Johannisberg

Riesling with a vintage or year mentioned on the label must contain at least
85 percent Johannisberg Riesling grape juice. The better growers, whether
or not they have a vintage year on the label, often increase the percentage
of varietal grapes beyond the requirements of the law. Their prices also
increase. Generics, on the other hand, are usually named for a famous wine
from another part of the world—"Chablis" and "Burgundy" are examples
—and the grapes used, often the cheaper kinds, are entirely up to the pro-
ducer's discretion. The wine that results seldom has any relationship in
flavor to its namesake nor, for that matter, does Mondavi's generic Chablis
have any necessary relationship to Sebastiani's Chablis. They both are white
and that's about it. The varietals offer not only better quality but, equally
important, some consistancy from brand to brand. An Almadén Pinot Noir
holds some hope of tasting like a Martini Pinot Noir simply because both
consist of at least half Pinot Noir grape juice. This is a gross oversimplifi-
cation, but in general, it works.

The rule, then, is to seek out the varietals for their quality and glimmer
of consistency. Which varietals, though? Here we take an even deeper dive
into the murky sea of the subjective; my opinions and tastes might be, and
are likely to be, quite different from yours. But, forewarned, here is my list
of favorite varietals for picnic purposes in order of preference. White:
Johannisberg Riesling (no relation to Grey Riesling), Chénin Blanc, Sauvignon Blanc and the cheaper Pinot Chardonnays. (Here in Idaho I have found
that Chappellet markets a fine Johannisberg, full of the fruit yet dry, and
that Robert Mondavi sells a fruity, ever so slightly sweet Chénin Blanc. But
in your area neither of these brands may be available, so I urge you to
taste different varietals.) Red: Zinfandel and the cheaper Pinot Noirs. I
don't like rosés, but Grenache has its advocates.

Imported Wines: Most European wine is varietal, but the custom there dic-
tates that the name of the place that made the wine, rather than the name of
the grape, becomes the name of the wine. The simple California rule of
discovering which grape has characteristics that appeal to you no longer will
work when you're dealing with such diverse-sounding wines as Puligny-
Montrachet, Les Pucelles and Bourgogne Blanc. But since large contiguous
areas of Europe use the same grape to produce their quality wine, there is
some hope of making broad sense out of what seems to be a muddle of
strange, complicated names.

German Mosel and Rhine wines, as well as the French Alsatian wines, are
almost all made from the Johannisberg Riesling grape, or as the growers
there would prefer to call it, the Riesling grape. The more expensive of these
wines—above eight dollars, usually—are likely to be sweet and not totally
appropriate for picnics, but the rest share the fruity dry taste common to

their California stepchildren. They make superb picnic wines, with the exception of Moselblümchen and Liebfraumilch, which I think are of poor quality for their price.

The Loire Valley of France also produces reasonably priced white picnic wines. The wine growers there use two grapes also popular in California—the Sauvignon Blanc grape, which is the principle ingredient of Pouilly-Fumé, and the Chénin Blanc, which is the principle ingredient of Vouvray. Unfortunately for those who enjoy Pouilly-Fumé, the recent rise in popularity and price of the similar-sounding Pouilly-Fuissé (made of Pinot Chardonnay grapes in southern Burgundy) has spread, so that Pouilly-Fumé can be expensive. On the cheaper side, Muscadet is another pleasant, though often extremely dry, Loire wine.

There are many, many more foreign wines suitable for picnics. Beaujolais is a good (and extremely gulpable) red. Graves is a very dry and good Bordeaux white wine, made mostly from Sauvignon Blanc grapes. Some of the South American Rieslings are good values. To go over them all is impossible and, given the lack of a good selection of imported wines in all but the larger cities and resorts, perhaps somewhat futile. (The list at the end of this chapter will give you additional information.)

Before finishing I want to suggest a very special wine for those few, really special picnics. Champagne it must be, and no one who has enjoyed a champagne picnic will call the choice prosaic. My favorites are Schramsberg Blanc de Blanc from California or any of the Bruts from France—my choice often depends on the state of my pocketbook. If you prefer a somewhat less dry and cheaper champagne, try an extra dry, which belies its name by its sweetness.

Finally, what should you do if the only store for miles has only three wines, say a too-sweet California Sauterne, a mediocre Vin Rosé and a 99¢ "red?" Complain firmly to whomever will listen and then buy a good beer. And to show you just how shaded by my own tastes and prejudices the specific wine recommendations have been and to encourage you to experiment with wines, I'll give you my beer suggestions: Of the imports, I prefer the German or Mexican beers to the Scandinavian or Dutch brews. And of the generally available domestics, Budweiser stands alone.

So find a nice wine that *you* like to drink, buy it the day before the picnic and chill it if necessary, drink the wine as something that really complements the taste and quality of the food, and don't forget in your euphoria to bring the bottle back out of the woods when your picnic's over.

—*Bruce LeFavour*
Robinson Bar Ranch
Clayton, Idaho

The following is a list of the most common domestic varietal wines with, opposite, the main areas outside of the United States growing the same type of grape along with names of representative wines produced there. Usually a family resemblance from domestic to foreign can be tasted (Riesling, Grenache), but different soils, methods and climatic conditions can produce wildly different results (Baco Noir, Sémillon). At any rate, the list could be of use to the picnicker or general imbiber who is already familiar with a domestic or foreign wine who might wish a reference point from which to expand his or her choices.

Grape names as used on California label	*European vineyard regions growing the same type of grape (with representative wines)*
WHITE:	
Johannisberg Riesling	Moselle and Rhine in Germany (Schloss Vollrads, Inc.), Alsace in France, and Chile (Riesling)
Pinot Chardonnay	Burgundy (Chablis, Meursault, etc.)
Chénin Blanc	The Loire Valley in France (Vouvray)
Gewürztraminer	Alsace in France (Gewürztraminer)
Folĺe Blanche	The Cognac district in France (brandy, country wines)
Sémillon (dry)	Bordeaux (sweet Sauterne)
Pinot Blanc	Burgundy (sometimes blended with Pinot Chardonnay), Champagne
Sauvignon Blanc	The Loire Valley in France (Pouilly-Fumé), Bordeaux (Graves)
RED:	
Cabernet Sauvignon	Bordeaux (Saint-Émilion, Lafite-Rothschild, etc.)
Pinot Noir	Burgundy (Vosne-Romanée, Côte de Beaune, etc.), Champagne
Gamay Beaujolais	Beaujolais region of France (Moulin-à-Vent, Beaujolais Villages, etc.)
Barbera	Piedmont province of Italy (Barolo, Barbaresco)
Zinfandel	No exact counterpart in Europe
Petit Syrah	Rhone Valley in France (Côtes du Rhône, Hermitage, Saint-Joseph)
Carignan	Roussillon region of France (country wines)
Baco Noir	Armagnac region of France (brandy)
ROSE:	
Grenache	Rhone Valley in France (Tavel)

TEN PICNICS

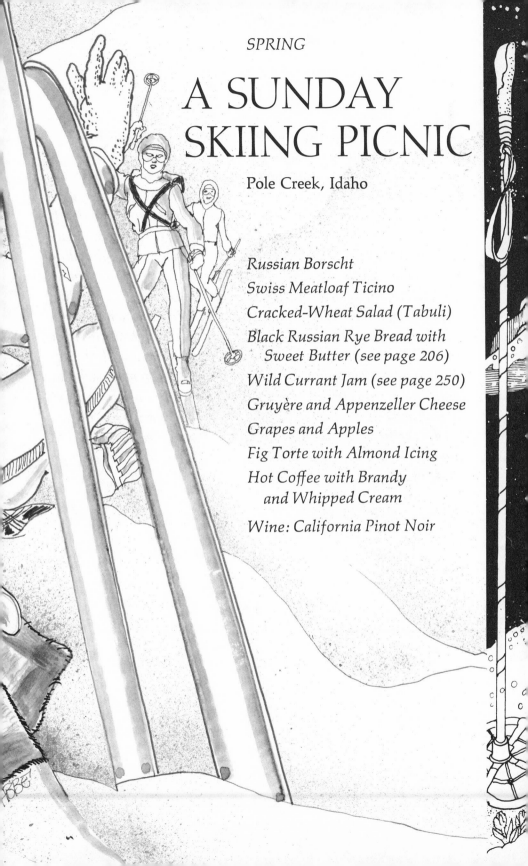

SPRING

A SUNDAY SKIING PICNIC

Pole Creek, Idaho

Russian Borscht

Swiss Meatloaf Ticino

Cracked-Wheat Salad (Tabuli)

Black Russian Rye Bread with
  Sweet Butter (see page 206)

Wild Currant Jam (see page 250)

Gruyère and Appenzeller Cheese

Grapes and Apples

Fig Torte with Almond Icing

Hot Coffee with Brandy
  and Whipped Cream

Wine: California Pinot Noir

It was one of those unbelievable spring days in April, cold enough for the snow to hold a good surface for skiing, but warmed by sunlight intensified many times by the whiteness of the open snowfields lying under a perfectly clear blue sky. We left our cars parked on the highway and cross-country skiied for two miles to a popular hot springs. The trek required some maneuvering on skis, since we had to pick our way through willow patches and search for a place to cross a partially frozen river.

We left our packs at the hot springs and continued climbing on the open hills ahead for an hour or so. We sat down to rest near a pine grove and enjoyed the magnificent view of the valley, defined on the opposite side by snow-covered Sawtooth peaks.

From where we stopped it was an easy glide on skis back down to the hot springs pool where we took a long leisurely dip. We then skiied out into the open field to settle down for our picnic.

We dug holes for our feet to dangle in as we sat on our skis and dined, feeling like a small band of Eskimo travelers on a great white plain.

RUSSIAN BORSCHT

Yield: 4 to 4½ quarts

There are so many shortcuts for making this rich soup that one tends to forget the superiority of the real thing made with fresh beets. Borscht is an elegant beginning to any picnic. In this case, we serve it hot to begin a picnic in the snow.

½ *cup shredded white cabbage*
4 *leeks, sliced*
2 *medium onions, peeled and chunked*
2 *cups chopped celery, including the leaves*
3 *whole cloves*
12 *whole black peppercorns*
3½ *quarts brown beef stock (see page 93)*
6 *medium beets*
½ *cup red wine*
4 *tablespoons butter*
2 *tablespoons good cider vinegar*
2 *tablespoons dry sherry* OR *Madeira*
2 *tablespoons instantized flour* OR *arrowroot*
2 *cups sour cream, at room temperature*

In a large pot, simmer the cabbage, leeks, onions, celery, cloves and peppercorns in the stock for about an hour. Let the stock cool, strain and refrigerate until ready to use.

Meanwhile, wash and scrub the beets with a stiff vegetable brush. Grate one-third of the beets finely and marinate them in the wine. Chop the remaining beets and sauté them in the butter in a large iron or enamel pot, stirring with a wooden spoon until heated through. Add the vinegar and sherry. Cover and simmer until tender (about half an hour). Mix the flour or arrowroot with a little cold water, and stir this gently into the beets. Slowly pour the vegetable stock into the beet mixture, stirring constantly. After the mixture thickens and all the stock has been added, add the marinated beets.

Pour a few teaspoons of the hot soup into the sour cream and blend; then slowly add the sour cream mixture to the borscht, stirring constantly. Serve the borscht hot for winter picnics or ice-cold in the summer.

This recipe makes 4 to 4½ quarts, which is more than one usually needs to take for a picnic. So pour some of the soup, hot, into a preheated thermos, and freeze or refrigerate the rest to save for another time.

SWISS MEATLOAF TICINO

Yield: 1 regular-size bread loaf or 2 small loaves

    2 *eggs, beaten*
    ¾ *cup soft bread crumbs*
    ½ *cup tomato juice*
    2 *tablespoons minced parsley*
    ½ *teaspoon dried oregano*
    ¼ *teaspoon each salt and pepper*
    1 *clove garlic, peeled and minced or put through a garlic press*
    2 *pounds lean ground beef*
    8 *thin slices baked ham* OR *prosciutto*
 1½ *cups grated Swiss cheese*
    3 *slices Swiss cheese, cut in half diagonally*

Oven temperature: 350°

Preheat oven. Combine eggs, bread crumbs, tomato juice, parsley, oregano, salt and pepper and garlic in a large mixing bowl. Add beef and mix well with your hands. On a flat surface covered with a piece of aluminum foil or waxed paper, pat the meat into a 12″ × 10″ rectangle. Arrange ham slices on top of the rectangle, leaving a small margin around the edge. Sprinkle the grated cheese over the ham. Starting at one of the short ends, carefully roll up meat, using the foil to lift. Seal the edges and ends by pinching together. Place roll, seam side down, in a bread-loaf pan, or (for backpacking) cut the loaf in half and use two small loaf pans.

Bake at 350° for one hour and fifteen minutes or until done. If the mixture is baked in small loaf pans, cooking time should be about 45 minutes. After 40 minutes test with a small sharp knife to see whether the meat is cooked through. The loaves will shrink slightly from the sides of the pan when done. (Don't overcook or the loaves will dry out.) Garnish with triangles of cheese overlapping and return to oven just to melt the cheese. Let cool and wrap the entire container in foil. The meat loaf can be served either in the pan or unmolded, cut in slices. Each slice has a spiral design of cheese and ham, very pretty.

CRACKED-WHEAT SALAD (TABULI)

Serves 8

This salad, a Middle Eastern hors d'oeuvre, is a wonderful accompaniment to many meat dishes, especially the spicy meatloaf we served for this picnic.

1 cup burghul (cracked wheat)
1 cucumber, peeled and finely diced
2 tomatoes, chopped
2 green peppers, washed, cored, seeded and finely chopped
4 tablespoons chopped parsley

¼ cup chopped fresh mint
OR
1½ teaspoons dried mint leaves

1 onion, peeled and finely chopped
½ cup olive oil
¼ cup lemon juice
salt
romaine lettuce

Wash the cracked wheat under cold water until the water runs clear. Put it in a bowl, cover it with boiling water and let stand one to two hours. Rinse with cold water and drain well, squeezing out the excess water with your hands. Place the wheat in a large bowl and add the cucumber, tomatoes, peppers, parsley, mint and onion. In a small bowl, mix the oil with the lemon juice and salt to taste. Pour the dressing over the wheat mixture and toss well.

Put the salad in a plastic container and chill in the refrigerator until ready to pack. Take romaine leaves packed in a separate plastic bag, a serving spoon and a small serving bowl. When ready to serve, line the bowl with the lettuce and pile the cracked-wheat salad in the middle. You can refill the bowl from the container of salad as necessary.

FIG TORTE WITH ALMOND ICING

5 eggs, separated
⅔ cup sugar
½ cup dry white bread crumbs
¾ cup dried figs, finely chopped
½ cup blanched almonds, very finely chopped
½ teaspoon cinnamon

¼ teaspoon each *nutmeg, allspice and cloves*
½ teaspoon baking powder
 1 teaspoon grated lemon rind
 1 tablespoon grated orange rind
 1 tablespoon brandy
10 whole almonds

Oven temperature: 325°

Preheat oven and line an 8-inch tube pan with greased wax paper. Beat the egg whites with a pinch of salt until stiff, and set aside. In a large mixing bowl beat the egg yolks until light in color. Add the sugar gradually and beat until well blended and thick.

Stir in the bread crumbs, figs and nuts, all of the spices, the baking powder, lemon and orange rind, and brandy. Lightly fold the egg whites into the batter.

Turn the cake into the prepared pan and bake for about 1 hour, testing for doneness with a toothpick. While the cake cools in the pan, prepare the icing:

 1 egg yolk
⅓ cup confectioners' sugar
½ teaspoon almond flavoring
½ teaspoon vanilla extract
 6 tablespoons butter, softened

Beat all the ingredients together in a small bowl with an electric beater until smooth. Chill.

Take the frosting and the whole almonds to the picnic in small containers, and wrap the cake and the pan in foil. Unmold the cake at the picnic, frost, and garnish with the nuts, or if you'd prefer, sprinkle the cake with confectioners' sugar instead of frosting it.

HOT COFFEE WITH BRANDY AND WHIPPED CREAM

Yield: 1 quart

 6 coffee measures freshly ground coffee
 1 half-inch piece vanilla bean
    Brandy or cognac to taste
½ pint whipping cream
    dash of vanilla extract
 2 teaspoons sugar

Cut the piece of vanilla bean in several small pieces and mix them with the ground coffee before brewing. Use your favorite method to brew 4 cups of coffee, using 6 coffee measures of a good blend to make the coffee extra strong. Add brandy to taste—up to 4 shots.

Whip the cream in a small bowl with an electric beater, adding the vanilla and sprinkling on the sugar while beating. *Beat only until thick and creamy, not stiff, so it still will run off a spoon.*

Take the coffee in a thermos and the cream in a separate container. Serve the coffee in small cups with a heaping tablespoon of cream on each serving. If you substitute Irish whiskey for the brandy, you have Irish coffee.

A PICNIC IN THE PARK OR LE DÉJEUNER SUR L'HERBE

Bois de Boulogne, Paris

Game Pâté

Cold Roast Tarragon Chicken

Haricots Potato Salad

*Raw Vegetables with
   Fresh Herb Dipping Sauce*

Cantal and Port Salut Cheese

Apple Gâteaux (see page 282)

Grapes and Peaches

*Wine: Château de la Chaize
      or any other nice Beaujolais*

A picnic in a city park? Why not. A very special picnic could take place in any city park—Golden Gate Park in San Francisco, Hyde Park in London, New York's Central Park, or the Bois de Boulogne in Paris.

The city has decided advantages. You can easily transport a basket laden with picnic delicacies bought that very morning from the best cheese shop, delicatessen and pâtisserie. Or you can make the recipes suggested here yourself.

We named this particular picnic after Édouard Manet's masterpiece Le Déjeuner sur l'Herbe, or "Lunch on the Grass." Our picnic also took place on the grass—in the Bois de Boulogne on a lovely warm sunny day in spring just as the tulips were coming into bloom. The idea of picnicking in the nude like the lady in Manet's painting was tempting. We had taken a typical French lunch: les charcuteries de France, le poulet, la salade, les fromages des provinces, la torte paysanne, les fruits and les vins de pays.

When we returned home, we adapted the French lunch menu.

GAME PÂTÉ

Serves 10

This recipe is adapted from Julia Child's Pâté de Veau et Porc avec Gibier. It is very popular with us, as we usually have game meat. The pâté can be made with any game birds or rabbit or venison meat. If you don't have game, veal liver is a successful substitute.

    thin slices of fresh pork fatback OR *salt pork, blanched,**
      OR *bacon, blanched*
1 *pound raw game meat, boned, skinned and cut into strips ¼ inch wide*
¾ *pound veal*
½ *pound pork*
½ *pound fresh pork fatback* OR *salt pork (blanched)*
2 *eggs, slightly beaten*

---

* To blanch salt pork or bacon, boil thin slices in 1 quart of water for 10 minutes, rinse and drain.

2 *tablespoons finely chopped shallots*
¼ *teaspoon dried thyme*
  pinch of allspice
1 *tablespoon finely minced parsley*
  salt to taste
  freshly ground black pepper to taste (about 1–1½ teaspoons)

Marinade

¼ *cup brandy*
4 *crushed juniper berries*
  pinch salt and freshly ground pepper
  pinch of allspice

Prepare enough slices of fatback or salt pork or bacon to line a six-cup terrine and to cover the entire surface of the pâté.

Soak about ¾ pound of the game meat in the marinade mixture of brandy and spices for 24 hours. The following day finely grind through a meat grinder or a Cuisinart the remaining game, the veal, pork and the pork fat. Stir in the eggs and the rest of the spices, salt and pepper. Drain the game strips, reserving the marinade. Stir the marinade into the ground meat mixture. This is the forcemeat. Refrigerate it for an hour.

Preheat oven. Line a six-cup terrine with the slices of pork fat or blanched salt pork. Put in a layer of forcemeat and arrange a layer of game strips on top of it. Again put in a layer of forcemeat and arrange a layer of game meat on top. Continue, ending with the forcemeat. Cover the top with strips of pork fat, then with foil. Put on the terrine lid, and put the whole terrine in a shallow pan. Pour boiling water into the pan to a level of 1½ inches. Bake for 1½ hours.

The pâté is done when it has shrunk away from the sides and the juices are no longer pink but are a clear yellow. When it is done, remove the lid of the terrine and take it out of the pan of water. Weight it down with a heavy object that fits inside the terrine, and let it cool several hours. Chill, still weighted, in the refrigerator.

Take the terrine to a picnic and slice. For a backpack, unmold it and wrap it in foil, then put it into a leakproof container or plastic bag. Slice and serve with French bread and cornichons. If there is any left over, it will keep well for 10-12 days wrapped in foil or plastic wrap and refrigerated.

COLD ROAST TARRAGON CHICKEN

Serves 5–6

1 3-pound roasting chicken
   fine crystal salt OR sea salt
   freshly ground black pepper
1 stick (¼ pound) butter
1 large bunch (1½ cups) fresh tarragon, chopped coarsely
   (save a few sprigs to garnish)

Oven temperature: 375°

Preheat oven. Salt and pepper the chicken inside and out. With stick of cold butter generously grease the outside skin of the bird.

Mash the remaining butter with the fresh tarragon leaves in a mixing bowl with a wooden spoon. Stuff the mixture inside the chicken.

Truss the chicken and place in a small roasting pan. Put it in the oven and cook for about 40 minutes. Baste the chicken with some of the tarragon butter which will have oozed out into the roasting pan. Turn up the heat of the oven to 400° and cook for about 15 minutes, turning the bird once. Test for doneness with a fork. If the juices run clear and the meat is tender, the bird is done.

Now turn on the oven broiler and crisp the skin under high heat for 3 to 5 minutes. Cool and refrigerate. Wrap in double-strength foil for basket or backpack picnicking. Serve on a bed of watercress, which you have carried separately, and with a few sprigs of tarragon as garnish. Remember to take poultry shears for carving.

HARICOTS POTATO SALAD

Serves 6–8

1½ pounds fresh green beans
 4 cups sliced, peeled boiled potatoes
    (about 3 potatoes)
 2 tablespoons sliced scallions (use some of green part)
⅔ cup French vinaigrette sauce (page 178),
    with 1 clove garlic, minced
⅓ cup sour cream
⅓ cup mayonnaise
¼ teaspoon each salt and pepper
 2 tablespoons pitted sliced black olives

Wash beans; cut off ends. Cut diagonally into 2-inch pieces. Cook beans in boiling salted water until just tender (20–30 minutes), rinse in cold water and drain. Combine the beans with the potatoes and scallions. Pour the vinaigrette over the mixture and toss lightly. Cover and chill several hours or overnight, stirring occasionally. To serve, drain the vegetables, reserving 2 tablespoons of the marinade and combining it with the sour cream, mayonnaise and salt and pepper. Toss lightly and garnish with olive slices.

Pack in a tight-fitting container. If you prefer, you can mix the sour cream and mayonnaise together and take them in a separate small container, then toss the vegetables with this mixture at serving time.

RAW VEGETABLES
WITH FRESH HERB DIPPING SAUCE

Serves 4–6

Choose any variety of your favorite vegetables:

1 *fresh medium zucchini, washed and cut into strips*
1 *big tomato, washed and cut into wedges*
2 *carrots, scrubbed, pared and cut into strips*
2 *celery hearts, washed and cut into sticks*
1 *piece of broccoli, washed and broken into flowerets*
¼ *whole cauliflower, washed and broken into flowerets*
1 *whole green pepper, washed, cored, seeded and sliced*

Arrange the vegetables in a tall plastic container or in a plastic bag. Prepare the dipping sauce:

1 *clove garlic, peeled and crushed*
¾ *cup sour cream*
½ *cup plain yogurt*
   dash fresh lemon juice
1 *tablespoon each minced fresh chives, parsley, dill*
   salt and freshly ground white pepper

Place all the ingredients in a bowl and mix thoroughly. Pack in a little plastic container.

Serve the vegetables on a plate with the sauce in the middle for easy dipping.

A BOATING PICNIC

The Havana Coast, Cuba

Gin with Fresh Coconut Juice

Spanish Peasant Soup

Marinated Oysters

Morro Crab with Mayonnaise

Cuban Potato Salad

Cuban Stuffed Avocados

*Cascos de Guayabe
    (Guava Fruit with
    Cream Cheese)*

Mary's Meringue Torte

*Wine: Marqués de Riscal, Tavel or
    any red Spanish table wine
    or Cerveza Hatuey Beer*

I've often told Connie of the long warm summer days out at sea, off the coast of Cuba, that we would spend fishing. My father and mother, Ernest, Mary and different friends would come along. Juan, the first mate, was also the cook, an expert chef and famous among us for his many specialties. Margot was just a baby then and remained back at the "finca" with a nurse. I must have been seven or eight, just at that age of insatiable curiosity, wiling away the day happily watching the grownups fish and asking Mary and Grandpapa endless questions about fishing and the sea. As a child one doesn't usually think about the prospect of a gourmet lunch, but I remember eating some strange and exotic dishes then as part of the unusual tropical meals on the Pilar. My grandmama Mary always invented great dishes and still has that rare ability to know how something will taste before she begins creating it. With a few basic ingredients you can continue to invent dishes in the way that she and Juan would. Here is a typically Cuban lunch, like the ones we used to have in those days.

GIN WITH FRESH COCONUT JUICE

Yield: 2 tall drinks

10 *ounces coconut juice, fresh or canned**
4 *ounces gin*
½ *cup crushed ice*

Put all the ingredients in a shaker and shake well, or stir the mixture vigorously in a large pitcher. Repeat the process as many times as necessary to make enough for all your guests. You can keep the mixture in a large pitcher in a cooler or take it in a thermos to your picnic.

* Coco Lopez makes a good product.

SPANISH PEASANT SOUP

Serves 8–12

This is the authentic way to make gazpacho, which was one of my grandfather's favorites.

2 *pieces day-old bread, with crusts removed*
3 *cloves garlic, peeled and put through a press*
2 *tablespoons vinegar*
3 *medium-size tomatoes, washed and*
 chopped coarsely
1 *green pepper, washed, cored, seeded*
 and sliced in thin slivers
1 *red pepper, washed, cored, seeded*
 and sliced in thin slivers
3 *medium-size cucumbers, scrubbed and cubed*
 to make 2 cups
6 *cups water and ice mixed*

In a large bowl, place the stale bread and 1 clove garlic. Add the vinegar and mix well. Let stand a few hours. Then add the chopped tomatoes, sliced peppers and cucumbers. Before serving, add the other two garlic cloves and ice water and chill. The soup can be put in chilled thermos at this point or in a large bowl in a cooler or a boat refrigerator. Serve with ice floating on top.

MARINATED OYSTERS

Serves 12

2–3 *dozen raw bluepoint oysters in season*
      (other varieties of oysters may be substituted) shucked and
      thoroughly cleaned of any grit
   2 *cups vegetable oil*, OR 1 *cup olive oil and 1 cup vegetable oil**
   3 *medium onions, peeled and thinly sliced*
   3 *tablespoons red wine vinegar*
   1 *tablespoon salt*
  ½ *tablespoon freshly ground white pepper*
      lemon wedges

Place all the ingredients in a tightly sealed container to marinate, and chill thoroughly.

Take a pretty plastic bowl to pour the oysters into at the picnic. Serve with lemon wedges and use large toothpicks to fish the oysters out of the marinade.

* This may sound like a lot of oil, and you can reduce it if you want, but the oysters will look beautiful if served this way.

MORRO CRAB WITH MAYONNAISE

Serves 6–12

Morro crabs, indigenous to deep reef waters in the Caribbean, are named after Morro Castle in Havana Harbor, where they are caught fresh daily. They are "stone shelled," with one claw much larger than the other. Substitute any variety of fresh crab available in your area.

   6 *fresh morro crabs*
      homemade mayonnaise

In a large pot, bring to a boil enough salted water to cover the crabs, perhaps two or three at a time. Place them in the pot and boil until they turn pink, about 20 minutes. Let them cool; then store in a cooler on a bed of ice until ready to serve.

At serving time, let each person crack his own crab or half a crab.

Have a small bowl of mayonnaise into which each person can dip the crabmeat.

CUBAN POTATO SALAD

Serves 8–12

4 *large potatoes, scrubbed*
1 *red onion, peeled and sliced thinly*
2 *tablespoons chopped fresh dill (and a few sprigs for garnish)*

Cook the potatoes in boiling salted water until they are just tender (about 20 minutes). Let them cool and then peel them. Cut them up into large cubes and place in a large bowl. Add the sliced onion (reserving one slice, separated into rings, for garnish) and fresh dill.

Make vinaigrette sauce:

3 *tablespoons fresh lemon juice*
1 *teaspoon salt*
1 *teaspoon pepper*
   dash of Tabasco sauce
⅔ *cup oil*

Combine the lemon juice, salt, pepper and Tabasco in a small bowl, and then add the oil slowly while beating vigorously with a fork.

Pour the sauce over the potato salad and toss gently. Cover the bowl with aluminum foil and refrigerate for about an hour. Then transfer the salad to a plastic container. To serve, turn it out into an attractive bowl; and don't forget a large serving spoon. Garnish with onion rings and fresh dill.

CUBAN STUFFED AVOCADOS

Serves 12

6 *small avocados*
2 *cups cooked chopped shrimp* OR *crabmeat*
¾ *cup finely chopped celery*
1 *cup basic blender mayonnaise, made with 2 tablespoons lime juice*
   instead of vinegar (page 177)
½ *teaspoon grated lime rind*
1 *teaspoon grated onion*
2 *hard-boiled eggs, sliced*

Cut each avocado in half and remove and discard the pits. Combine the cooked shrimp or crab with the celery, mayonnaise, lime rind and grated onion. Fill the cavities of the avocados with the mixture and garnish with egg slices. If you're hiking, carry the whole avocados, cut them in half at the site, and fill with the premixed filling. Be sure to include spoons.

CASCOS DE GUAYABE

Serves 12

6 *ripe guavas*
2 *cups cream cheese*

Guavas are a sweet fruit and need no sugar. Cut them in halves and remove the seeds. Whip the cheese with a beater until creamy and then stuff the guavas with it. Pack in a plastic container and refrigerate before serving. For a hiking picnic bring the cream cheese in a separate container and stuff the guavas at the site.

MARY'S MERINGUE TORTE

1 *paper-thin prebaked pie crust*
7–8 *egg whites*
1 *cup chopped candied fruit*
    (*cherries, oranges, lime, citron, grapefruit*)

Oven temperature: 350°

Beat the egg whites until stiff. Fold in the candied fruit and place the mixture in the prebaked pie crust. Bake for 25–30 minutes in a moderate oven. This dessert should be served in very small wedges like a confection, rather than in large wedges like a pie.

Basic Crust

1½ *cups all-purpose flour*
¾ *teaspoon salt*
½ *cup shortening*
3–4 *tablespoons ice water, approximately*

Oven temperature: 375°

Sift together the flour and salt. With a pastry cutter or fork, work in the shortening until it resembles coarse meal. Sprinkle the ice water on the mixture, using as little as possible—enough so that the flour holds together and can be formed into a ball. Refrigerate for 15 minutes. On a floured board, roll out the dough into an even, thin circle. Fold gently in half, place it in the pie pan and unfold it. Fit it loosely without stretching over the rim of the pan. Trim with a knife. With the tines of a fork or the edge of a knife make slits to allow steam to escape. Bake for 10–12 minutes until lightly browned.

SUMMER

A FOURTH OF JULY PICNIC

Trail Creek, Idaho

Fresh Strawberry Daiquiris

Steak Tartare with Sour Cream and Caviar

Mushroom-Stuffed Eggs

Fried Chicken

Ranch-Style Sliced Tomatoes

Idaho Potato Salad

Mountain Bread, Butter and Huckleberry Jam (see page 210)

Old-Fashioned Chocolate Cake

Burnt-Sugar Ice Cream

Lemonade

Spiked Iced Coffee

A Keg of Beer

The Fourth of July is the time to have an old-fashioned picnic in the American tradition. We organize this picnic family style, like a potluck dinner. We all bring our children and dogs.

The menu is usually comprised of typical dishes that our mothers and grandmothers cooked for Sunday picnics. The menu is updated a bit: we never started with strawberry daiquiris when we were kids, since strawberries were to be eaten with cream and maybe shortcake. The deviled eggs are also not the same as our mothers made, but they're delicious. The rest of the menu, except the bread, is tried and true. The sliced tomatoes, fried chicken, potato salad, and chocolate cake are just as good as they ever were. Instead of the white rolls or biscuits of our childhood we serve our Mountain Bread, a modern, earthy, wholegrain bread which is wonderful with wild-fruit jams.

We usually go to a Forest Service area with tables, benches, and a fireplace for this picnic, because there are a lot of people, kids, dogs, Frisbees, fireworks, excitement, and confusion. This particular picnic took place at a picnic area along Trail Creek, a few minutes' drive from Sun Valley and the town of Ketchum. With the prospect of a very short drive home, we could linger around the fire having coffee and a last piece of chocolate cake.

FRESH STRAWBERRY DAIQUIRIS

Yield: 2 quarts

2 *pints fresh strawberries, washed and hulled*
8 *shots light rum*
   juice of two fresh limes
6 *tablespoons sugar syrup* OR *honey*
1 *cup crushed ice*

Mix half of all the ingredients in a blender; then repeat the process. Pour the mixture into two prechilled thermoses.

STEAK TARTARE
WITH SOUR CREAM AND CAVIAR

Serves 8–10

  1 *pound lean top sirloin* OR *lean rump roast*
  ½ *onion, minced*
1½ *teaspoons minced parsley*
  1 *teaspoon Dijon mustard*
  ¾ *teaspoon salt*
  ½ *teaspoon freshly ground black pepper*
  1 *fresh raw egg yolk*
1½ *tablespoons brandy (preferably cognac)*
  1 *cup sour cream*
  ½ *cup black caviar*
   lettuce leaves OR *watercress*

Grind the meat twice through a meat grinder (or have your butcher do it for you) or once through a Cuisinart food processor. Using a fork, mix the ground meat with the onion, parsley, mustard, salt, pepper and egg yolk in a large bowl. Add the brandy and blend gently but thoroughly with a fork, folding in all the ingredients just until the meat is of a light texture.

Form the meat into 1-to-1½-inch round balls. Roll first in sour cream, then in caviar. Chill in the refrigerator before packing into a plastic container. Serve on a bed of lettuce or watercress. If you prefer, the steak tartare may be served alone, without sour cream and caviar. Form it into a loaf pan or mold and serve with thinly sliced black bread. To pack, wrap the loaf pan in heavy plastic. Take the lettuce or watercress separately in a plastic bag.

MUSHROOM-STUFFED EGGS

Serves 12

6 *hard-boiled eggs*
¼ *cup minced fresh raw mushrooms*
1 *tablespoon mayonnaise*
1 *teaspoon Dijon mustard*
   salt and pepper
   dash cayenne pepper
   minced parsley

Halve the eggs lengthwise. Remove yolks and mash them in a bowl with the mushrooms, mayonnaise, mustard, salt and pepper to taste, and dash of cayenne. Stuff the mixture into the egg whites and sprinkle with minced parsley.

Pack closely together in an airtight container. When packing in a backpack, make sure the eggs are in an upright position and the container is flat and secure in the pack.

FRIED CHICKEN

Serves 5

Buy the best-quality fryer you can find. If you live near a poultry market, buy a freshly killed chicken.

1 *fryer, cut up*
½ *lemon*
3 *cups milk*
1 *pound shortening*
1⅔ *cups all-purpose flour*
3 *teaspoons salt and pepper, mixed*
¼ *teaspoon sage*
   bacon grease (optional)

Wipe the chicken pieces off with a damp tea towel. Rub each piece of chicken quickly all over with half a lemon to flavor it. Then soak the chicken in milk one to two hours, or overnight. Drain the pieces of chicken well on paper towels.

Start heating the shortening in a large, deep frying pan. Mix the flour, salt, pepper and sage in a good-sized paper bag. Then add chicken to the bag, several pieces at a time, and shake to coat the pieces evenly with the flour mixture. Shake off excess flour as you take the pieces from the bag. Repeat until all pieces are floured.

After the shortening is heated to the point of sizzling, you can add a little bacon grease for flavor. Reduce heat a little and, using tongs, put in the chicken, legs and thighs first. Reduce heat to medium. Cook uncovered for 15 to 20 minutes. Lower heat, turn all the pieces over, and cook uncovered for 15 minutes more. Take the pieces out with tongs and lay them on paper towels to drain and cool. Do not cover or put in the oven. When cooled, put chicken in a container to carry, then arrange on a platter at picnic time, garnished with parsley or watercress.

The fried chicken can be kept in the refrigerator, but do not cover it at any time or it will lose its crispness.

RANCH-STYLE SLICED TOMATOES

Serves 8

Make this dish with big beefsteak tomatoes in season, fresh from the garden if possible.

    4   *large beefsteak tomatoes*
    2   *teaspoons sugar*
        salt and freshly ground pepper
    ¾   *cup vegetable oil*
    3   *tablespoons cider vinegar*
    3   *scallions, finely chopped*
    2   *tablespoons finely chopped parsley*

Wash and slice the tomatoes and put them in one or two layers in a large shallow glass dish. Sprinkle them with sugar, salt and pepper. Mix the oil and vinegar and pour over them. Sprinkle with half the scallions and parsley. Let the tomatoes marinate overnight. Place the tomatoes carefully in an attractive shallow plastic container with marinade and secure the lid well. Take the reserved scallions and parsley (wrapped in plastic wrap) to use as a garnish.

IDAHO POTATO SALAD

Serves 6–8

4 *hard-boiled eggs*
1 *small green pepper*
4 *large Idaho potatoes, boiled, cooled, peeled and thinly sliced*
1 *yellow onion, peeled and finely chopped*

2 *tablespoons finely minced fresh dill*
   OR
2 *teaspoons dried dill weed*

½ *cup chopped parsley*
   salt
   freshly ground black pepper
⅓ *cup vegetable* OR *olive oil*
3 *tablespoons wine vinegar*
½ *cup homemade mayonnaise mixed with ⅓ cup yogurt*

Peel and chop three of the hard-boiled eggs. Wash, core and seed the green pepper; finely chop half of it, and slice the other half in thin strips. Toss the potato slices in a large bowl with the onion, dill, parsley, chopped eggs, finely chopped green pepper, salt, pepper, oil and vinegar. Let this mixture marinate several hours or overnight.

Fold in the mayonnaise and yogurt and pack in a plastic container to travel. Take the egg and the pepper strips wrapped in plastic wrap. Peel and quarter the egg and garnish the salad with the egg alternating with strips of green pepper. Serve directly from the container if it's attractive, or spoon the salad out onto a plate or into a large wooden or plastic bowl. Don't forget a large serving spoon.

OLD-FASHIONED CHOCOLATE CAKE

Serves 8–10

⅔ *cup butter, softened*
1¾ *cups sugar*
2 *large eggs*
1 *teaspoon vanilla*
3 *1-ounce squares unsweetened chocolate*
2½ *cups sifted cake flour*
1¼ *teaspoons baking soda*
½ *teaspoon salt*
1¼ *cups ice water*

Oven temperature: 350°

Preheat the oven; butter and flour two 8-inch round cake pans.

Cream the butter and the sugar in a large mixing bowl, then add the eggs and vanilla, beating until fluffy. Melt the chocolate. When it has cooled, blend it into the butter mixture. Sift the dry ingredients together and add them to the butter mixture alternately with the ice water, beating after each addition. Pour the batter into the pans and bake for 40 minutes or until a knife inserted comes out clean. Let the cakes cool a bit before removing from the pans, then place on wire racks and allow to cool completely before filling and frosting with:

Chocolate Icing

6 *ounces semisweet chocolate (squares or bits)*
¼ *cup water*
¼ *cup confectioners' sugar*
4 *egg yolks*
6 *tablespoons butter, cut into pieces*
1 *teaspoon vanilla extract*

Melt the chocolate, water, and powdered sugar in the top of a double boiler over simmering water. Remove from heat, let cool to lukewarm, and then add the yolks one at a time. Stir in the butter a piece at a time. Add vanilla and mix until smooth. Cool and spread on the bottom layer. Place top layer on the cake and frost.

The chocolate cake should be carefully transported to the picnic in a container that will protect it, such as a cardboard box or an unbreakable platter covered with a plastic cake cover. Keep cool in the shade until ready to slice and serve.

To take in a pack, cut the cake into serving-size wedges, wrap each one in plastic wrap and put them into a hard-sided container.

BURNT-SUGAR ICE CREAM

Yield: 1½–2 quarts

10 *egg yolks*
¼ *teaspoon salt*
1 *cup sugar*
½ *cup water*
3½ *cups milk*
1 *cup heavy cream*

Put the egg yolks and salt into a mixing bowl and beat until pale yellow and creamy.

In a medium-size saucepan over medium heat, boil the sugar with ¼ cup water until it is a golden-brown syrup. Remove from heat. In another pan bring the other ¼ cup of water to a boil and then add it to the syrup, being careful not to burn yourself as it spatters. Put the burnt-sugar syrup back on moderate heat, scraping the sides and bottom of the pan as you bring the mixture back to a boil for a few minutes.

With a wire whisk, beat this hot syrup into the egg yolks a little at a time until the mixture is creamy. Let it cool.

In a large pot, scald the milk and cream (bring it just to the point of boiling and then turn off the heat). Mix several spoonfuls, one at a time, of the scalded milk-cream into the egg mixture. Then stir the egg-sugar mixture back into the pot of milk-cream and cook this over low heat, stirring constantly with a wooden spoon until the custard coats the spoon.

Let cool and refrigerate in a large plastic container to chill thoroughly before putting it into an ice cream freezer. Take the mixture to your picnic in a cooler.

Packing an old-fashioned ice cream freezer with rock salt and ice, and then cranking it until the ice cream is ready, is a great part of the fun of a summer picnic. The reward of homemade ice cream is worth the trouble.

LEMONADE

Yield: 1 gallon

If taking lemonade to a picnic by car, make it in a cooler with a spigot so that everyone can help himself. If you'll be hiking to a site that has good fresh water, icy cold from a stream or spring, make the base concentrate in a blender as described below and add the water when it's served.

fresh lemons, enough to yield 3 cups of juice
2 *cups honey*
1 *cup cold water*
1 *lemon, sliced thinly, for garnish*
  fresh mint sprigs, for garnish

In a blender mix the lemon juice, honey and water together for 2 minutes. Put this mixture in a cooler or a large container and add chopped ice and cold water to it to make 1 gallon of lemonade. To make a quart of lemonade, use 1 cup of freshly squeezed lemon juice, ½ cup of honey, and 1 cup of water for the base liquid. Remember to carry a pitcher along to get water from the stream.

SPIKED ICED COFFEE

Yield: 3 quarts

8 *cups strong coffee, made with a freshly ground good blend*
  honey to taste
⅛ *teaspoon (2 drops) almond extract for each cup of coffee*
½ *cup evaporated milk for each cup of coffee*
1 *shot cognac for each cup of coffee*

Blend 1 or 2 cups of coffee at a time with the other ingredients in a blender or cocktail shaker. Pour into a jug or thermoses with a few ice cubes. Stir well before serving.

Take a quart of milk in the cooler to thin the mixture if it is too strong. Also, take extra ice cubes in the cooler and add to the coffee when serving.

When backpacking, serve the coffee directly from the thermos.

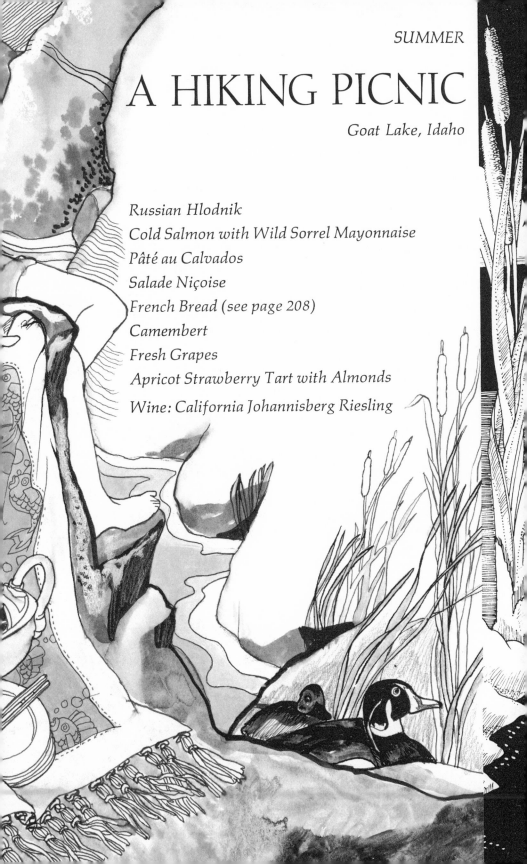

A HIKING PICNIC

Goat Lake, Idaho

Russian Hlodnik

Cold Salmon with Wild Sorrel Mayonnaise

Pâté au Calvados

Salade Niçoise

French Bread (see page 208)

Camembert

Fresh Grapes

Apricot Strawberry Tart with Almonds

Wine: California Johannisberg Riesling

T

his trip began in a busy parking lot and culminated three hours later at a spectacularly beautiful alpine lake—very deep, turquoise and still, with a large ice mass or two moving slowly, never melting the entire summer. On one side of the lake, a very steep, high, solid rock backdrop reaches to the sky. We chose a mossy meadow on the opposite side of the lake as our picnic spot. There were large, smooth granite boulders to lounge on and to dive from if we cared to brave the icy waters, full of golden trout.

A natural route up the snowfield behind our picnic site led to a chain of smaller lakes ranging from pools in huge rock slides to idyllic deep little lakes in mossy alpine meadows.

After lunch we climbed up the snowfield and continued on, exploring almost to the top of the ridge which separates this basin from the next valley. We returned late to Goat Lake, where we had left most of our packs. We had had the foresight to save a thermos of coffee and the apricot strawberry tart. We consumed them with gusto to reinforce us for the long walk still ahead of us down to the car. We left Goat Lake just as it began to get dark, but the trail was good and our path was easy to see. We walked by moonlight and remained in a state of enchantment for some time.

RUSSIAN HLODNIK

Yield: 2 quarts

A cold beet soup.

½ cup tiny shrimp
1 cup finely chopped cooked beets (either 2 medium-sized beets with their greens, OR 1 small can—8¼ ounce size—diced beets)
2 cups beet pot liquor
2 cups water
1 cucumber, peeled, seeded and finely chopped
2 radishes, washed and thinly sliced

2 *scallions (with a little of the green part), finely chopped*

2 *large sprigs fresh dill, finely minced,*
   OR

1 *teaspoon dried dill weed*

¼ *teaspoon sugar*

2 *cups sour cream*

1 *tablespoon lemon juice*

2 *tablespoons red wine vinegar*
   salt and pepper to taste

If you are using fresh shrimp, shell and devein enough shrimp to make ½ cup, then cook them in boiling salted water for 3–5 minutes until tender. Rinse in cold water and set aside. If using canned (we prefer Pacific Pearl brand), rinse and drain the shrimp from one small can and set aside.

Use fresh beets if possible, since they have a superior flavor. Scrub the beets and cook them with their greens in 2 cups of lightly salted boiling water until tender (about 20 minutes). (You may substitute canned diced beets in this recipe, in which case use all the beet liquid in the can, adding water to make 2 cups of beet "juice" and still using the additional 2 cups of water called for in the recipe.)

Reserve the pot liquor and rinse the beets quickly under cold water. Chop them finely, greens and all, and combine them in a large pot or bowl with 2 cups of the pot liquor, 2 cups water, the cucumber, radishes, scallions, dill and sugar.

Using a fork, blend the sour cream with the lemon juice and vinegar in a bowl; then stir this into the beet mixture, ½ cup at a time, mixing thoroughly after each addition. Stir the shrimp in at this point, or take them in a separate container, putting 1 heaping teaspoon of shrimp into each cup as the soup is served. Chill the soup thoroughly before pouring it into a chilled thermos.

COLD SALMON
WITH WILD SORREL MAYONNAISE

Serves 4–8

Gathering wild sorrel on summer hiking trips is one of our favorite pastimes. You can make a salad with it on the spot and also gather enough to take home for making mayonnaise, sorrel sauce or soup.

You can use domestic sorrel in place of wild. It's easy to grow and can also be bought during the summer in some markets and at special greengrocers.

Court-bouillon

- 2 *cups water*
- 6 *black peppercorns*
- 1 *bay leaf*
  sprig of parsley
- ½ *onion, peeled and cut in chunks*
- 1 *small carrot, scrubbed and cut in chunks*
- 1 *cup dry white wine*
- 4 *small thick filets of fresh salmon,*
  each 3–4 inches square
- 1 *cup homemade wild sorrel mayonnaise (page 178)*
  several sprigs of sorrel

Make the court-bouillon in a medium-sized saucepan by first bringing
the water to a boil, then adding the herbs, vegetables and wine. When the
mixture boils again, reduce the heat and simmer for 30 minutes to an
hour.

Place the salmon in a fish poacher or on a rack in a deep frying pan with
a lid and pour in the court-bouillon so that the filets are partially immersed
in the liquid. Cover and simmer the fish until it is just tender and flakes off
easily with a fork—about 10 minutes. Do not overcook. Let the filets cool
in the liquid, then remove them with a slotted spoon. Let cool and chill them
in the refrigerator. Decorate each filet with a sorrel leaf or a bay leaf and a
peppercorn. Wrap individually in plastic wrap and pack in a hard-sided
plastic container to put in a pack or a cooler to take in the car. Take the
mayonnaise in a separate container and take a spoon to serve it with. The
salmon can be arranged decoratively on a paper plate with extra sorrel
leaves as decoration and the mayonnaise on the side. To serve more people
(up to eight) cut each filet in half.

PÂTÉ AU CALVADOS

Serves 6

- 1 *pound chicken livers*
- 19 *tablespoons butter*
- ½ *cup finely chopped onions*
- 1 *small green apple, peeled, cored and chopped*
- ¼ *cup Calvados* OR *applejack, warmed*
- 2 *tablespoons heavy cream*
- 1 *teaspoon lemon juice*
- 1½ *teaspoons salt*

freshly ground pepper

2 *small truffles, very thinly sliced,*

OR

2 *mushrooms cut in thick slices and sautéed in butter*

parsley
butter squares

Wash the chicken livers, pat dry and chop coarsely. In a frying pan melt 3 tablespoons butter, add the chopped onions, and cook over medium heat for five to seven minutes, or until the onions are soft. Mix in the green apple and cook three or four more minutes, until soft. Transfer the mixture to a blender.

Fry the livers in 4 tablespoons of hot butter over a medium-high heat. Cook and turn until they are browned, but still pink on the inside. Remove from heat, add the warmed applejack or Calvados and ignite. Let the brandy burn itself out. Add the livers and liver juices to the blender with the cream and blend at high speed; add more cream if necessary. Let cool completely.

In a medium mixing bowl beat 1½ sticks (12 tablespoons) of softened butter until smooth. Beat in the cold liver paste a tablespoon at a time. Stir in lemon juice and about 1½ teaspoons of salt and some freshly ground black pepper. Fold in truffle slices or mushrooms, pack the pâté in two small molds, and refrigerate. When ready to serve, unmold and garnish with parsley and iced butter squares.

Take the butter in a little plastic container. Put it in a cooler to transport or, if hiking, put it in a snow patch or in icy water as soon as you arrive at your destination. Take the parsley in a plastic bag. Put the molds, which you have carried wrapped in foil, upside down on a plate in the sun. Let them sit and tap the tops after 15 minutes to unmold.

SALADE NIÇOISE

Serves 8–12

During August, when there are fresh green beans in the market, we always take some version of a *salade Niçoise* on our hikes.

1 *pound fresh green beans*
2 *cups sliced cold boiled potatoes*
1 *cup vinaigrette sauce (page 178)*
3 *tablespoons chopped parsley*
2 *tablespoons chopped mixed green herbs (a combination of any of the following: chives, thyme, basil, chervil, summer savory, rosemary)*

      salt and pepper
      romaine leaves, washed
3–4 *fresh tomatoes*
  3 *hard-boiled eggs*
  1 *can water-packed tuna*
 20 *anchovy filets, drained and patted dry*
  1 *small green pepper, washed, cored, seeded*
     and sliced thinly
 15 *black olives (we like the Mediterranean type*
     best for this salad)

String the beans, breaking off the ends but leaving them whole. Boil the beans 10–15 minutes in plenty of boiling salted water (they should be slightly crisp). Drain them and rinse in cold water. Set aside.

Mix the potatoes with ⅓ cup vinaigrette, parsley, herbs, salt and pepper, pack into a plastic container and chill. Pour ⅓ cup vinaigrette over the green beans. Put them into another container and chill.

Sprinkle the romaine leaves with water and put them in a plastic bag. Take the tomatoes in a hard-sided container. Pack the can of tuna. Wrap the anchovy fillets in plastic wrap. Carry the rest of the vinaigrette in a little container with a tight lid. Take the eggs, the anchovies, green pepper, and the olives in a plastic container.

Assemble the salad at the site. (Make sure someone's bringing a thin, oval wooden platter and a can opener.) Using the romaine leaves as a bed, arrange the potatoes and beans on top of it and then put slices of green pepper around the edge. Peel and quarter the eggs and quarter the tomatoes; arrange these on top of the other vegetables along with chunks of tuna (drained) and black olives, using the anchovies as the final decoration. Serve with vinaigrette in individual enamel, plastic or paper bowls. Take plastic forks or chopsticks to eat it with.

Niçoise is traditionally a mixed vegetable salad which includes tuna, black olives and anchovies; otherwise the vegetable combination can include anything you like. You can use cold cooked rice instead of potatoes.

APRICOT STRAWBERRY TART WITH ALMONDS

Yield: 1 8-inch tart

Make half a recipe of *pâte sucrée*. Roll the pastry dough out with a rolling pin into a 9-inch round. Line an 8-inch tart pan with it. Prick the bottom and the sides of the pastry with a fork. Bake the shell at 375° for 15 minutes, until very slightly browned. Reserve.

Apricot Strawberry Filling

½ cup slivered almonds
1 cup washed, sliced fresh strawberries
10 ripe fresh apricots, peeled, halved, and pitted,
      then pan-boiled 15 seconds and drained
¾ cup sugar
1 teaspoon almond extract
2 tablespoons lemon juice
    butter

Oven temperature: 375°

Place ¼ cup sliced almonds on the bottom of the partially baked pie shell. Place a layer of half the sliced strawberries over the almonds. Sprinkle them with ¼ cup sugar. Sprinkle the rest of the almonds over this, then the rest of the strawberries and another ¼ cup sugar. Place the halved apricots on top, cut side up. Combine the lemon juice and almond extract and sprinkle over the apricots, then sprinkle on the rest of the sugar and dot with pieces of butter. Bake for about half an hour until the fruits look syrupy. Cool and cover with apricot glaze if you like. Simply rub apricot jam* through a sieve with a wooden spoon. Discard the apricot pieces in the sieve. (This is easier to do if the jam is heated.) Use a pastry brush to paint on the glaze.

Pack very carefully in foil or heavy plastic. If using a pan with a removable bottom, tape the bottom. Place in the top part of the pack in a horizontal position, wedged in place by other items.

* We like to use homemade crabapple, wild currant or rose-hip jams to glaze tarts. The color is lovely and the taste is piquant. You can melt down homemade crabapple jelly, page 249, adding a few cut-up dried or canned apricots to flavor. Let the mixture sit about 30 minutes, and then rub it through a sieve.

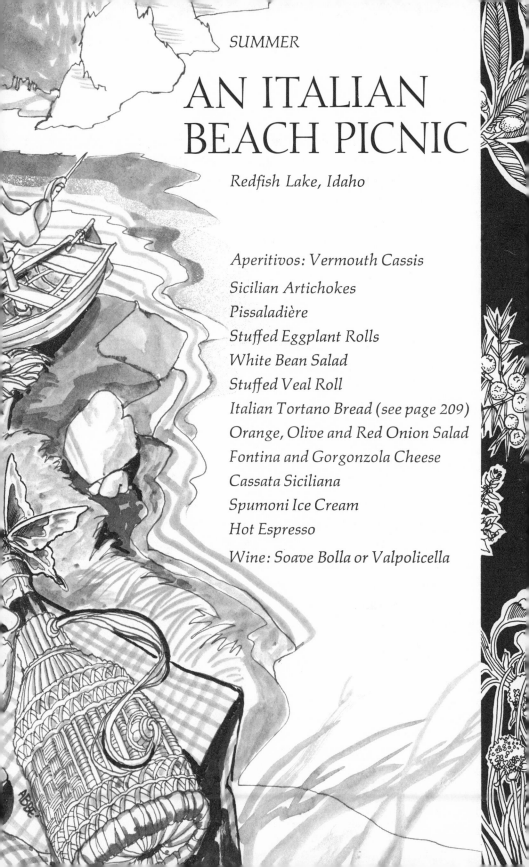

SUMMER

AN ITALIAN BEACH PICNIC

Redfish Lake, Idaho

Aperitivos: Vermouth Cassis

Sicilian Artichokes

Pissaladière

Stuffed Eggplant Rolls

White Bean Salad

Stuffed Veal Roll

Italian Tortano Bread (see page 209)

Orange, Olive and Red Onion Salad

Fontina and Gorgonzola Cheese

Cassata Siciliana

Spumoni Ice Cream

Hot Espresso

Wine: Soave Bolla or Valpolicella

The summer doesn't quite seem complete without a glorious Italian picnic. Usually a well-planned feast with lots of people and the best of food, it has become a tradition. The Italian cooking tradition offers the most exciting range of foods for picnicking, perhaps because there are so many dishes which are meant to be eaten "at room temperature." There are countless Italian recipes for cooked vegetables—zucchini, eggplant, artichokes, etc.—that are ideal for picnicking; and a whole world of stuffed meat rolls, not to mention the desserts.

Redfish Lake is an hour's drive from Sun Valley with spectacular views along the way—mountains, sheltered green valleys, crystal streams, bird and game. There are open fields of wild mountain ranges. From here you can spot Mount Heyburn, the daisies and purple lupines. Halfway there, we reach Galena summit, which overlooks what seems a never-ending expanse of most impressive peak of all, overshadowing Redfish Lake, our destination.

Easily accessible by car, our beach is only a short walk from the parking spot, so we can take coolers, umbrellas, radios—all the paraphernalia for a day at the beach, including a folding table to spread the picnic on. One can sail, water-ski, fish and swim. The meal is leisurely, of course; the picnic is pleasantly time-consuming in the European tradition, served in a series of courses. The food is so good, and the setting so seductive, we usually spend the rest of the day lolling about in the sun sipping wine, napping or watching boats sail by.

SICILIAN ARTICHOKES

Serves 6–12

Each Sicilian cook claims to know the best way to prepare these stuffed artichokes, and there are variations for every region, house and mood.

6 *artichokes, with their stems*

Stuffing:

1 *cup fresh white bread crumbs*
1 *egg*
½ *cup finely minced fresh parsley*
3 *large cloves garlic, peeled and mashed*

1 *small fresh red pepper, finely minced,*
OR
3–4 *dried red peppers, seeds removed, soaked in hot water for*
30 minutes and then chopped finely*

salt and freshly ground pepper
6 *tablespoons of fresh green herbs—rosemary, mint, chervil,*
sage, thyme, or chives—minced
3 *tablespoons freshly grated Parmesan*

juice of 2 large lemons
3 *tablespoons olive oil*
1 *large clove garlic, peeled and cut in half*
salt and pepper to taste

Cut about ½ inch from the tough end of the artichoke stalks. Cut off the stems at the base of the artichokes and cook them in salted, boiling water in a medium-sized saucepan until tender (15–20 minutes). Drain and purée them in a blender with a little of the liquid in which they were cooked. Reserve. Pull out the center leaves of the artichokes, and scrape the central hairy part away from the base (or heart) with a spoon. (A grapefruit spoon works well, or a knife if the artichoke is very tough.)

Mix all the stuffing ingredients except the cheese together with a fork in a large mixing bowl. Add the purée from the stems, mixing well. Add enough liquid—milk, oil or water—a little at a time until the mixture has a

* If red peppers are unavailable, use green peppers and add a dash of Tabasco.

pasty consistency. Stir in the Parmesan.* Using a spoon and your fingers, sparsely fill the spaces between the leaves of the artichoke and the central cavity with the stuffing. After stuffing, push all the leaves gently inward and upward.

Heat the olive oil in a pot. Use a heavy-bottomed pot large enough to hold all the artichokes placed tightly side by side. Brown the artichokes quickly on all sides, three at a time. Pack the artichokes tightly upside down and side by side, in the pot. Add enough water to cover the artichokes one-third of the way up, add the lemon juice to the water, cover, bring to a boil, turn down the heat and simmer, tightly covered, until tender, 30 minutes to one hour. The time varies depending on the tenderness of the raw vegetable. Test for tenderness by prodding with a fork around the base or heart. Remove the cooking liquid, and let cool at room temperature. Boil down the cooking liquid with the garlic and seasoning to 1½–2 cups of dipping sauce.

Pack the artichokes in tightly secured plastic bags, and make sure they are propped right side up in your pack. Carry the sauce in a separate container. Serve each artichoke in a bowl in a pool of sauce in which the leaves can be dunked.

You can make this recipe several days in advance and refrigerate the artichokes, but be sure to bring them to room temperature before serving.

* If you have a Cuisinart or other food processor, blend all the ingredients for the stuffing just long enough to blend them.

PISSALADIÉRE

Serves 8–12

This dish, the precursor of pizza, comes from the south of France. It's actually an onion and tomato pie or tart. It's excellent picnic food—easy to pack, wonderful to eat, tepid or cold, and beautiful to look at.

Make one-half recipe of *pâte brisée* (page 152). Chill and roll out the dough to 12 inches in diameter. Line a 10-inch tart pan or a pie tin. Press a piece of buttered foil gently into the pan and against the sides, buttered side down. Bake 10 minutes in a preheated 425° oven, then remove foil. Bake 5 minutes more. Remove from oven and let cool. Pierce any bubbles in the pastry with a sharp-pointed knife.

    4 *tablespoons butter*
    2 *pounds (about 4 large) onions, peeled and finely chopped*
       to make 6 cups

2–3　*cloves garlic, peeled and pressed to make*
　　　1 tablespoon
　2　*pounds (about 4 large) fresh tomatoes*
　3　*tablespoons olive oil*
　2　*tablespoons tomato paste*
　2　*tablespoons finely chopped fresh basil leaves*
　　OR
　2　*teaspoons dried basil*
　2　*tablespoons finely chopped fresh parsley*
1½　*teaspoons dried oregano*
　1　*teaspoon salt*
　　freshly ground pepper
　1　*tablespoon dry bread crumbs*
20　*flat anchovies, drained well on paper towels*
20　*black Mediterranean-type olives*

　　　Oven temperature: 375°

Melt the butter in a large skillet; put the onions in the skillet, cover it, and
sauté them slowly over low heat for 10 minutes, stirring occasionally. Uncover, add the garlic, and cook 30 minutes more, stirring occasionally, until
the liquid in the pan has all evaporated and the onions are soft but not
brown. Reserve this mixture.

Blanch the tomatoes quickly in a pot of boiling water; cut them in half
and gently squeeze out the seeds and juice. Peel them and chop coarsely. In
another large skillet heat 2 tablespoons of the olive oil, add the tomatoes
and quickly bring them to a boil; continue to boil, uncovered, watching that
they don't burn and stirring frequently until the liquid has *all* evaporated
and the tomatoes are a thick pasty consistency.

Take off heat and mix in tomato paste, basil, 1 tablespoon parsley, and
the oregano. Combine the onion mixture and the tomato mixture in a mixing bowl, seasoning all with the salt and pepper.

Sprinkle the pastry shell with the bread crumbs to absorb any excess
moisture. Spoon the onion-tomato mixture into the shell, smoothing the top
with the back of a spoon. Arrange the anchovies over the top in an attractive
lattice type pattern. Arrange the olives between the anchovy strips. Sprinkle
1 tablespoon olive oil over all. Bake 30–40 minutes. Sprinkle with the rest
of the parsley when done.

Cool. Wrap the whole tart in foil to take to a picnic. Make this recipe in
two small 5-to-6-inch round tins or several smaller tart pans to carry in a
pack.

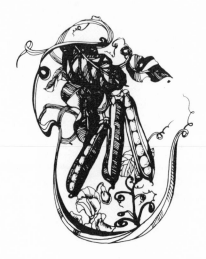

STUFFED EGGPLANT ROLLS

Serves 8

1 *large eggplant* (OR *2 small ones*)
   salt
½ *cup peanut* OR *vegetable oil*
½ *pound Ricotta cheese*
¼ *cup grated Parmesan*
   freshly ground pepper
2 *tablespoons chopped parsley*
1 *small clove garlic, peeled and minced*
⅓ *cup finely chopped walnuts*
1 *tablespoon olive oil*
2 *teaspoons red wine vinegar*
2 *teaspoons dried oregano*
1 *large can whole Italian plum tomatoes*
   salt and pepper
   Romano cheese, grated

Oven temperature: 325°

Slice the eggplant in quarter-inch slices. Sprinkle them with salt and let drain in a colander for half an hour. Thoroughly wipe the salt off with damp paper towels. Heat 3 tablespoons oil in a large skillet and fry the eggplant slices in the oil until soft and just golden brown, about 1 minute on each side, adding more oil as needed, a little at a time. Drain the eggplant on a paper bag as you continue to fry the remaining slices. Set them aside as you prepare the filling and preheat the oven.

Filling

In a small bowl combine the Ricotta and Parmesan cheeses. Add pepper to taste, 1 tablespoon of chopped parsley, garlic, walnuts, olive oil, vinegar and 1 teaspoon of the oregano. Mix well.

Spread a generous amount of this stuffing over each fried eggplant slice and fold it up. Arrange the rolls in a baking dish seam side down, and spread the tomato sauce over them.

Tomato Sauce

Put the Italian plum tomatoes in a 1-quart saucepan. Add salt and freshly ground black pepper to taste and the other teaspoon of oregano. Mix well, and with a metal spoon, mash the whole tomatoes up a bit.

Pour this mixture over the eggplant rolls and sprinkle with freshly grated Romano cheese and 1 tablespoon of chopped parsley. Bake for 45 minutes.

This dish is best served at room temperature. You may want to transfer the hot eggplant rolls right from the oven to your picnic container by placing them side by side in rows one on top of the other. You may refrigerate them before picnic time, but allow them to return to room temperature before serving.

WHITE BEAN SALAD

Serves 6

1 *cup dry white navy beans,*
   OR
1 *large can cooked white navy beans, drained and rinsed*

1 *bay leaf*
1 *small onion*
3 *cloves*
1 *slice bacon* OR *salt pork*
1 *tablespoon chopped parsley*

2 *tablespoons chopped fresh basil*
   OR
1 *teaspoon dried*

⅓ *cup olive oil*
2 *tablespoons wine vinegar* OR *lemon juice*
   salt and freshly ground pepper

If you're using dried beans, wash and drain them, then soak in water to cover overnight or for several hours. Drain, reserving liquid. Put beans in a 2½-quart saucepan. Add reserved liquid to measure 1½ quarts. Add the bay leaf, a small onion peeled and stuck with cloves, a slice of bacon or a piece of salt pork. Bring the beans to a boil and simmer slowly only until tender, about 1½ hours. (If you use canned beans, heat them up with the ingredients you cook dried beans with.) Do not overcook.

Drain them, rinse with cold water quickly, and while they are still warm, mix them in a bowl with the remaining herbs, oil and vinegar. Let them sit an hour at room temperature before chilling or pack them directly into a container to take for a picnic.

Variation: This bean salad is very good as it is. In Italy, it's often served with chunks of tuna tossed in it. Use water-packed tuna that will absorb the olive oil in the salad.

STUFFED VEAL ROLL

Serves 4–6

An Italian meat roll in the style of Parma.

> ½ *cup sliced large raw mushrooms*
> 1 *tablespoon butter*
> 1 *teaspoon lemon juice*
>   *salt and pepper*
> 2 *pounds of veal, from the leg, well-trimmed and flattened*
>   *pinch of sage*
>   *pinch of ground cloves*
>   *salt and pepper*
>   *grated rind of 1 lemon*
> 3 *thin slices of prosciutto* OR *baked ham*
> 3 *small hard-boiled eggs, peeled and sliced*
> 2 *tablespoons olive oil*
> ¾ *cup good dry white wine*

Sauté the mushrooms in a small frying pan over low heat in the butter with the lemon juice, salt and pepper to taste.

Season the veal by rubbing it with the sage, cloves, salt and pepper and lemon rind. Cover first with the ham, then the mushrooms, then the eggs. Roll up the meat and tie it securely with string. Tie the roast at one-inch intervals crosswise. Tuck the ends of the meat in and tie the roll length-

wise twice. Brown the meat in heated olive oil in a deep heavy pan. Pour
the wine in, reduce heat to low, and simmer, covered, for 2 hours.

Let the roll cool completely before slicing, then carve into pieces about an
inch thick. Wrap the stuffed veal roll into a double thickness of foil, and let
each person help himself or herself at the picnic site. It's a lovely picnic
entrée served chilled or tepid.

ORANGE, OLIVE, AND RED ONION SALAD

Serves 12

6 *oranges, peeled (take off both the skin and the white part)
   and sliced*
2 *medium-sized red onions, peeled, sliced thinly, and separated in rings*
2 *dozen Mediterranean-type black olives
   romaine lettuce*

Dressing:

¾ *cup olive oil*
3 *cloves garlic, peeled and minced
   juice of ½ a lemon
   salt and freshly ground black pepper*

Mix all the dressing ingredients in a small bowl.

Wash and dry some lettuce leaves, put them in a plastic bag and refrigerate.

In a medium bowl toss the orange slices and onion rings lightly with the
dressing. Put in a plastic container and refrigerate until time to pack.

Take olives and lettuce separately.

At serving time, line a large platter with the lettuce leaves. Arrange the
orange and onion slices on the bed of lettuce. Drain and scatter the olives
over all. Don't forget to take salad servers.

CASSATA SICILIANA

Yield: 1 cake

This is a delicious cake for any picnic, but it's become mandatory for our Italian ones. Its flavor mellows with age, so it tastes best a couple of days after it's baked. If you're in a hurry you can make it with a pound or sponge cake from a bakery, or even a frozen pound cake.

Start by making either a sponge or a pound cake.

Italian Sponge Cake (Pan di Spagna)

    8 *eggs, separated*
    1 *cup sugar*
    1 *cup cake flour, sifted*
    ½ *teaspoon salt*
    1 *tablespoon white wine*
    1 *teaspoon vanilla, rum* OR *brandy*
    1 *tablespoon lemon juice*
    1 *teaspoon grated lemon peel*

    Oven temperature: 350°

Preheat oven. Grease and flour the sides, but not the bottom, of a 9-inch tube pan. Beat the egg yolks with sugar until creamy. Gradually add the rest of the ingredients, beating constantly with an electric mixer. In another bowl, beat the egg whites until stiff and fold gently into the first mixture. Turn the batter into the pan and bake for 45 minutes. (In a high altitude, add 2 tablespoons flour and bake for 55 minutes.) Test with a toothpick for doneness.

Invert the cake pan, propping it up so that air can circulate between the cake and the countertop. Let the cake cool in the inverted pan, and remove it by loosening the edges with a knife and tapping the bottom of the pan.

Pound Cake

    1   *cup butter, softened*
    1½ *cup sugar*
    1   *teaspoon grated lemon rind*
    5   *eggs*
    1   *teaspoon vanilla extract*
    2   *cups cake flour, sifted*
    ¼   *teaspoon cream of tartar*
    ¼   *teaspoon salt*

    Oven temperature: 300°

Grease and flour a 9-inch tube pan. Do not preheat the oven.

With an electric mixer, cream together the butter, sugar and lemon rind until creamy and well blended. Beat in the eggs one at a time. Add the vanilla. Resift the flour with the cream of tartar and salt. Stir it into the batter a little at a time, and blend slowly. Beat the batter at a slow speed for two minutes.

Turn into the greased pan, and put into a cold oven. Set the oven at 300° and bake for 2 hours. (In a high altitude, increase the flour by two tablespoons and bake slightly longer.) Cool in the pan for about 10 minutes and turn out on a wire rack to finish cooling.

When the sponge or pound cake is completely cooled, carefully slice it into three thin layers, using a bread knife.

Make the following filling:

Filling

    1 *pound Ricotta, at room temperature*
    ½ *cup grated bitter chocolate*
    ½ *cup chopped candied fruit*
    ½ *cup chopped almonds*
    1 *ounce orange-flavored liqueur*
    ½ *teaspoon grated orange rind*

Mix the Ricotta with a wooden spoon for a few minutes until soft and creamy, and then mix in all the other ingredients until well blended. Spread between the layers of the cake, leaving the top and sides bare. Frost the top and sides with the following chocolate frosting.

Chocolate Frosting (Glassatura al Cioccolato)

    1½ *cups sugar*
    1½ *cups hot water*
    2 *ounces grated unsweetened chocolate*
    ⅓ *cup cornstarch*
    ¼ *cup cold water*
    1 *teaspoon vanilla extract* OR *almond flavoring*

Mix sugar, hot water and chocolate in saucepan over heat, stirring constantly until the sugar dissolves. Boil for 5 minutes, stirring the entire time. Dissolve the cornstarch in the cold water. Over medium heat, add to the chocolate mixture and slowly stir until thick and creamy. Remove from heat, add the flavoring and beat until cool enough to spread.

This cake can be taken in a picnic basket, or even in a pack if you put it into a hard-sided container or a small shoe box.

SPUMONI ICE CREAM

> Yield: 1½–2 quarts

   5 *egg yolks*
1½ *cups sugar*
   3 *cups milk*
   1 *cup heavy cream*
   3 *tablespoons cornstarch*
   3 *tablespoons chopped candied fruits*
   1 *ounce unsweetened chocolate, grated*
   3 *tablespoons unsalted pistachio nuts, chopped*

Beat the egg yolks until creamy pale-yellow, and mix in sugar.

Mix 2½ cups milk and the heavy cream in a large saucepan. In a small bowl, blend the cornstarch with ½ cup cold milk and stir it into the milk-cream mixture. Cook this mixture over a low flame for about 10 minutes, until the mixture is almost at the boiling point, but *do not boil*.

Stir a few spoonfuls, one at a time, of the milk mixture into the egg-sugar mixture, mixing well with each addition. Then add the egg-sugar mixture to the pan of milk and cook over low heat, stirring constantly with a wooden spoon, until the mixture coats the spoon. Remove from heat.

Stir in the fruits, chocolate and nuts, and let cool. Pour into a large plastic container and refrigerate to thoroughly chill mixture. Take this container to a picnic in a cooler. (The custard must be chilled when it's poured into the ice cream freezer.) Follow the instructions for your type of ice cream freezer.

It takes only about half an hour to make the ice cream, and volunteers can take turns cranking while the picnic is being laid out.

HOT ESPRESSO

With your favorite espresso maker, make enough good Italian espresso to serve each picnicker a 3-ounce cup. Pour boiling water into a thermos to heat it. Let it sit 5 minutes and then empty. Pour in the hot coffee.

Take lemon-peel twists, wrapped in plastic wrap, to be served with each cup of coffee.

If there is a fireplace with a grill for cooking at your picnic site, it is easier to take powdered instant espresso and a pouring pot in which to boil water. Each picnicker can then have second cups of coffee with their spumoni and cassata.

AUTUMN

A ROADSIDE PICNIC

A Highway in Nevada

Fresh-squeezed Orange Juice,
    Packed with Ice in a Thermos
Cold Green-Pepper Soup
French Omelette Picnic Loaf
Pâté Maison
Pickled Mushrooms
Fig, Fresh Fruit and Walnut
    Plate, served with
    Cookies and Chocolate
Café au Lait

Take a picnic basket and a small cooler for drinks and perishable food whenever you're traveling by car. Though it's awfully easy, it's never really gratifying to stop at a drive-in or greasy spoon. We always try to prepare a delicious home-made meal that we can eat whenever our appetites and the scenery concur that it's time for lunch.

We took this "brunch" picnic on an autumn trip through the Nevada desert. Having left Sun Valley early in the morning, we stopped for brunch just before noon when we found a roadside table with a remarkable view of the open desert and sky.

We carried cold soup in a thermos, and mushrooms made days in advance. The French Omelette Picnic Loaf we had is a wonderful peasant concoction that travels easily, stores well, and provides enough leftovers for the next day's lunch as well. Carrying stuffed bread loaves like this, or Torta Rustica (see page 172), is common practice for travelers in Spain and Italy.

If you don't have the time to prepare a picnic loaf, substitute a good fresh loaf of French bread, and the best cheese, sausages and cold cuts you can find. You can often buy fresh fruit at roadside stands, but plan to take along extras like dried figs and walnuts. This picnic could turn out to be the highlight of your trip.

COLD GREEN-PEPPER SOUP

Serves 6

2 *green peppers, washed, cored and seeded*
1 *stalk celery, with leaves, scrubbed*
1 *small onion, peeled and thinly sliced*
1 *cup water*
2 *cups good vegetable* OR *chicken broth*
2 *tablespoons arrowroot* OR *instantized flour*
1 *cup light cream*
  salt
  pepper
  pinch thyme

Chop the peppers finely. Reserve and wrap in plastic wrap about 2–3 tablespoons of the chopped pepper for a garnish. Combine peppers, onion, celery stalk and water in a large (2½ quart) saucepan. Bring to a boil, reduce heat and simmer uncovered fifteen minutes. Cool and take out the celery and put the rest of the mixture into a blender; blend for a few seconds. Put the broth and the pepper mixture in a saucepan. In a small bowl, mix the arrowroot or flour with ¼ cup water to form a thin paste. Stir this mixture into the pepper broth and heat to boiling, stirring constantly. Then take off heat and stir in the light cream and seasoning, chill thoroughly, and pour into a cold thermos. When serving, top with a few bits of chopped pepper.

FRENCH OMELETTE PICNIC LOAF

Serves 6–8

This recipe is best when made with homemade French bread (see page 208), which keeps the omelette wonderfully moist. If you'd prefer, you can use any good round French or sourdough bread. Since you can keep the omelette warm by wrapping it in several thicknesses of foil, it's equally good for any season's picnic.

1 *large round loaf of French bread*
2 *tablespoons olive oil*
5 *tablespoons butter*
10 *ounces ham, chopped*
1 *large new potato, cooked, peeled and sliced*
    (see "To Boil Potatoes," page 287)
1 *pound mushrooms, wiped clean and chopped*
1 *onion, peeled and finely chopped*
2 *cloves garlic, mashed*
1 *green pepper, washed, cored, seeded and chopped*
9 *eggs*
1 *teaspoon salt*
½ *teaspoon pepper*
1 *tablespoon milk*
1 *cup grated Gruyère or Swiss cheese*

Oven temperature: 300°

Split the bread in half horizontally and hollow out the loaf, leaving a one-inch thickness of bread lining the loaf. Brush the cut surfaces with a tablespoon of the olive oil and place the two halves together. Wrap in foil and keep warm in the oven while preparing the omelette.

In a large omelette pan, sauté the ham, potato, mushrooms, onion and garlic over high heat in the remaining olive oil and 2 tablespoons of butter until all ingredients are slightly browned, about 3 minutes. Add the green pepper and cook 5 minutes longer. Remove mixture to a plate.

With a wire whisk, beat the eggs with the salt and pepper and a little milk. Use an omelette pan about the same size or smaller than the loaf of bread. Over a very high flame heat the omelette pan to hot with 2 tablespoons butter. Pour in the eggs and cook 1 minute. Lower heat to moderate. Distribute the vegetable mixture over the eggs and sprinkle the grated cheese on top. As the edges begin to set, push the part that is already set toward the center and shake pan vigorously to allow the uncooked egg to flow underneath. Cook omelette until the top is just set but appears moist, and the bottom is golden brown (about four more minutes). To turn the omelette, run a large metal spatula around the edge and under it to loosen. Place a plate over the pan and invert the pan quickly. Add another tablespoon of butter to the pan and gently slide omelette back into the pan. Cook another minute and a half until almost brown on the other side; remove from heat. Fill the hollowed bread loaf with the omelette by inverting the pan over one half of the bread loaf. Replace the top half of the bread and wrap in several thicknesses of foil to keep warm up to four hours.

PÂTÉ MAISON

Serves 8–10

The chicken liver pâté here is a thick mixture, and a good spread for toast and crackers.

1½ *tablespoons butter*
¼ *pound salt pork, diced*
1 *onion, peeled and minced*
1 *pound chicken livers, washed, drained and coarsely chopped*
2 *whole cloves*
1 *bay leaf*
¼ *teaspoon nutmeg*
salt and freshly ground black pepper to taste
3 *tablespoons dry sherry*
1–2 *tablespoons cream*

Melt the butter in a medium-sized skillet. Add the salt pork, onion and chicken livers, cloves, bay leaf, nutmeg, salt and pepper. Cook over medium heat, stirring until the liver is just tender, still slightly pink inside. Add the sherry, turn off the heat, and stir. Let the mixture cool. Put it in a blender with the cream and blend until smooth. Store in a heavy crock.

When using a picnic basket, take the whole crock and some small squares of toast or thinly sliced French bread on which to spread the pâté. If backpacking, take the pâté in a small plastic container, and serve from a small wooden bowl.

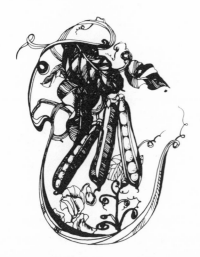

PICKLED MUSHROOMS

Yield: 2 pints

3 *cups white wine*
4 *tablespoons Japanese rice vinegar* OR *cider vinegar*
2 *stalks celery, scrubbed*
4 *tablespoons olive oil*
4 *teaspoons salt*
2 *cloves garlic, peeled and crushed*
1 *pound fresh mushroom caps, wiped clean with a damp cloth*

Clean two pint-size canning jars and lids by running them through a dish-washer cycle or by immersing in boiling water.

Simmer all the ingredients except the mushroom caps in a 2-quart sauce-pan for 10 minutes. Strain the liquid and return it to the pan. Add the mushrooms and simmer for 3 to 5 minutes. Pour the mushrooms into the jars, being careful to screw the lids down tightly. Refrigerate. When pack-ing for your picnic, transfer as many as you'll need to a small plastic con-tainer. Store in your cooler, since these are best when served quite cold.

FIG, FRESH FRUIT AND WALNUT PLATE, SERVED WITH COOKIES AND CHOCOLATE

On a plate arrange some fresh fruit, such as a sliced apple, some fresh halved apricots, or a bunch of Concord grapes. On the same plate put sev-eral dried figs and some walnut halves. With the fruit plate, serve small squares of semisweet chocolate and petite beurre biscuits or shortbread cookies.

CAFÉ AU LAIT

Serves 4

3 *cups strong coffee*
1 *half-inch vanilla bean*
1 *cup milk*
   dash cinnamon
   honey to taste

Brew 3 cups of good, strong coffee using 3 measures of a good blend and one measure of espresso, freshly ground if possible. Put the vanilla bean in with the ground coffee before brewing. Keep the coffee hot while heating milk to a simmer in a small pan. Stir the hot milk vigorously with a whisk, adding a dash of cinnamon.

Have a preheated thermos ready. Pour the hot coffee and the milk into it. Pass around a small container of honey at the picnic.

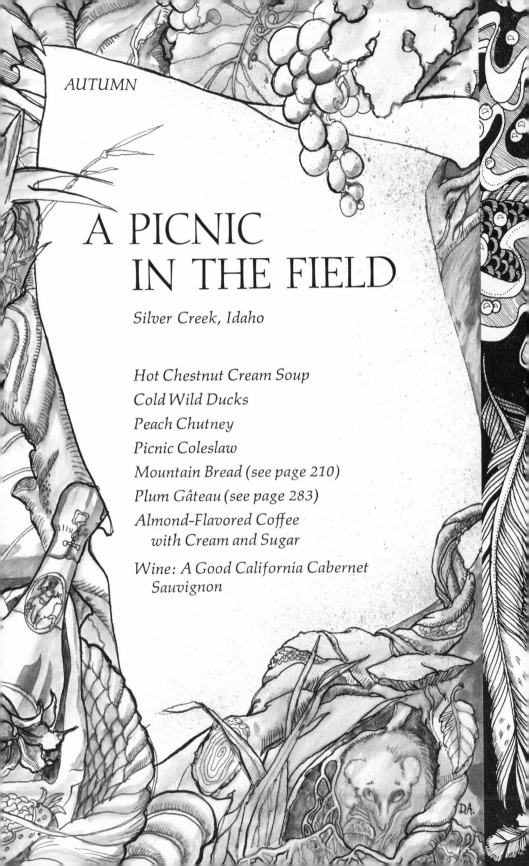

AUTUMN

A PICNIC
IN THE FIELD

Silver Creek, Idaho

Hot Chestnut Cream Soup

Cold Wild Ducks

Peach Chutney

Picnic Coleslaw

Mountain Bread *(see page 210)*

Plum Gâteau *(see page 283)*

Almond-Flavored Coffee
    with Cream and Sugar

Wine: *A Good California Cabernet*
    Sauvignon

One of the most delightful of all occasions counting in the pattern of life is a hunting luncheon. . . . After several hours of exercise, the most vigorous hunter feels a need for rest; his face has been caressed by the early-morning breeze; his skill has served him well on occasion; the sun is about to stand at its peak in the sky; it is time for the sportsman to stop for a few hours. . . . A bit of shade attracts him; the grass is soft beneath him, and the murmur of a nearby stream suggests that he leave cooling in it the flask meant for his refreshment. . . . These pleasures are immeasurably heightened if several friends share them; for, in this case, a more copious feast is brought along in one of the old military cook-wagons now put to a gentler use. Everyone chatters eagerly about this chap's skill and that one's bad luck. . . . There are certain days when our wives, our sisters and our pretty cousins and their equally pretty friends are invited to share our amusements.

—Brillat-Savarin

W*e share Brillat-Savarin's sentiments, but the military wagon is now a Jeep or Land-Rover and ladies are included in the hunting party instead of being imported to decorate the luncheon.*

We leave the house in the predawn hours in order to arrive at a blind or other advantageous position before the ducks' first morning flight. Those of us who don't hunt think it's worth the trip just to witness this sight.

Since we leave so early, lunch must be completely prepared the night before. Our menu, consisting of fall delicacies, is perfect for the long, golden days.

HOT CHESTNUT CREAM SOUP

Serves 8–10

2 *tablespoons butter*
2 *carrots, scrubbed, pared and cut into chunks*
2 *stalks celery with leaves, washed and coarsely chopped*
2 *onions, peeled and coarsely chopped*
1 *veal knuckle, cracked (your butcher will do this for you)*
6 *cups boiling water*
1½ *cups dry white wine*
½ *tablespoon salt*

1 *pound fresh chestnuts*
    OR
2 *15-ounce cans fresh chestnut purée*

2 *whole cloves (tied in cheesecloth)*
½ *cup heavy cream*
¼ *cup brandy*
salt and freshly ground pepper
chopped parsley

Melt the butter in a large, heavy-bottomed kettle, and cook the carrots, celery and onions over medium heat for about 10 minutes, stirring occasionally. Add the veal knuckle, water, wine and salt. Bring to a boil, adjust heat, cover and simmer for 2 hours.

Peel the chestnuts by slitting the flat side of each one. Place them in a saucepan and cover with boiling water. Continue boiling until soft (about 20–25 minutes). Drain the chestnuts, and while still warm, remove the loosened shells and skin.

After the stock has simmered for 2 hours, take it off the heat and let it cool. Remove the veal knuckle and any meat, skin or excess fat. Strain the stock, reserving the vegetables. Return the vegetables to the pot with 4 cups of the stock, the peeled chestnuts and the cloves. Cover and simmer for 20 minutes. Remove the cloves. Purée the mixture a little at a time in a blender, food mill, or Cuisinart food processor until it is smooth.

If using canned chestnut purée, which will make excellent soup, purée the soup vegetables in a blender after straining the stock. Add this mixture with the canned chestnut purée to the strained stock, stirring well. You do not need to simmer or purée the broth again—just stir well with a whisk and continue with the last step.

Return the mixture to the pot and add the cream and brandy, bringing soup to a simmer. Add more salt and pepper, if needed. Pour the hot soup into a preheated thermos.

Carry the thermos of soup to your picnic, and take parsley wrapped in plastic wrap separately. When ready to serve, sprinkle each serving with parsley. One large thermos will serve four nicely, so you can freeze the other quart of soup for another outing.

COLD WILD DUCKS

Serves 4

Use this recipe for wild duck only, since it is served medium rare. It is the simplest, and one of the very best, ways to prepare wild ducks.

    2 *wild ducks*
    ¼ *pound salt pork cut in small strips (optional)*
    3 *tablespoons gin*
    4 *tablespoons soy sauce*
      salt and pepper
    4 *tablespoons oil*
    1 *tablespoon melted butter*
    2 *shallots, cut up*
    2 *small onions, peeled and coarsely chopped*
    2 *small apples, coarsely chopped*
      some celery leaves
    2 *ounces brandy*
      watercress
      wild mint

   Oven temperature: 450°

Preheat oven. Pluck and clean the ducks. If you wish, you can lard the breasts at this point. (Boil the salt pork for 10 minutes and drain. Rinse with cold water. Use it in a larding needle to lard the duck breasts.) Mix the gin and the soy sauce and rub part of this mixture into the ducks. Salt and pepper well, then let them rest in the remaining sauce thirty minutes at least, and preferably several hours. In a large heavy skillet, heat the oil and butter together until sizzling. Brown the ducks quickly on all sides until a dark-golden color.

Have the oven hot. Put a shallot, an onion, an apple, and some celery tops into each cavity loosely—don't truss—and bake the ducks in an open roasting pan for 35 minutes (45 minutes in higher altitudes). Baste a couple of times with the butter-oil mixture in which they were browned, melting more butter in the pan if necessary. Test for doneness. Wild duck should always be served pink or medium rare. In fact, many people prefer wild duck as rare as steak, in which case cook them 20 to 25 minutes only. Pour 2 ounces warmed flaming brandy over them.

If you can resist eating them now, let them cool to room temperature and cut them into serving pieces with poultry shears. Pack the pieces in a plastic container. Since you will want to serve the duck pieces on a bed of watercress and wild mint, take these greens, or others, along in a small plastic bag, unless you're sure you can pick them along the way. Serve the duck with both sweet and sour condiments, such as peach chutney (see below) and pickled onions (see page 246).

PEACH CHUTNEY

Yield: 2 quarts

½ cup chopped onion
½ pound raisins
1 clove garlic
4 pounds peaches, washed, peeled,* pitted and
    cut in small pieces
⅔ cup fresh ginger root
    OR chopped candied or powdered ginger to taste
2 tablespoons chili powder
2 tablespoons mustard seed
1 tablespoon salt
1 quart cider vinegar
1½ pounds brown sugar

* It's easier to peel peaches if you blanch them in boiling water.

Put onion, raisins and garlic through food chopper, using medium blade, or chop by hand. Mix with peaches and all the spices, vinegar and sugar in a large kettle.

Bring mixture to a boil, turn down heat, and simmer for 1 hour or longer until the mixture turns a rich brown color and becomes fairly thick. Pour into washed and scalded jars and seal. Pour melted paraffin over the top to seal, just as in jam-making.

PICNIC COLESLAW

Serves 6–8

3 cups shredded cabbage (½ head)
1 cup shredded carrot
½ small red onion, peeled, thinly sliced and separated into rings
½ cup sour cream
1 tablespoon sugar
2 tablespoons tarragon vinegar
½ teaspoon salt

Combine cabbage, carrot and onion with the sour cream, sugar, vinegar and salt in a large bowl. Toss the slaw to coat thoroughly, and chill before picnic time. Carry the slaw in a plastic container, and take a pretty bowl and a large spoon for serving.

ALMOND-FLAVORED COFFEE WITH CREAM AND SUGAR

Serves 4

4 cups coffee
3 drops almond extract
  cream to taste
  sugar to taste

Brew 4 cups of your favorite blend of coffee. Just before pouring into the thermos, carefully add 3 drops (no more than ⅛ teaspoon) of almond extract, using an eyedropper or your finger on the bottle opening to let a drop at a time escape.

Take cream and sugar cubes separately in little jars. Take enamel cups and plastic spoons for serving.

A CROSS-COUNTRY SKIING PICNIC

Fox Creek, Idaho

Cabbage Soup Supreme

Rice Salad Vinaigrette

Smoky Eggplant

Sourdough Rye Bread
  (see page 214)

Rolled Stuffed Flank Steak

Cocoa Bars

Honey Cream-Cheese Cake

Hot Tea with Lemon and Honey

Wine: Zinfandel

This was more than a typical winter cross-country skiing picnic. Eight of us had to cross the Wood River to gain access to a lovely narrow valley full of elk, deer, rabbit and mink tracks. One man wearing rubber fishing waders stood in a shallow place in the river and pulled each person with skis, packs, etc., across in a little rubber boat. It was a bright, beautifully sunny day. Breaking trail through the willows of Fox Creek, we made our way up a narrow canyon to the top of a ridge with an expansive view across a shallow white basin to the snow-covered rolling hills beyond. There were several groupings of small evergreen trees; otherwise the landscape was entirely white, open and undisturbed.

It was very cold by the time we reached a desirable picnic spot. The picnic began immediately, as all winter picnics must, with hot, hot soup from a thermos. We quickly built a fire and sat on logs and mats and passed the food. We ate with big gloves on, but that did not detract from the enjoyment of the food at all.

CABBAGE SOUP SUPREME

Yield: 2 quarts

¼ *head white cabbage, finely chopped*
¼ *cup heavy cream*
   pinch of nutmeg
   dash white pepper
1 *cup milk*
1 *quart duck soup (page 97)*
     OR *chicken stock (page 93)*

Boil the cabbage in a pot of water until it is tender (about 20 minutes). Drain the cabbage and add the cream, nutmeg and pepper to the pot. Turn off the heat and let the cabbage-cream mixture cool. Then purée it in a blender. Add the milk and blend a few minutes more. Taste for seasoning.

Add this mixture to the basic duck soup or any good white stock, and bring it to a simmer, being careful not to let it boil. This is an outstanding hearty hot first course.

To transport, pour the soup into a large, 2-quart thermos or two 1-quart ones. Heat the thermoses with hot water before pouring in the soup.

Variations: Substitute cauliflower or celery for the cabbage.

RICE SALAD VINAIGRETTE

Serves 10

3 *cups cooked rice*
1 *cup minced red onion*
½ *cup chopped green pepper*
½ *cup chopped red pepper*
½ *cup cooked sliced green beans*
⅓ *cup vinaigrette sauce (page 178)*
¼ *cup chopped pimento*

Combine the first five ingredients and toss with vinaigrette. Place in attractive plastic picnic container, and take the pimento in a separate container. At the picnic, serve onto individual plates. Garnish with pimento. Take a serving spoon and forks for each person.

SMOKY EGGPLANT

Serves 6

1 *large eggplant*
1 *small onion, peeled and finely chopped*
1 *small green pepper, washed, cored, seeded and finely chopped*
3 *tablespoons olive oil*
2 *cloves garlic, peeled and mashed*
1 *teaspoon salt*
  freshly ground pepper
1 *tablespoon lemon juice*

Oven temperature: 350°

Roast the whole eggplant over a charcoal grill, or directly over the flame on a gas stove, charring the skin until it is black. Bake the whole eggplant for twenty minutes in preheated oven. Let it cool, then peel it. Coarsely chop the pulp, place it in a bowl, add the onion, green pepper, olive oil, garlic, salt, pepper and lemon juice, and mix well.

Put in a plastic container to take to a picnic. If the container is not attractive enough for serving, take a wooden bowl. Serve as a very special dip, condiment, or side dish.

ROLLED STUFFED FLANK STEAK

Serves 6–8

1–2½ *pounds flank steak*
  2 *tablespoons butter*
  ¼ *cup chopped mushrooms*
  1 *fresh shallot, chopped*
  ½ *cup chopped pecans*
  2 *tablespoons chopped parsley*
  ¾ *cup bread cubes, made from dry Italian or French bread*
  ½ *teaspoon salt*
    freshly ground black pepper to taste
  1 *cardamom pod, crushed,* OR *a pinch of dried cardamom*
    pinch of ground cloves
    a few shavings of fresh OR *frozen ginger root*

1 *egg*
½ *cup orange juice*
½ *cup dry vermouth* OR *bouillon*

Oven temperature: 350°

Preheat oven. Pound the steak and score it lightly on both sides. In a skillet, heat the butter; add mushrooms and shallot and cook 3 minutes. Turn off heat and add nuts, parsley, bread cubes, salt, pepper, cardamom, cloves, ginger and egg; mix well. Spread mixture over the top of the steak. Roll the meat up from the narrowest end, like a jelly roll, and tie with string at two-inch intervals. Tuck the ends in. With another string, tie lengthwise twice. Brown on both sides in a little fat in a skillet or Dutch oven. Add orange juice and vermouth, cover and cook 2 hours. Let cool.

To serve, cut into slices less than one inch thick. Put roll back together and wrap tightly in foil while still warm. Take a plastic jar full of the cooking sauce to pour over the meat as it is served. Place the roll, slices overlapping, on a plastic or paper plate on the picnic "table." Garnish with watercress or parsley.

We usually make a double portion of this recipe. Have one roll for dinner the same night you make it, or refrigerate it and then heat it up for the next day's dinner. Wrap the other roll for the picnic.

COCOA BARS

Yield: 15 bars

¼ *cup butter* OR *margarine, softened*
1 *cup sugar*
1 *teaspoon vanilla extract*
2 *eggs*
¼ *cup milk*
1 *cup sifted all-purpose flour*
2 *tablespoons cocoa*
¼ *teaspoon salt*
½ *cup chopped walnuts*

Oven temperature: 375°

Cream butter and gradually add sugar and vanilla, creaming all together well. Beat in eggs one at a time. Stir in milk. Sift together dry ingredients and stir into creamed mixture. Add nuts. Spread into a greased 9 × 9 × 2 inch pan. Bake for 20 minutes or until done. Frost cake with:

Cocoa Frosting

1½ *tablespoons cocoa*
1 *tablespoon milk*
¼ *teaspoon vanilla extract*
1½ *tablespoons butter, softened*
⅔ *cup sifted confectioners' sugar*

With spoon, blend cocoa, milk, vanilla, butter and sugar. Cool iced cake and cut into bars.

Wrap the bars individually in foil or plastic wrap and carry them in a hard-sided plastic container.

HONEY CREAM-CHEESE CAKE

Makes 15 squares or 1 loaf

¼ *cup butter* OR *margarine, softened*
½ *cup sugar*
½ *cup all-purpose flour*
½ *teaspoon ground cinnamon*
1 *pound cream cheese, at room temperature*
½ *cup honey*
4 *eggs*
½ *cup lemon juice*
⅛ *cup finely grated lemon peel*
1 *teaspoon vanilla extract*
1 *tablespoon all-purpose flour*

Oven temperature: 375°

Preheat oven. Butter a 9-inch square cake pan.

In a medium-size mixing bowl, cream butter and stir in ¼ cup of the sugar. Add the ½ cup of flour and the cinnamon and mix until ingredients are well blended. Pat mixture evenly and firmly into the bottom of the prepared pan. Bake 15 minutes or until crust is lightly browned; remove pan from oven. Turn oven up to 500°.

In the large bowl of an electric mixer, beat cream cheese until light; add honey and the remaining ¼ cup of sugar and beat until light and fluffy. Add eggs one at a time, beating well after each addition. Add remaining ingredients and beat until well blended. Pour cheese mixture evenly over crust in pan. Bake 12 minutes. Turn oven down to 300° and bake 30 minutes longer. Turn oven off. Leave cake in oven with door closed for 30 minutes. Remove cake from oven, let cool completely, and then cover with foil and chill in refrigerator at least several hours, or up to two days.

It is now ready for your backpack or basket. You can carry the loaf whole, and cut into small squares at the site, or cut the cake into 3-inch squares and wrap individually in plastic wrap. Carry these squares in a hard-sided container.

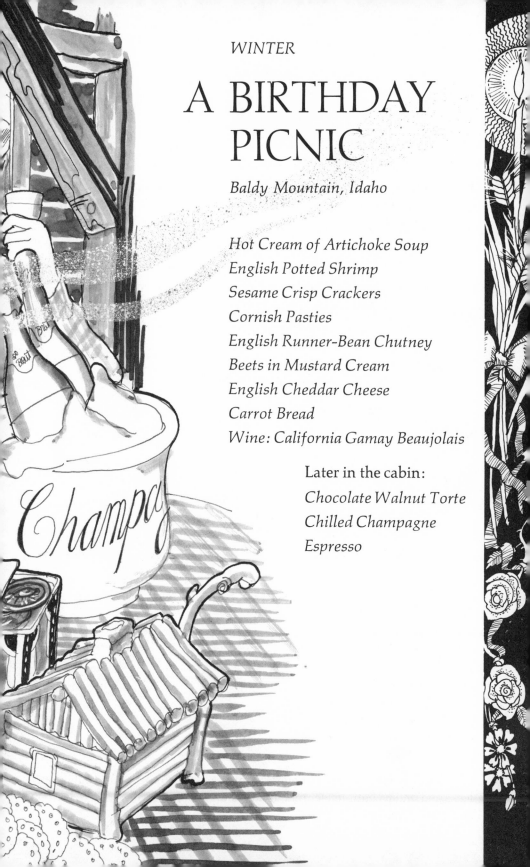

A BIRTHDAY PICNIC

Baldy Mountain, Idaho

Hot Cream of Artichoke Soup
English Potted Shrimp
Sesame Crisp Crackers
Cornish Pasties
English Runner-Bean Chutney
Beets in Mustard Cream
English Cheddar Cheese
Carrot Bread
Wine: California Gamay Beaujolais

Later in the cabin:
Chocolate Walnut Torte
Chilled Champagne
Espresso

During a day of alpine skiing, a picnic lunch at a table strategically placed for maximum sun exposure is a great treat. We held this particular picnic in midwinter on Baldy Mountain. The occasion was our friend Karin's birthday, and the flavor was English in honor of Karin's English husband.

The sun was shining and skiing conditions were excellent. Exhilarated by several runs before lunch, everyone enjoyed the meal so much that we had very little to carry down. The birthday cake, a delectable walnut torte, chilled champagne and espresso waited for us at a friend's cabin in the valley below.

HOT CREAM OF ARTICHOKE SOUP

Yield: 2 quarts

Vary this recipe by changing the vegetable. It is also good served cold in summer.

4 tablespoons butter
2 leeks, sliced, including a little of the greens
2 yellow onions, peeled and sliced
4 tablespoons all-purpose flour
6 large fresh artichokes
  OR
2 small cans of artichoke hearts or bottoms packed in water,
   not pickled

1 cup water
2 cups chicken stock (homemade or the equivalent made with
   2 chicken bouillon cubes or canned bouillon)
3 cups milk
  pinch of sugar
2 teaspoons salt
½ teaspoon white pepper
1 cup heavy cream

In a large heavy-bottomed pot over low heat melt the butter; then sauté the leeks and onions until tender (about 20–30 minutes). Add the flour and stir a few minutes.

While the onions are cooking, boil the artichokes in a large pot with water to cover for about 30 minutes, or until tender. When cool enough to handle, remove bottoms and edible parts of leaves. (Cut away all the leaves and the hairy center, leaving the heart or bottom. Cut the hearts into pieces, and cut off the tender bases of the leaves.) If using canned artichokes, drain the hearts. Place all the pieces in a blender with the water and purée. Place puréed liquid in the pot with the onions, leeks and flour, stirring to mix. Add stock, milk, sugar, salt and pepper. Cook until slightly thickened.

When ready to serve, mix cream into soup. Heat, but do not boil. Place soup in 2 large (1 quart) thermoses. Each thermos will serve six.

ENGLISH POTTED SHRIMP

Serves 6–10

 2 *cups small shrimp, rinsed, shelled and deveined*
½ *pound butter*
½ *teaspoon mace*
¼ *teaspoon nutmeg*
 1 *teaspoon lemon juice*
½ *teaspoon salt*
½ *teaspoon finely minced chives*
½ *teaspoon finely minced chervil or parsley*

Cook shrimp by dropping them into a pot of boiling water. Boil until pink, a few minutes. Melt butter in a small saucepan, add all the rest of the ingredients, and turn off the heat. Drain the shrimp, rinse with cold water and put back in the pan. Pour some of the butter mixture over the shrimp, coating all of them; then pack the mixture snugly, but taking care not to crush the shrimp, in a small mold, and pour the rest of the butter over them and chill well in the refrigerator. Use as a spread on bread or crackers. For a picnic unmold the shrimp on a small plate lined with lettuce. For backpacking, wrap the mold in an unbreakable container in a leakproof plastic bag, tie securely and set squarely horizontal in a pack. Bury in the snow to solidify before unmolding. It was served with sesame crisp crackers for this picnic, but is also wonderful served with thinly sliced black Russian rye.

SESAME CRISP CRACKERS

Yield: 3–4 dozen

1½ *cups whole-wheat flour*
¼ *cup soy flour*
¼ *cup sesame seeds*
¾ *teaspoon salt*
¼ *cup oil*
½ *cup water*

Oven temperature: 350°

Stir flours, seeds and salt together; pour in oil and blend well. Add enough water to the dough to make it pie-dough consistency. Gather the dough into a ball, then roll it to ⅛ inch thick. Cut it in circular cracker shapes and place on an ungreased baking sheet. Bake about 20 minutes or until crackers are crisp and golden. Pack crackers carefully in a hard plastic container or a can so that they will not get broken in transit.

CORNISH PASTIES

Serves 6

This recipe found its way to Idaho in the late 1800's during mining days and is still popular today. It tastes good at any temperature and is particularly hearty and satisfying for a winter picnic entrée.

Cornish Pasty Filling

1 *pound sirloin tip cut into ¼-inch cubes*
3 *raw potatoes, washed, peeled and chopped finely*
5 *green onions, minced (green parts, too)*
salt and pepper

Pasty Crust

Yield: 10–12 pasties

1 *cup lard* OR *shortening*
1 *tablespoon butter*
4 *cups flour*
2 *tablespoons salt*
½ *teaspoon baking powder*
2–3 *tablespoons ice water*

1 *egg, slightly beaten*
1 *tablespoon cream*

Oven temperature: 425°

Put meat and vegetables in a bowl. Add seasoning to taste and mix well.

Cut the fats into the flour mixed with salt and baking powder, and add just enough ice-cold water to make a stiff dough. On a floured board roll out to about ⅛ inch thick and cut circles about 5 inches in diameter.* (A bowl or a funnel turned upside down works well for this.)

Into the center of each circle, put a mound of filling ingredients. Moisten around the edge of the pasty and fold in half, pressing the edges together with a fork. Brush the pasties with a mixture of 1 egg and 1 tablespoon of cream beaten together. Make a small hole in each one to allow the steam to escape. Bake for 1 hour. (Cover with foil if crust browns too quickly.)

To pack, lay them one on top of the other in a hard-sided container deep enough to hold them stacked so they won't be broken en route.

* You might want to cut slightly larger 6-inch circles if you'll be serving these pasties at home.

ENGLISH RUNNER-BEAN CHUTNEY

Yield: 5–6 pints

2 *pounds fresh runner beans (green beans), with ends snapped*
    and loose strings peeled off
3 *medium-size onions, peeled and coarsely chopped*
3 *cups cider vinegar*
2 *pounds dark-brown sugar*
1½ *tablespoons cornstarch*
1½ *tablespoons turmeric*
1 *teaspoon dry mustard*
    dash of salt

Wash and sterilize 6 pint jars and their lids in a dishwasher or in boiling water for 10 minutes. In a large saucepan cook beans in salted water to cover over medium heat for 20 minutes or until tender. Drain, rinse in cold water, chop coarsely, and return to saucepan.

In another saucepan boil onions in 1 cup vinegar for 5 minutes. Add the onion and vinegar mixture to the beans. Add 2 more cups of vinegar, brown sugar, cornstarch, turmeric, mustard, and salt. Boil gently for 10 minutes. Ladle mixture into jars, wiping off rim of jar with clean damp cloth before placing on lids. Fill jars only to within ½ inch of the top. Screw caps on as tightly as you can. Place in boiling water bath to cover for 5 minutes to insure sealing. (That is, bring enough water to a boil in a big pot with a rack in the bottom to cover the top of the jars by one inch. Cover and boil 5 minutes.) Take out the jars with tongs and set them on a towel to cool. Take the amount you want for the picnic in a plastic container.

BEETS IN MUSTARD CREAM

Serves 8–10

1   *pound fresh beets (about 4 medium)*
    pinch of salt
2   *tablespoons Dijon mustard*
1   *tablespoon tarragon vinegar*
½   *teaspoon salt*
½   *teaspoon freshly ground pepper*
¼   *cup olive oil*
1   *cup plain yogurt*

Cut off the tops and roots of the beets and scrub them under cold water with a vegetable brush. Boil them in a saucepan filled with cold water and a good pinch of salt, for about a half-hour or until beets are just tender. Put them in a colander and rinse with cold water. Slice them thinly, leaving the skins on, into a medium-sized bowl.

In a smaller bowl, thoroughly combine the mustard with the vinegar, salt and pepper. Add the olive oil slowly, beating with a whisk, as in making mayonnaise. Stir in the yogurt to finish the sauce. Pour the mustard cream sauce over the beets, toss, cover and refrigerate before packing into a plastic container to travel.

CARROT BREAD

Makes 3 small loaves (5″ x 2½″ x 2″) or
1 medium loaf (9¼″ x 5¼″ x 3″) or
1 round loaf (baked in a 1-lb. coffee can)

2   *cups unsifted all-purpose flour*
1¼   *cups sugar*
2   *teaspoons cinnamon*
2   *teaspoons baking soda*
½   *teaspoon salt*

½ cup grated coconut
½ cup currants
½ cup chopped pecans
2 cups grated carrots
1 cup bland vegetable oil, such as corn oil
3 eggs
2 teaspoons vanilla extract

Oven temperature: 350°

Preheat oven. Grease pans. In a large bowl, combine the flour, sugar, cinnamon, baking soda and salt. Add the coconut, currants and pecans and mix. Add the grated carrots, oil, eggs and vanilla. Mix together with a wooden spoon and bake for 1 hour. The bread is done when it shrinks slightly from the sides and is firm to a gentle pressure, or when a wooden toothpick inserted in the center comes out clean. Cool in the pan for 10 minutes. Turn out on racks and cool thoroughly. Wrap and store in the refrigerator for up to two weeks, or freeze. Slices best if one day old.

These breads can also be left in the pans for easy packing. If baked in a coffee can, use a can opener to open the bottom of the can. The bread may then be gently pushed through, and you have a pretty round loaf to slice at the picnic.

CHOCOLATE WALNUT TORTE

This is a special birthday cake made from an old family recipe. Though not easy to take on a hike, it can be served outdoors if protected by a cake cover and taken in a car to the picnic site. You can take the Chocolate Whip Topping in a separate container if you prefer. In this case, wrap the torte in plastic wrap and frost it at the picnic, keeping it cool in an ice pack or cooler until it is time to frost the cake.

½ cup shortening
½ cup sugar
½ teaspoon vanilla extract
4 egg yolks
1 cup all-purpose flour
   dash of salt
1 teaspoon baking powder
⅓ cup milk
   walnut meringue

Oven temperature: 300°

Preheat oven and grease and flour two 8-inch round cake pans. Cream shortening and sugar. Add vanilla and egg yolks, one at a time, beating after each addition. Sift flour with salt and baking powder, and add alternately with milk. Pour into pans. Now spread the unbaked cakes with Walnut Meringue:

   4 *egg whites*
   1/8 *teaspoon cream of tartar*
   1 *cup sugar*
   3/4 *cup finely chopped walnuts*

Put the egg whites and the cream of tartar in the large bowl of an electric mixer, and beat at high speed, adding the sugar two tablespoons at a time. When stiff peaks form, fold in the walnuts. After spreading the cakes with the meringue, bake for 1 hour. Cool layers. Frost with Chocolate Whip Topping:

   1/3 *cup cocoa*
   3/4 *cup sugar*
   1 1/2 *cups heavy cream*
       several walnut halves

Add cocoa and sugar to heavy cream, stirring well. Let this mixture stand 1 hour, then with an electric mixer beat at high speed until stiff. Garnish frosted torte with walnuts.

SOUP

S oup is the most comforting of foods, the most heartening, and often the most digestible. It subtly prepares our palates for the meal to come.

Soup is also a perfect beginning for a picnic served from a backpack. In summer, after a long, hot, sometimes dusty trail, an icy-cold cup of soup delights and refreshes.

In cold weather, especially on midwinter cross-country trips, a steaming hot cup of soup warms our bones as well as our hearts. We pour the hot soup into enamel or tin cups as soon as we stop, sometimes even before taking off our skis. Then we build a fire, if it's terribly cold, and quickly lay out the rest of the meal.

We often serve soup as the first course at a more conventional picnic, when we take the food in baskets and travel by car to our site. The comforting qualities of the soup are not so important, since we have not been exerting ourselves as much, and warm or cool shelter is not far away, but a flavorful soup always carries a promise of an out-of-the-ordinary, delectable meal.

Most of the soup recipes here call for chicken or beef stock. Bouillon cubes or canned stock can be substituted, but the finished product is much better when made with homemade stock. You can make a reasonable stock in half an hour by using canned bouillon and adding a few chopped vegetables, a carrot, some onion, a piece of celery, and some parsley and herbs. You can also make stock whenever you have the ingredients on hand, then freeze it, or refrigerate it. You can keep a stock in the refrigerator for two weeks; but you should take it out of the refrigerator every four days, bring it to a boil briefly, then cool it and refrigerate again. We start our soup section with recipes for basic beef and chicken broths. You can alter proportions somewhat and substitute ingredients, but you should try to use most of the basic ingredients in the recipes to make really good stocks. Duck Soup can also be used as a basic stock to create other soups, and the broth left from boiling a chicken (see Cold Chicken with Walnut Sauce, page 122) is a chicken stock par excellence.

A soup's delicate blend of flavors and textures reflects the sensitivity of the cook's hand. And attention to details like garnishes can make a world of difference. As good as the Strawberry Soup (page 116) is, it tastes better when served with a small dollop of sour cream topped with chopped, toasted almonds.

Pack your garnishes in small jars or plastic bags and your soup in thermoses. Heat or cool your thermos before pouring in the soup. Put it into the refrigerator to cool, or run hot tap water into it to warm.

Stocks

BEEF STOCK

Yield: 4 quarts

A base for making the best of soups.

2 pounds meat scraps, mostly beef
   (you can also use some veal and/or chicken)
4 pounds beef bones, including a beef shank,
   sawed into pieces by your butcher
1 teaspoon salt
2 medium-sized onions, peeled and stuck with
   several cloves
2 stalks celery with leaves, washed
1 bay leaf

1 bouquet garni, including a sprig of thyme, a large sprig of parsley,
   a sprig of rosemary and a sprig of chervil tied together in a bunch
   OR
½ teaspoon of each in dried form, tied in a little piece of cheesecloth

1 parsnip (optional), scrubbed and pared
1 turnip (optional), scrubbed and pared
2 carrots (optional), scrubbed and pared
2 leeks (optional), halved lengthwise and rinsed under
   cold running water

Wash the meat and bones and put them into a large stockpot. Add cold water until about 2 inches above the level of the meat and and bones. Bring slowly to a simmer, and skim foam from the top with a slotted spoon. Add the salt, onions, celery, bay leaf, bouquet garni, and other suggested vegetables if you wish. Add boiling water until at least 1 inch above the level of the new additions to the pot. Bring to a simmer, skim the top, and partially cover the pot. Maintain a gentle simmer for four to five hours or even longer, until the stock has a strong flavor.

If you ever need to add more liquid, use boiling water. Do not let the stock itself boil. Do not cover the stockpot tightly at any point, including when it's finished and cooling. When cool, strain and degrease the stock either by spooning the grease off and running paper towels over the surface or by refrigerating the stock and waiting for the grease to harden on the surface to be easily lifted off.

This stock can be used immediately, frozen for up to two months or stored in the refrigerator for up to two weeks. If stored in the refrigerator, the stock should be taken out and brought to a boil every four days, then cooled and put back in the refrigerator. This will keep the stock fresh and prevent spoilage.

BROWN BEEF STOCK

Yield: 4 quarts

This is a variation to use as a base for richer soups such as Russian Borscht.

Oven temperature: 450°

Put all the vegetables and meats listed in the Beef Stock recipe into a hot oven for about 30 minutes or until well browned. Some of the vegetables may brown quicker than the meat, so take them out earlier.

Now follow the instructions for making Beef Stock in the recipe just preceding.

CHICKEN STOCK

Yield: 4 quarts

1 *4-to-5-pound chicken*
2 *pounds chicken giblets and parts (wings, backs, etc.)*
2 *carrots, scrubbed and pared*
1 *onion, peeled and stuck with cloves*
1 *bouquet garni including a sprig of thyme, a large sprig of parsley,*
  a sprig of rosemary and a sprig of chervil tied together in a bunch
  OR
½ *teaspoon of each in dried form, tied in a little piece of cheesecloth*

  a large bay leaf
8 *peppercorns*
2 *teaspoons salt*

Wash chicken pieces and pat dry. Put all the above ingredients together in a large stockpot and fill it with water until about 2 inches above the level of the mixture. Bring slowly to a boil, skimming off the scum as it rises; then reduce the heat to maintain a steady simmer. Do not let the mixture boil. Partially cover the pot and continue to cook for at least 3 hours or until the stock has a good strong flavor. Skim it several times more. The large pieces of chicken can be removed after 1½ to 2 hours to be used in any dish call-ing for cooked chicken.

Cool the stock *uncovered* and then refrigerate it until the fat rises to the top and congeals. Then lift off the fat. Chicken stock can be frozen for up to two months, or kept in the refrigerator up to two weeks if you take it out of the refrigerator and bring it to a boil every four days.

Hot Winter Soups

BLACK BEAN SOUP

Yield: 4 quarts

3 tablespoons butter
2 large onions, peeled and coarsely chopped
2 cloves garlic, peeled and mashed
2 leeks, well washed and coarsely chopped
1 stalk celery, washed and finely chopped
2 teaspoons all-purpose flour
4–5 quarts water
1½ pounds smoked ham hock OR split ham shank with bone and rind
3 pounds beef bones, cracked and sawed
   in pieces by your butcher
2 bay leaves
2 cloves
8 peppercorns
2 cups dried black beans, soaked overnight in water to cover
salt
freshly ground black pepper
½ cup Madeira

Melt the butter in a large heavy-bottomed pot. Add the onions, garlic, leeks and celery, and sauté over low heat for ten minutes. Blend in the flour and cook gently for 2 minutes, then stir in the water. Add the ham hock or shank, beef bones, bay leaves, cloves and peppercorns. Bring the water to a boil, skim off the scum, reduce the heat and simmer for 4 to 6 hours, partially covered, skimming off the scum from time to time.

Drain the beans and add them to the stock. Simmer 2½ hours more, stirring occasionally. Add more liquid if needed. Remove and discard the ham shank and rind and the beef bones. Put the soup through a food mill to purée the beans and vegetables. Taste carefully for seasoning, adding the salt and freshly ground pepper. Return the soup to the pot and add Madeira, then bring soup to a boil and pour the amount you wish to take into a thermos, freezing or saving the rest for another meal.

CREAM OF WILD ASPARAGUS SOUP

Yield: 6 quarts

When asparagus grows wild in the spring, and you have eaten your fill from platters piled high with fat, tender spears soaked in beurre noir and topped with fresh grated Parmesan, make asparagus soup. This recipe freezes well, so we include the soup in summer or even fall menus. Buy fresh asparagus from the market if you're not near a place where it grows wild.

- 1 *medium onion, peeled and chopped*
- 4 *tablespoons butter*
- 25 *large spears of asparagus (or an equal amount of smaller spears)*
- 4½–6 *cups asparagus water* OR *chicken stock*
- 4 *tablespoons all-purpose flour*
- ½ *cup heavy cream*
- 2 *egg yolks*
- 2 *teaspoons salt*
- 1 *piece of butter to enrich (1–2 tablespoons)*

Sauté the onion in the butter slowly in a large (3 to 4 quart) heavy-bottomed pot for about 10 minutes over low heat.

Fill a large pot (5½ quarts at least) with water and bring it to a boil. Put in the asparagus and reduce heat slightly, maintaining a slow boil for 5–10 minutes with the pot uncovered.

Drain the asparagus (reserving the water) and chop it coarsely. Add to the onion mixture, cover and cook slowly 5 minutes. Add flour to this mixture and mix it in, cooking slowly and stirring for a few minutes more. Blend in ½ cup of the water the asparagus was cooked in; then gradually add 4 more cups of this water and simmer, partially covered, for half an hour. (You can use chicken stock instead of the water here for a richer soup.)

When the soup is done, let it cool and put it through a food mill. A food mill is quick, easy and does the best job on stringy vegetables like asparagus. If you prefer, you can purée the soup in a blender, and then put it through a mesh sieve to eliminate the stringy fibers. Stir and push the blended soup through the sieve with a wooden spoon. Correct seasoning.

When serving hot, mix the cream and egg yolks together and slowly stir this mixture into the soup as it heats. Do not let it boil. Next add the salt and taste for flavor. Put in a piece of butter and let it melt just before pouring into a warmed thermos. To serve cold, eliminate the egg yolks and butter and add a little more salt. Chill thoroughly before pouring into a thermos. Save the little tender heads which break off the asparagus, cook them quickly in a little boiling water and use them to garnish each serving.

CREAM OF WILD MUSHROOM SOUP

Yield: 2 quarts

3 *cups wild mushrooms,* finely chopped*
6 *tablespoons butter*
1 *tablespoon lemon juice*
4 *tablespoons finely minced fresh parsley mixed with fresh minced*
     chervil OR *½ teaspoon dried chervil*
6 *scallions, coarsely chopped*
3 *tablespoons all-purpose flour*
6 *cups chicken stock (page 93),*
     OR *canned chicken bouillon or bouillon cubes to make 4 cups stock*
     salt and freshly ground pepper to taste
¼ *teaspoon thyme*
     piece of bay leaf
½ *cup heavy cream*

Before you chop the mushrooms, wipe them off with a damp cloth. If they
are a species with a lot of folds, immerse them in salted water a few
minutes, then drain on paper towels and pat dry. Melt 2 tablespoons of butter in a medium-sized skillet. When it's foaming, put in the mushrooms,
lemon juice, 2 tablespoons parsley and chervil and cook over low heat, stirring with a wooden spoon, for about 5 minutes or until lightly browned.
The time will vary depending on the type of mushrooms used. Reserve.

In a large heavy-bottomed pot, sauté the scallions and mushroom stems
in the remaining 4 tablespoons of the butter until the scallions are soft and
transparent. Add the flour and stir until the mixture thickens, about one
minute. Boil the stock and add it to the pot, stirring well. Add the salt and
pepper and herbs. Simmer the soup for 20 minutes. Strain it and return to
the pot and add the mushrooms and continue to cook 5 minutes more. Add
the cream slowly, mixing well. Taste for seasoning. Serve very hot from a
thermos and garnish with the remaining parsley and chervil.

* The type of mushrooms used will determine the texture and flavor of the soup. You
can use fresh mushrooms from the market instead of wild mushrooms.

DUCK SOUP

Yield: 3 quarts

This recipe is adapted from Harriet Barnett's recipe in her *Game and Fish
Cookbook*. There is no better method for extracting the last bit of flavor
from duck carcasses or those of other game fowl.

2–3 *duck carcasses*
    OR *several carcasses of other game birds*
1 *cup dry red wine*
2 *tablespoons vinegar*
1 *cup dry sherry* OR *Madeira*
1 *teaspoon salt*
6 *peppercorns*
6 *whole cloves*
1 *bay leaf*
1 *turnip, scrubbed and chopped*
2 *onions, peeled and chopped*
2 *carrots, scrubbed, pared and chopped*
2 *stalks celery with leaves, scrubbed and chopped*
1 *small bunch parsley, chopped*
1 *teaspoon marjoram*
   water to cover
¼ *pound smoked ham, cut into strips*

Place all ingredients except the ham in a large soup pot, fill with cold
water to two inches above the contents and cover the pot. Bring it to
a boil, reduce heat and simmer for 3–4 hours or longer. Strain the liquid
through a double thickness of cheesecloth and let it cool. Remove the fat by
running paper towels across the top. Return to pot and add the cooked ham;
heat almost to boiling. The soup is ready to be poured into a thermos. You
will have enough left for another meal.

You can use this stock as a base for cream of vegetable soups such as
Cabbage Soup Supreme (page 75).

HOT CHEDDAR CHEESE SOUP

Yield: 1 quart

This is a simple but very tasty cheese soup. Its flavor depends on the cheese
you use.

2 *tablespoons butter*
1 *large onion, peeled and finely chopped*
2 *tablespoons all-purpose flour*
2 *cups milk*
2 *cups shredded mild yellow Cheddar of good quality*
    OR *half sharp and half mild Cheddar*
   pinch white pepper
   salt to taste

Melt the butter in a large heavy-bottomed saucepan and sauté the onion until transparent (about 10 minutes). Sprinkle on the flour and mix well, browning lightly. Add the milk slowly, mixing well with a wooden spoon or a wire whisk. Now add the cheese, still mixing, and heat until blended. Be very careful *not to boil* the soup or it will curdle. Add salt and white pepper to taste. Serve very hot. Heat to just below boiling before pouring into a hot thermos.

You can use a combination of sharp white or yellow Cheddar and mild yellow Cheddar for a tangier taste.

HOT TOMATO SOUP WITH VODKA

Makes 2 quarts

The vodka in this recipe flavors, but does not dominate, the wonderful tomato taste.

8–10 *large ripe tomatoes*
   4 *tablespoons olive oil*
   1 *tablespoon finely chopped fresh green herbs, a combination of any*
      of the following: thyme, parsley, chives, scallions, basil, chervil
      salt and pepper to taste
   2 *cups tomato juice, canned*
   2 *cups beef bouillon, canned or made with beef bouillon cubes*
   2 *shots of vodka*

Blanch the tomatoes one or two at a time by dropping them into briskly boiling water for a minute and then taking them out with a large spoon. Cut off both ends and gently but firmly squeeze out the seeds and excess liquid. Peel and chop the tomatoes finely. Sauté tomatoes and fresh green herbs in olive oil in a large heavy-bottomed pot over medium heat for 5 minutes.

Let the tomatoes cool for about 10 minutes and put them through a food mill, not a blender. (If you don't have a food mill, simply mash the tomato mixture well with a fork.) Return the tomatoes to the pot, add salt and pepper to taste and the tomato juice and beef bouillon. Heat to steaming, add vodka, taste for seasoning and pour into a preheated thermos.

Variation: For a quick and good version of this soup, use canned tomato soup instead of the fresh tomatoes.

Following the directions on the can, mix the soup with one can of water and heat through. Add the herbs, tomato juice, bouillon, vodka and salt and pepper to taste.

ITALIAN SPRING VEGETABLE SOUP

Yield: 2 quarts

½ onion, peeled and thinly sliced
½ leek (white part), well washed and thinly sliced
1 small clove garlic, peeled and minced
1 tablespoon butter
1 quart chicken stock
1 potato, peeled and grated or finely cubed
1 small zucchini, washed and thinly sliced
1 cup finely shredded spinach
1 cup finely shredded fresh garden lettuce

1 tomato, peeled, seeded and chopped
   OR
1 cup canned Italian plum tomatoes

   freshly grated Parmesan cheese
   minced parsley

Slowly cook the onion, leek and garlic until soft, not brown, in the butter in a large heavy-bottomed pot. Add the chicken stock, potato, sliced zucchini, shredded spinach, lettuce and tomato. Cook slowly for 45 minutes at a simmer.

Season to taste. Pour into a hot thermos and take some grated Parmesan and minced parsley to pass when the soup is served.

LENTIL SOUP

Yield: 4 quarts

This is a very warming, filling, wonderful, wintery soup.

1 package dried lentils (1 pound)
4 quarts water
1 whole medium onion, peeled and stuck with cloves
3 carrots, scrubbed and pared
1 bouquet garni consisting of about ½ teaspoon each rosemary,
   marjoram and thyme and a few sprigs of parsley tied in a piece
   of cheesecloth OR mixed herbs of your choice
1–3 stalks celery, scrubbed and cut in large chunks
6 peppercorns
1 bay leaf
2 ham hocks

4 *tablespoons tomato paste*
  juice of 1 lemon
2 *cloves garlic, peeled and put through a press*
  salt and pepper to taste

Soak lentils overnight. Bring a large pot of water to boil (about 4 quarts)
and add everything except last three ingredients. Turn heat to simmer for
about 1½ hours or until lentils are tender and the meat comes off the ham
hocks. Remove onion, celery and bay leaf with slotted spoon and discard.
Also remove ham hocks. Allow them to cool a bit, then remove lean meat
from bone, chop the meat into small pieces and reserve.

Next blend about three-fourths of the soup, including all the carrots, in
a blender, 1 to 2 cups at a time. Return to pot with the unblended soup and
stir. Add the chopped ham with the lemon juice, garlic, salt and pepper.
Simmer about ½ hour more and pour into a warm thermos.

MUSHROOM CONSOMMÉ

Serves 6–8
Yield: 1½ quarts

3 *tablespoons minced shallots* OR *scallions*
3 *tablespoons butter*
1 *pound fresh mushrooms, very finely chopped*
4 *cups fresh chicken stock*
    OR *the equivalent made with canned broth or chicken bouillon*
    cubes
½ *teaspoon salt*
1 *teaspoon lemon juice*

Sauté the shallots or scallions in the butter in a large heavy-bottomed pot
over low heat, 5–10 minutes, until transparent and soft. Then add the mushrooms and simmer for another five minutes. Add the stock and continue
simmering for about half an hour. Strain the soup after it has cooled
slightly by pouring it through a wire mesh strainer. Add the salt and lemon
juice and taste for seasoning. Bring the soup again to a boil and pour it
into a large preheated thermos for the picnic.

SPINACH AND CHARD SOUP WITH PINE NUTS

Yield: 1½ quarts

½ *cup pine nuts*
4 *tablespoons butter*
1 *onion, peeled and finely chopped*
1 *cup fresh spinach, well washed and finely shredded*
    with a cleaver or large chopping knife
1 *cup fresh chard, well washed and finely shredded*
    with a cleaver or large chopping knife
3 *tablespoons all-purpose flour*
⅛ *teaspoon of ground nutmeg* OR *a grating of fresh nutmeg*
2 *cups fresh chicken stock*
    OR *its equivalent made with canned broth or chicken*
    bouillon cubes
2 *cups milk*
1 *teaspoon salt*
    freshly ground black pepper

Sauté the pine nuts lightly in 1 tablespoon butter, in a small skillet over moderate heat until golden. Set aside 3 tablespoons of the nuts for last-minute garnish.

Sauté the onion in the remaining 3 tablespoons butter in a large heavy-bottomed pot until they are transparent. Add the spinach and chard to the onions and continue to cook over low heat for about 5 minutes, just until the greens are wilted. Sprinkle on the flour and stir with a wooden spoon. Add the nutmeg and continue stirring. Mix in the stock and simmer for 10 minutes, then add the milk and simmer 5 more minutes, but don't let the soup boil. Add the salt and a little pepper, and taste for seasoning. Serve hot from a thermos and garnish with the rest of the nuts.

TORTILLA SOUP

Yield: 3 quarts

This wonderful Mexican soup is a good beginning to a winter's meal.

4 *corn tortillas*
¼ *cup oil*
1 *onion, peeled and minced*
½ *cup tomato purée*
2½ *quarts chicken* OR *beef broth, fresh or canned*

1 *tablespoon fresh cilantro (coriander leaves), chopped*
OR
1 *teaspoon dried coriander*

   salt and pepper to taste
1 *tablespoon finely chopped mint leaves*
⅓ *cup grated Monterey Jack*

Cut tortillas into thin strips and fry until crisp in oil in a large heavy-bottomed pot. Drain the strips on absorbent paper. Sauté the onion over moderate heat for about 5 minutes (being careful not to brown) in the same oil that the tortillas were fried in. Add the tomato purée to the onions. Add the stock and tortilla strips. In a bowl mash the cilantro with a wooden spoon, then add about ½ cup of the broth. Strain this mixture through a wire sieve into the soup.

Simmer, uncovered, for ½ hour, adding the salt, pepper and chopped mint leaves the last 10 minutes. Heat almost to boiling before pouring into a warmed thermos. This recipe makes about 3 quarts, so you can freeze or save the remainder for another meal. Put the grated cheese into a little plastic bag and take along to garnish. Monterey Jack cheese is usually served with this soup, but you can use another white mild-flavored cheese.

WILD SORREL SOUP

   Yield: 2 quarts

½ *onion, peeled and finely minced*
3 *tablespoons butter*
4 *cups fresh sorrel*
½ *teaspoon salt*
3 *tablespoons all-purpose flour*
5 *cups chicken stock*
1 *egg yolk*
½ *cup light cream*

Sauté the onion in the butter over medium heat in a large heavy-bottomed pot (2½ to 4 quart) until tender (5–10 minutes). Wash the sorrel in a colander and pat dry on a towel. A handful at a time, roll the sorrel into a cigarlike shape and slice it very thinly with a sharp knife. Add it to the onions and cook until just wilted, about 5 minutes. Add salt. Now add the flour and stir until a thick pasty consistency develops. Cook for 2–3 minutes. Stir in the chicken stock slowly and bring the mixture almost to the boiling point. Simmer 5 more minutes and then take the pot off the heat.

Mix the egg yolk and light cream together in a separate small bowl. Add a little of the warm soup to it, stirring well, then pour all the cream-yolk mixture back into the rest of the liquid. Return the pan to the heat on medium and cook, stirring constantly. Don't let it come to a boil. The soup will thicken after about 5 minutes. Pour into a warmed thermos to pack.

Note: Sorrel soup does not need to be put through a strainer or a sieve (like asparagus or watercress, for instance) because sorrel is tender, and not fibrous or stringy in texture.

ZUPPA DI PESCE

This soup is rich and hearty, nice to begin a fall or winter picnic menu.

Yield: 2½–3 quarts

2½ *pounds bass or other white firm-fleshed fish,*
including the head and tail, washed and cut into chunks
2 *pounds fish heads and bones*
1 *8-ounce bottle clam juice*
1 *small can minced clams, with juice*
2 *pounds (3 large) onions, peeled and sliced*
2 *carrots, scrubbed, pared and cut in pieces*
1 *stalk celery, scrubbed and sliced*
2 *tomatoes, peeled, seeded and chopped*
1 *bay leaf*
6 *sprigs parsley*
1 *clove garlic, peeled and minced*
   salt and pepper to taste
   dash of cayenne pepper
1 *teaspoon saffron*
1 *egg yolk, lightly beaten*
1 *cup light cream*
1 *tablespoon each butter and flour,*
   rubbed together with fingers to make a beurre manié

Put all the ingredients except the last three in a large pot and cover them with cold water to come about 2 to 3 inches above the contents of the pot. Bring the water to a boil and continue to boil vigorously for 10–15 minutes or until the pieces of fish are cooked and flake easily with a fork. Remove all the pieces of fish, discarding the skin and bones, and reserve them. Lower the heat and simmer about 40 minutes uncovered. Then strain the soup through a sieve lined with cheesecloth, pressing hard with a spoon to extract all the juices. Discard everything but this vegetable fish broth. Rinse out the pot and pour the broth back into it. Beat the egg yolk and cream together in a medium bowl and add some of the warm broth to it, a spoonful at a time, stirring constantly so the egg-cream mixture will not curdle. Now add it all to the broth in the pot, stirring constantly while pouring slowly. Next add the pieces of fish that were reserved. Heat slowly, adding bits of the beurre manié to thicken the broth to a desired consistency. Do not let the soup come to a boil. When very hot, place in two large thermoses, and serve at the beginning of the picnic meal.

Cold Summer Soups

CHILLED CREAM OF CHIVE SOUP

Yield: 1 quart

- 3 tablespoons butter
- 3 tablespoons all-purpose flour
- 2½ cups chicken stock
- 1 bay leaf
- 2 tablespoons finely snipped chives
- 1 cup light cream
  salt
  white pepper

In a saucepan over medium heat, melt the butter and blend in the flour. Add the chicken stock (undiluted), bay leaf and chives. Cook and stir over medium heat until mixture bubbles and thickens. Remove bay leaf. Stir in the cream and taste for seasoning, adding salt and white pepper as needed. Chill thoroughly and pour into a cold thermos.

CHILLED PEA SOUP

Yield: 2 quarts

- ½ cup chopped onion
- 1 tablespoon butter
- 5 pounds fresh peas, shelled
  OR
- 3 10-ounce packages of frozen peas
- 1¼ cups beef stock OR condensed canned bouillon
- 4 cups water
- 1 teaspoon dried chervil
- 1½ teaspoon salt
  freshly ground pepper to taste
  several leaves finely chopped fresh mint
- ½ cup chilled dry white wine
- 2 cups light cream (half-and-half OR milk and cream)

Sauté onion in butter in a large heavy-bottomed pot until onion is soft and transparent (about 10 minutes). Add peas, bouillon, water, chervil, salt and pepper and bring to a boil. Reduce heat and simmer, uncovered, until peas are very soft—about 30 minutes. Purée the soup in a blender or food mill. Strain it, add the mint leaves and chill at least three hours. Before serving, stir in wine and cream, and correct seasoning, tasting for salt. Place in chilled thermos.

CHILLED SALMON BISQUE

Yield: 1–1½ quarts

1 *small onion, peeled and chopped*
½ *cup finely minced green pepper*
1 *clove garlic, peeled and crushed*
1 *tablespoon butter*
¾ *pound of salmon, freshly poached*
　OR
2 *6-ounce cans salmon, drained and broken up into small pieces*
2½ *cups light cream* OR *half milk and half cream*
¼ *cup snipped fresh dill*
　OR
1 *teaspoon dried dill weed*
¼ *teaspoon Worcestershire sauce*
¼ *teaspoon salt*
⅛ *teaspoon pepper*
2 *tablespoons dry sherry*
1 *tablespoon lemon juice*

In a medium skillet, sauté the onion, green pepper and garlic in hot butter until golden—about 5 minutes. Combine the salmon and sautéed vegetable mixture, cream and dill, Worcestershire sauce, salt and pepper in a blender at high speed for about one minute until smooth. If using a piece of fresh salmon, poach it lightly, just until tender, in a little simmering water in a small frying pan, covered. Remove and discard the skin and bones and flake the salmon with a fork into small pieces. Refrigerate until chilled. Stir in the sherry and lemon juice and taste for seasoning, before pouring into a cold thermos.

COLD CREAM OF WATERCRESS SOUP

Yield: 1½–2 quarts

We often make this soup in the middle of summer, when the flowers bloom-
ing on the watercress give the cress a more peppery taste.

1½ *tablespoons butter*
¼ *cup minced onion (½ medium onion)*
5 *cups watercress, well washed and patted dry*
1½ *tablespoons flour*
3 *cups* boiling *chicken stock*
½ *teaspoon salt*
1 *egg yolk*

¼ *cup cream*
   OR
½ *cup light cream or milk*

Melt the butter in a large (2½ to 4 quart) heavy-bottomed pot. Over low
heat sauté the onions in the butter for about 10 minutes, or until just transparent. Turn up the heat a bit and stir in the watercress, which will cook
and wilt almost like spinach, so the whole 5 cups can be added to the pan.
After 5 minutes turn the heat up to medium, add the flour and stir another
5 minutes. Next add the hot chicken stock and stir. Let the soup cool.
Now purée the mixture in either a food processor or blender, then again
through a food mill or fine sieve. (This step is to break up the stringy
consistency of the watercress. Putting it through a blender is not enough.
You can eliminate the blender step but not the food-mill process.)

Return to the pot and add the seasoning, tasting if more salt is required.
Often a soup like this will need more salt to bring out the flavors after it is
finally chilled, as food tastes more bland when cold. Now mix the egg yolk
and light cream together in a bowl. (For a thicker version, heavy cream may
be used. Use milk for a lighter refreshing soup.) Add some of the hot puréed
liquid, spoonful by spoonful, to the bowl, until there is about a cup of soup
mixed well with the cream and yolk mixture. Add this to the rest of the
liquid in the pot. Simmer 10 minutes, but don't let the soup come to a boil.
Set aside to cool and refrigerate for 3 hours before pouring into a thermos.
Decorate each serving with watercress leaves and their flowers.

Watercress Soup (Quick Blender Version)

Make 3 cups hot chicken bouillon from a can or cubes. Chop a large bunch
of watercress (about 2 cups) and simmer it in the bouillon with half an
onion, a bay leaf and a squeeze of lemon juice for 5–10 minutes. Take out

the onion and bay leaf. Cool the soup by adding one cup cold cream or half-and-half and purée in a blender. Put through a strainer or food mill to eliminate stringy stems.

Variation: Use chopped fresh spinach or chard.

COLD CUCUMBER SOUP

Yield: 1½–2 quarts

1 *tablespoon butter*
3 *cucumbers: 2 peeled and sliced; 1 peeled, seeded and grated*
1 *tablespoon chopped fresh dill* OR *mint*

1 *leek, sliced (white part)*
   OR
¼ *cup chopped onion*

1 *bay leaf*
1 *tablespoon all-purpose flour*
3 *cups fresh chicken stock* OR *canned chicken broth*
1 *teaspoon salt*
1 *cup light cream*
   juice of ½ a lemon
1 *tablespoon honey (optional)*
   white pepper to taste (optional)

Heat the butter in a large heavy-bottomed saucepan and sauté the two sliced cucumbers gently over low heat for a few minutes. Add the dill, leek and the bay leaf and cook over low heat until tender (about 20 minutes). Stir in the flour and cook a few minutes, stirring; then add the stock and salt and simmer gently 30 minutes more.

Let the mixture cool slightly and purée it in a blender, half at a time. Return to the pan, adding white pepper if desired. Add the cream, lemon juice and honey if desired, and taste for seasoning. Stir in the grated cucumber last; chill until ready to put into a chilled thermos to take to a picnic.

COLD CURRIED CREAM SOUP

Yield: 2 quarts

This soup cools more than any soup recipe we offer, so serve it as the first course on a hot day.

- 2 *fresh tomatoes*
- 2 *medium-size onions, peeled and chopped*
- 1 *tablespoon butter*
- 1 *tablespoon all-purpose flour*
- 1 *clove garlic, peeled and minced*
- ¼ *teaspoon chopped fresh ginger root*
- 1 *pinch each of powdered cardamom, cinnamon, cloves, cumin*
- 1 *quart chicken stock (page 93)*
- 1 *green cooking apple (very tart), peeled, cored and minced*
- ½ *green pepper, washed, cored and finely chopped*
- 2 *teaspoons grated coconut*
  juice of ½ lemon
- 1 *cup cream*
- 1 *cup milk*

Blanch the tomatoes quickly in boiling water, put under cold water, cut off both ends and gently squeeze out seeds, peel and chop. In a large heavy-bottomed pot, lightly sauté onion over low heat in butter just until transparent; add flour, garlic and ginger and cook a few minutes until the aroma rises, then add other spices and cook a few minutes more. Be careful not to put in too much ginger or it will dominate.*

Add the chicken broth, apple, green pepper, tomatoes, coconut, and lemon to the pot you sautéed the onion in. Cover and simmer for 1½ hours. Strain and cool. Add the cream and the milk. Cool the soup and chill thoroughly before pouring it into a chilled thermos.

* I find the ginger root keeps very well for some time in the freezer and a shave or so can be taken from the frozen piece as needed.

ICED AVOCADO CREAM

Yield: 1½–2 quarts
Serves 4–6

- 2 *medium-ripe avocados, peeled and sliced*
- 2 *tablespoons lemon juice*
- 1 *small onion, peeled and sliced*

2 *tablespoons dry vermouth*
1½ *cups fresh chicken broth*
    OR *the equivalent made with canned bouillon or cubes*
 ¾ *cup milk*
 ½ *cup heavy cream*
    salt
    dash white pepper

Put avocados into blender (reserving several slices for garnish) with lemon juice, onion, vermouth and broth. Blend until smooth. Combine blender contents with milk, cream, salt and pepper to taste. Dice the reserved avocado slices, toss with a little lemon juice and add to the soup. Chill well and pour into a chilled thermos to take to a picnic.

ICED TOMATO SOUP ROMANOFF

Yield: 1 quart

 6 *tomatoes*
 3 *green onions, minced*
 ½ *teaspoon salt*
 ½ *teaspoon sugar (or honey)*
    dash pepper
 ¼ *teaspoon each marjoram and thyme*
 2 *tablespoons lemon juice*
 1 *teaspoon grated lemon peel*
 1 *cup fresh chicken stock*
    OR *the equivalent made with canned broth or a bouillon cube*
 ½ *cup sour cream mixed with 1 teaspoon minced parsley for garnish*

Blanch the tomatoes one at a time in boiling water. Rinse in cold water, cut off both ends and gently squeeze out the seeds. Peel and chop the tomatoes and put them through a food mill over a large saucepan. Add the green onions, salt, sugar or honey, pepper, herbs, lemon juice, peel and stock. Bring the mixture just to a boil. Turn off the heat and cool. Taste for seasoning and refrigerate until ready to pour into a cold thermos. When serving into each individual cup, garnish with a spoonful of the sour cream and parsley mixture (which you may transport separately in a small container).

ORANGE–APRICOT–YOGURT SOUP

Yield: 2 quarts

1 *16-ounce carton of plain yogurt*
5 *ripe apricots, pitted and mashed*
1 *cup milk*
½ *cup orange juice*
6 *thin slices orange*
6 *sprigs mint*

Combine the yogurt, apricots, milk and orange juice in a blender and blend at medium speed 1 minute. Refrigerate until well chilled and pour into a chilled thermos. Carry orange slices and mint separately, and float in the soup to serve.

PLUM POTAGE

Much like a refreshing fruit juice, this soup is very light because there is no cream or broth. It's especially nice in hot weather. Try making it with blueberries, fresh apricots, peaches or cherries, or a combination of different fruits.

Yield: 1½–2 quarts

1 *pound fresh purple plums, pitted and halved*
   grated peel of ½ lemon
5 *cups water*
½ *cup dry vermouth*
3 *tablespoons honey*
3 *whole cloves*
¼ *cup fresh orange juice*

Put all ingredients in a large saucepan and cook over medium heat until fruit is soft and mushy. Take out the cloves, cool the mixture and purée it in a blender 1 cup at a time. Chill thoroughly before pouring into thermos.

This recipe is also good with fresh red sweet cherries, washed and pitted. Use red sweet vermouth or port wine instead of vermouth and add honey only to taste.

Peaches, peeled, pitted and cut up, or apricots, pitted and halved, may be substituted for the plums, in which case use dry vermouth as called for here.

POTAGE D'ABRICOTINE

Yield: 1 quart

5 *ripe apricots*
1 *16-ounce carton of plain yogurt*
1 *cup milk*
½ *cup fresh orange juice*
6 *sprigs mint*
6 *thin slices of orange, peeled and quartered*
2 *teaspoons abricotine liqueur*
   OR *apricot brandy (optional)*

Wash and pit unpeeled apricots and cut them up coarsely. Combine the yogurt, apricots, milk and orange juice in a blender and blend at medium speed 1 minute. Stir in the liqueur if desired. Refrigerate until well chilled. Pour into a cold thermos. Float orange sections and mint in the soup to serve.

QUICK CHILLED BORSCHT

Yield: 1½–2 quarts

1 *cup chopped cabbage*
   (¼ wedge of a small head of cabbage)
1 *medium onion, peeled and thinly sliced*
1 *cup water*
1 *can condensed beef bouillon*
1 *can water*
1 *tablespoon minced fresh dill*
   OR
½ *teaspoon dried dill weed*
1 *small can diced beets, with juice from the can*
   salt and white pepper to taste
1 *cup sour cream*

Combine the cabbage and onion slices with 1 cup of water in a medium saucepan. Bring to boiling over medium heat; reduce heat and simmer, covered, 10–15 minutes until tender. Add the beef bouillon, water, dill and beets. Purée, 1 cup at a time, in a blender and chill thoroughly. Taste for seasoning, adding salt and pepper, and pour into a chilled thermos. Take the sour cream in a separate container and put a dollop on each cupful as it is served.

SENEGALESE SOUP

Yield: 2 quarts

   3 *tablespoons butter*
   1 *medium onion, peeled and chopped*
   1 *carrot, pared and diced*
   1 *stalk celery, scrubbed and sliced*
   2 *tablespoons curry powder*
1½ *tablespoons all-purpose flour*
   1 *tablespoon tomato paste*
   2 *cups chicken stock*
   2 *cups water*
   1 *tablespoon almond paste*
   1 *tablespoon red currant jelly*
 10 *whole cloves*
   1 *cinnamon stick*
1½ *cups heavy cream*
   2 *tablespoons shredded coconut*

Melt the butter in a large heavy bottomed pot and sauté the onion, carrot, and celery over moderate heat until golden. Remove from heat. Stir in curry powder and flour until well blended. Add tomato paste and cook, stirring, 1 minute. Gradually stir in chicken stock and 2 cups water. Bring to a boil, stirring occasionally.

Stir in almond paste and jelly; add cloves and cinnamon stick. Simmer about 30 minutes, stirring occasionally. Strain, cool, then refrigerate until well chilled. When ready to serve, lift off any surface fat with a spoon. Blend in the cream and pour into chilled thermos. When serving, sprinkle coconut into each bowl or cup.

SIMPLE "GAZPACHO"

Yield: 1 quart

   3 *large ripe tomatoes, peeled, cored and seeded*
      OR
   1 *large can of tomatoes*
3–4 *scallions, chopped*
  ½ *green pepper, washed, cored, seeded and chopped*
   1 *large stalk celery, scrubbed and finely chopped*
      salt to taste
      pepper to taste

1 *teaspoon dried dill weed*
1 *teaspoon good wine vinegar*
1 *teaspoon olive oil*
  freshly ground black pepper
1 *teaspoon salt*
  garlic croutons

Blend all ingredients except garlic croutons together briefly in a blender. Chill well and pour into a chilled thermos. Garnish with croutons.

SPRING TONIC

Yield: 1½ quarts

This easy soup, good either hot or cold, will have a tonic effect on any weary hiker.

4 *cups brown beef stock (page 93)*
    OR *canned bouillon or bouillon cubes to make 6 cups beef stock*
3 *pounds (8 medium-sized) fresh tomatoes, coarsely chopped*
2 *stalks celery, with leaves, scrubbed and coarsely chopped*
2 *carrots, scrubbed, pared and coarsely chopped*
1 *green pepper, washed, cored, seeded and coarsely chopped*
1 *large onion, peeled and coarsely chopped*
3 *peppercorns*
2 *whole cloves*
1 *teaspoon salt*
½ *teaspoon dried basil leaves*
  pinch sugar
1 *tablespoon fresh lemon juice*
¼ *cup port wine* OR *Madeira* OR *dry sherry*
5 *sprigs parsley*
  several additional parsley sprigs to garnish

Bring the stock to a boil in a large 3 to 4 quart pot. Add all the chopped vegetables and all the other ingredients except the lemon juice, wine and fresh parsley sprigs. Turn down the heat until the mixture is just simmering. Leave the pot, uncovered, on low heat, simmering for 1 hour. Let the mixture cool in the pot, then pour it through a wire mesh strainer and add the port wine and lemon juice. Taste for seasoning. Refrigerate. Reheat the soup and pour it into a warm thermos if you want to serve it hot, or pour it into a chilled thermos to serve cold. Take fresh sprigs of parsley for a garnish in either case.

STRAWBERRY SOUP

Yield: 1½ quarts

Without reservation, our summer picnic favorite.

1 *large box (1 quart) fresh strawberries, washed and hulled*
½ *cup unsweetened pineapple juice*
1 *large ripe peach, peeled, pitted, and sliced*
2 *cups good chicken broth*
½ *cup sour cream*
2 *tablespoons chopped toasted almonds*

Put half the strawberries and the pineapple juice in the blender and purée; then add the rest of the berries with the peach, and blend all together for 30 seconds. Add this mixture to the bouillon and beat with a wire whisk. Chill thoroughly and pour into a cooled thermos. Garnish with a large dollop of sour cream and toasted almonds. (The almonds should be toasted by putting them in a pan in the oven at 350° for a few minutes. Watch them carefully and take them out as soon as they are light brown. Chop them on a board.)

Quick Version:

Also quite good.

2 *chicken bouillon cubes*
2 *cups boiling water*
1 *12-ounce package frozen sliced peaches, thawed*
1 *10-ounce package frozen sliced strawberries, thawed*
½ *cup unsweetened pineapple juice*
½ *cup sour cream*
2 *tablespoons chopped toasted almonds*

Dissolve bouillon cubes in water. Put fruits and juices from both packages in blender, cover and blend 30 seconds at high speed. Add bouillon and pineapple juice. Blend 10 seconds at low speed. Chill until ice-cold, and garnish with the sour cream and toasted almonds.

YOGURT SOUP WITH MINT

Yield: 2 quarts

A refreshing and nourishing soup for a summer hike.

¼ *cup pearl barley*
4 *cups chicken broth*
2 *tablespoons minced onion*
½ *cup finely chopped fresh mint*
3 *cups plain yogurt*
¾ *teaspoon salt*
   freshly ground pepper

Place the pearl barley in a small bowl; add water to cover and soak overnight. The next day, drain the barley in a strainer and rinse well. Then put it
into a medium-sized saucepan with the chicken broth and the minced onion.
Bring it to a boil, lower heat and simmer 15 minutes, or until barley is
tender. Then remove from heat. Add the mint to the cooling barley, then
add the yogurt, and stir until the soup is smooth. Add the salt and pepper
to taste. Chill and place in chilled thermos.

MAIN DISHES

A picnic is a merry-go-round of food with the main dish as the nucleus, the balancing point for the whole movable feast. When the food is laid out on the cloth and the dishes are arranged with thought to color and design, the main dish is the center. We might set the dessert nearby on a log or flat rock, or the white wine in a stream or lake to chill, but the main dish always remains in the middle of things.

The main dish is also the most substantial one of the picnic. It can be very grand—a tenderloin of beef stuffed with pâté, a whole baked salmon with homemade green mayonnaise, or an elegant terrine of pheasant. Or the main dish can be very simple—a selection of cheeses served with good bread and condiments like mustard pickles and antipasto can be the focal point of a very satisfying picnic lunch.

Fowl and Fish

CHICKEN SEBASTIANO

Serves 6

 1 *large fryer, cut up*
    juice of ½ lemon
¼ *cup olive oil*
½ *cup butter*
 8 *large cloves garlic, peeled and minced*
 1 *teaspoon oregano*
    salt and pepper

Oven temperature: 350°

Preheat oven. Using poultry shears, cut the standard pieces of chicken up into several sections each. (For example, each thigh should be cut into two pieces and each leg cut in half.)

Rub all these pieces first with lemon juice, then olive oil. Put them in a roasting pan large enough to spread out the pieces in one layer. Melt the butter in a saucepan with the garlic, oregano, and salt and pepper to taste, and baste each piece of chicken thoroughly with this sauce several times during cooking. Roast for one hour and fifteen minutes, until chicken is crisp and brown. At high altitudes increase the oven heat to 375° for one hour.

CHICKEN SHANGRI-LA

Serves 6–8

The most popular main course of our early picnic menus. Though we named it for a favorite place in the mountains, its name is appropriate for the hot and spicy, exotic flavor.

 1 *3½–4-pound fryer, cut up*
 1 *egg white*
    juice of 3 limes OR *lemons*
 1 *tablespoon paprika*
 1 *teaspoon cayenne pepper*
 4 *cloves*
 6 *chili tepines*
    large pinch of cilantro (dried coriander leaves)
 2 *medium onions, peeled and thinly sliced*

   2 *cloves garlic, peeled and minced*
  ½ *cup peanut* OR *vegetable oil*
   1 *cup flour*
  ½ *cup chicken bouillon*

   Oven temperature: 375°

Beat the egg white until foamy and add the lime or lemon juice and all the spices, including the onions and garlic. Marinate the chicken pieces in this mixture several hours or overnight.

Heat oil in a large frying pan. Roll the chicken in flour and brown in the oil. Transfer the chicken to a medium casserole and bake it covered for 30 minutes. Add the marinade sauce and ½ cup chicken bouillon. Bake 10 minutes more. Let the chicken cool. Put the chicken in a strong leakproof plastic bag (two thicknesses are best) and secure it well with rubber bands to avoid having any of the sauce dripping out en route.

At the picnic site, arrange the chicken pieces on a platter and garnish them with fresh mint leaves picked en route or around the picnic site. It's a little messy, but fun to eat with your fingers.

COLD CHICKEN WITH WALNUT SAUCE

   Serves 6–8

This Turkish dish is really elegant picnic fare. It requires a bit more preparation than most picnic food, and can be reserved for the "special occasion." It's well worth the trouble.

   1 *large stewing hen*
   1 *cup wine—dry white Chablis* OR *dry vermouth*
   1 *large onion, peeled and cut in chunks*
   2 *medium carrots, scrubbed, pared and cut in chunks*
   4 *celery stalks with leaves, scrubbed and cut in chunks*
   4 *leeks (if available), well washed and cut in chunks*
      salt and pepper
      bouquet garni in a piece of cheesecloth containing: 2–3 whole bay
         leaves, 1 bunch fresh parsley, and 1 teaspoon dried thyme
         OR *1 tablespoon fresh thyme (add any other fresh or dried herbs*
         you prefer to the bag)
      watercress for garnish

Put whole chicken in a large deep pot, big enough for plenty of stock and vegetables. Fill the pot with freshly drawn cold water, the wine or vermouth, the vegetables and the bouquet garni bag. Bring to a boil, immediately turn down to a bare simmer and cook partially covered until the chicken is tender. Test with a fork and by slicing off a piece to taste. The time depends on the age and size of the chicken, and doneness should be tested starting at one hour (cooking time may be up to three hours). Let the chicken cool in this broth. Take out chicken and vegetables. Strain the broth and reserve. This makes an excellent stock, and you will have enough left for soup or other dishes. If the chicken was very fatty you may have to degrease the stock. Refrigerate it until the fat congeals so that it can be lifted off, or run paper towels over the surface and spoon off excess fat without cooling it.

Cut all the meat from the chicken into pieces three inches long and one inch wide, as much as possible. Place in a good sealing container with a bit of broth to keep moist.

Make this sauce separately:

- ¼ *pound blanched almonds*
- ½ *pound shelled walnuts*
- 3 *tablespoons butter*
- 2 *medium onions, peeled and finely chopped*
- ½ *pint pure walnut oil*
- 4–5 *slices good white bread, crusts removed*
- ½ *cup milk*
- 3 *cups clear hot chicken broth*
  - *salt*
- 3 *tablespoons Hungarian paprika*
  - *pinch cayenne pepper*

Put all the nuts into a blender and blend only until powdery (be careful not to blend too much or they may turn to paste). Put the nuts into a large mixing bowl.

In a medium-size frying pan sauté onions in butter over medium heat just until transparent. Blend into nuts. Pour the walnut oil slowly in a stream into the mixture, beating constantly with a wire whisk until smooth. Soak bread slices in milk and mash with a wooden spoon; then squeeze the bread dry with your hands and work into nut mixture with your hands. Season to taste with salt, paprika and cayenne pepper. Mix all vigorously with a wooden spoon, until mixture is quite smooth.

Begin blending in the hot chicken broth by spoonfuls until the mixture has a texture between a paste and a sauce too thick to pour. Put the sauce in its own nonbreakable container, and secure tightly.

This wonderful dish is traditionally decorated with a thick paprika sauce, which is made separately from the walnut sauce:

1 *tablespoon paprika*
   pinch of cayenne
¼ *cup walnut oil*

Mix all the ingredients vigorously with a wire whisk or electric blender and store in a small container. Take watercress in a separate plastic bag for garnish.

At the picnic site, arrange the chicken pieces in a dome-shaped mound on a platter. Spoon the sauce over the chicken and smooth with the back of a large serving spoon until all pieces are coated. Pour the paprika sauce in a thin stream in an interesting design to decorate the mound. Garnish with watercress and *voilà*!

You could also totally assemble this dish before the picnic and carry carefully in a suitably sized box or basket. Don't let a protecting cover, such as a dish towel or plastic wrap, touch the design.

CURRIED CHICKEN DRUMSTICKS

Serves 8–10

½ *cup fine dry bread crumbs*
2 *teaspoons onion powder*
2 *teaspoons curry powder*
¾ *teaspoon salt*
½ *teaspoon dry mustard*
1 *clove garlic, peeled and minced*
¼ *teaspoon paprika*
2½ *pounds chicken drumsticks, washed and patted dry*
1 *cup milk*

Oven temperature: 375°

Preheat the oven.

In a bowl, mix together the bread crumbs, onion powder, curry powder, salt, mustard, garlic and paprika. Dip the chicken pieces in the milk, then in the crumb mixture, and place in a greased shallow baking dish in the preheated oven for one hour, or until crisp and done, turning once during baking. Refrigerate until picnic time, and pack in a plastic bag to transport.

RED PEPPER CHICKEN

Serves 6

This is a Chinese Szechuan dish, very spicy, good served tepid in summer or winter.

10 *small, dried red-hot chilis*
2 *chicken breasts, washed and patted dry*
2 *tablespoons soy sauce*
2 *tablespoons cornstarch*
2 *egg whites*
4 *cloves garlic, peeled and pressed*
6 *tablespoons salad oil*
⅔ *cup peanuts, chopped*
2 *small green peppers, washed, cored, seeded and cut into thin strips*

Put dried chilis to soak in a cup of warm water. Take the skin off the breasts and cut the meat from the bone with a small sharp knife. Then cut the meat into strips about ½ inch wide.

Mix the soy sauce, cornstarch, egg whites and garlic. Add the chicken, mixing well. Chill in refrigerator, covered, at least half an hour. Meanwhile, prepare this sauce:

½ *teaspoon chopped fresh ginger*
2 *tablespoons dry sherry*
4 *tablespoons soy sauce*
1 *tablespoon honey*
2 *tablespoons rice vinegar*
¼ *cup red wine*

Mix ginger into sherry. Add rest of ingredients and set aside.

Drain the dried chilis, slit them, and take out the seeds. Cook the chilis lightly with the peanuts in a frying pan or wok in the oil, which has been heated to very hot. Stir and cook until the peanuts are browned and the peppers turn black. Watch carefully. Take out the peanuts with a slotted spoon and drain on a paper towel. Discard peppers.

Now drain chicken pieces. Reheat oil to very hot, add chicken, and stir for 2 minutes. Add green peppers and cook, stirring, 2 minutes more. Add ginger sauce and cook, stirring, until it all comes to a boil. Then stir in peanuts. Remove from heat and let the mixture sit until room temperature. Then put into a plastic container to pack for a picnic.

We like to serve this with Syrian pita bread (page 217). It's also very good served alone, or accompanied by grapes or melon and cheese. Take a serving spoon and chopsticks or forks for each person.

ROAST CHICKEN
WITH WILD GARLIC AND HERBS

Serves 4–6

A beautifully browned roast chicken is a classic picnic entrée. This one is unique and can be served from a pack or basket.

1   *3½-pound roasting chicken*

5   *cloves wild garlic, peeled and cut in halves*
    OR
3   *domestic cloves garlic, peeled and cut in thirds*

    salt and freshly ground pepper
2   *tablespoons vegetable oil*
¼   *cup chicken stock (page 93)*

Stuffing:

¼   *pound (1 stick) butter*

4–5   *cloves wild garlic*
      OR
2–3   *cloves domestic garlic, peeled and sliced*

5   *scallions, minced*
1   *small celery stalk, with leaves,*
       washed and finely chopped

1   *tablespoon each fresh chives, chervil and parsley*
    OR
½   *teaspoon each of dried*

½   *teaspoon dried thyme*
1   *chopped chicken liver*
2   *tablespoons brandy*
1   *cup day-old bread, finely cubed*
    salt and freshly ground pepper

    Oven temperature: 350°

Prepare the stuffing first. Cream the butter in a large bowl with an electric mixer or wooden spoon, softening it until it's creamy. Add the garlic, scallions, celery and all the herbs. Mix together with your fingers. Purée the chicken liver and brandy in a blender, and combine with ½ cup of the bread. Add to the butter mixture and blend together, using a wooden spoon. Add the remaining ½ cup bread, and salt and pepper to taste.

Preheat the oven. To prepare the chicken, stuff the remaining garlic cloves under the skin of each thigh and on down the leg as well. Also place pieces under the skin of the neck opening.

Sprinkle the chicken inside and out with salt and pepper and stuff the cavity with half the stuffing. Starting with the neck cavity, stuff the chicken under the skin as well, working the stuffing up under the skin to make a mound on the breast. Truss with skewers or tie with string so that the chicken keeps its shape while roasting.

In a bit of oil, brown the chicken on all sides in a roasting pan. Add the chicken broth. Lay the chicken on its side and roast in the preheated oven for about 1½ hours, or until tender and the juice runs clear when the bird is pierced with a fork. You may have to cook it for 2 hours at higher altitudes.

Let the chicken cool and wrap in foil. Refrigerate until time to place in a picnic basket or into a heavy drip-proof plastic bag for a journey in a back-pack. Take poultry shears along for carving the bird. Remember to bring separately some watercress or romaine leaves on which to place the stuffed bird before carving.

SPICY CHICKEN CROQUETTES

Serves 5–6

1 *pound cooked, boned chicken breasts, ground in a meat grinder*
    (see "To Cook Chicken," page 287)
1 *thick slice wheat or white bread,*
    with crusts trimmed off
1 *egg*
2 *teaspoons chopped parsley*
¼ *teaspoon turmeric*
    salt and freshly ground black pepper
4 *teaspoons oil*
    lemon juice to taste

Put the ground chicken into a bowl. Soak the bread in a little water, squeeze it dry and add it to the chicken, with the egg, parsley, turmeric and salt and pepper to taste. Mix and knead the ingredients well together and shape into small, marble-sized balls.

Heat the oil in a large frying pan. Add the chicken balls and fry, turning them frequently until they are golden-brown. Drain on paper towels. Arrange the chicken balls in a picnic container and sprinkle with lemon juice.

LEMONY WILD DUCK WITH CANAPÉS

Serves 4–6

1 *duck*
   salt and pepper
3 *tablespoons peanut oil*
5 *tablespoons (1 stick) butter*
5 *ounces salt pork*
       OR *raw ham* OR *bacon*
1 *medium onion, peeled and finely chopped*
5 *shallots or scallions, minced*
       (3 for sauce, 2 for liver spread)
1 *carrot, scrubbed, pared and chopped*

2 *sprigs fresh thyme*
   OR
1 *teaspoon dried thyme*

1 *bay leaf*
2 *cloves garlic, peeled and minced*
   a sprinkle of flour
1 *teaspoon tomato paste*
1 *cup dry white wine*
1 *cup bouillon* OR *water*
2 *chicken livers*
4 *thin slices French bread*
2 *lemons*
1 *bunch watercress for a serving bed*

Oven temperature: 375°

Prepare the duck by plucking its feathers and cleaning and trussing it. Rub lightly with salt and pepper. Cut off the neck and wing tips. Reserve the liver and the giblets. Preheat oven.

To make the sauce, heat 1 tablespoon of the oil and 4 tablespoons butter in a large heavy skillet and place in it the neck, salt pork, wings, and the gizzard, immediately followed by the chopped onion, 3 minced shallots and carrot. Add the thyme, bay leaf and garlic. When mixture is a deep golden brown, sprinkle a little flour over it all. Let it cook a few minutes to mix all the juices and ingredients together. Now add the tomato paste, white wine and bouillon or water. Lightly salt and pepper this mixture. Bring it to a strong boil for a few more minutes, lower the heat and simmer gently for a full hour. Remove the foam on top from time to time. While cooking, prepare the canapés and the roast duck.

The Canapés

Wash the duck liver, adding one or two chicken livers, and cook it in a
skillet with a tablespoon of butter and one of oil, plus the last 2 minced
shallots. Sauté the liver slowly, about 4 minutes on each side. Raise the heat
and mash the liver and shallots together in the pan with a fork. Continue
mashing with a spatula until it reaches the consistency of a purée. Let
cool, place in a small container, and refrigerate.

Toast the thin slices of French bread. Cut each piece of bread into quarters and put in a plastic bag.

The Duck

About 30 to 40 minutes before the sauce is fully cooked, rub the trussed
duck with the remaining tablespoon of peanut oil, salt and pepper, and
place in a roasting pan. Put it in the oven for 30 to 35 minutes until cooked,
but still rare inside. Cooking time depends on the size of your bird and
your tastes, so check doneness and cook 15 minutes more if too rare. Cut up
the bird, slicing pieces of the filet onto a plate, and leaving the wings and
thighs whole. Cool the pieces and pack in a leakproof plastic bag to travel.

Using a metal spatula, loosen the little pieces of meat on the bottom of
the roasting pan and add the juice of one lemon, stirring well. Pass sauce
base through a sieve and add it to the roasting pan. Bring it all to a boil for
a few seconds and add the grated rind of one lemon. Put the sauce in a
plastic container, and also take along some watercress chilled in a separate
bag. This recipe is wonderful cold, served with slices of buttered toast
spread with the duck liver pâté at the last minute. At the picnic site, put the
pieces of duck on a bed of watercress on a paper or plastic serving plate,
arranging the legs and wings around the duck. Pour a little of the sauce over
it, and pass the rest of it separately. Decorate the platter with slices of
lemon around the dish.

PIGEON COMPOTE

Serves 6

- 6 *pigeons* OR *any small game bird**
- 5 *tablespoons butter*
- 3 *tablespoons peanut oil*
   salt and pepper
- 8 *medium-sized onions, peeled and finely minced*

---

* Pheasants are good, but prepare 1 for every two people.

1 *bouquet garni (1 bay leaf, parsley sprig, pinch thyme,*
    pinch rosemary, tied in a cheesecloth bag)
8 *cloves garlic, peeled and put through a press*
2 *cups dry white wine*
⅔ *cup white raisins*

Oven temperature: 325°

Preheat oven. Clean and truss the pigeons. Brown the birds on both sides in 3 tablespoons butter and the oil in a large heavy pan over high heat. Add salt and pepper, and cover the pigeons with the onions, bouquet garni and garlic.

Bake just until the onions become transparent. Add the wine and continue to cook until the breast meat is tender when pierced with a fork, about 25–30 minutes.

Sauté the raisins lightly in the remaining two tablespoons of butter in a small saucepan. Let the bird cool and put it in a leakproof plastic bag. Mix the raisins in the pan juices and take this sauce in a leakproof container. Take poultry shears to carve.

To serve, place the bird on a serving plate, surround it with the onion-raisin sauce.

CHINOOK SALMON BAKED WHOLE WITH OYSTER STUFFING

Serves 10–12

One of the most delicious dishes in our picnic repertoire, the whole salmon also makes a spectacular display. If you can get an ocean troll salmon, all the better, for salmon caught in upstream fresh waters have lost 20 to 30 percent of their body fat in the long hard struggle up the river.

8 *tablespoons (1 stick) butter*
1 *small yellow onion, peeled and minced*
½ *cup finely diced celery*
¼ *cup finely minced fresh parsley*
1 *tablespoon minced fresh tarragon*
1 *tablespoon minced fresh thyme*
3 *cups bread crumbs, made from day-old French bread*
1 *pound fresh whole oysters, cleaned and shucked*
  salt
  freshly ground pepper
1 *whole fresh salmon (head and tail left on), about 4½ pounds*

½ *cup dry white wine*
14 *slices bacon*
    blender green mayonnaise
    lemon slices
    parsley

Oven temperature: 375°

Preheat oven. In a large frying pan, melt 4 tablespoons of butter, add the onion and celery and cook over medium heat for 3 or 4 minutes, then add the parsley, tarragon, thyme and bread crumbs. Stir thoroughly, then add the oysters and their liquid. Season with salt and pepper. Set the mixture aside.

Wash fish inside and out under cold running water; pat dry with paper towels. Sprinkle salt lightly on the inside cavity of the salmon. Lightly pack the stuffing mixture in it, then close the cavity with skewers and tie with string. Place six pieces of bacon over the top of the fish. Wrap loosely in foil, folding the ends together at the top so that you can easily unfold it to baste the fish. Place in a large shallow roasting pan in a preheated oven.

Melt 4 tablespoons of butter in white wine to use for basting. Baste through the opening at the top of the foil by squirting the liquid onto the fish with a basting bulb. (If you don't have a basting bulb, pour a few spoonfuls over the fish through the same opening.) Reclose the foil.

After 20 minutes, test the fish for doneness with a fork. It is done when the meat flakes off easily near the backbone. A 4–5 pound salmon should be done in about 30 minutes.

You can also cook the salmon on an outdoor barbecue grill. Prepare coals for a barbecue. Wrap the stuffed salmon in a double layer of foil. When the coals are ready, lay the salmon on the grill and close the lid. Cook 1 hour or until the salmon meat flakes with a fork. Let cool and refrigerate overnight.

Fry the remaining pieces of bacon until crisp, drain. Prepare blender green mayonnaise (page 178). Crumble and add the bacon to the mayonnaise. Place this mixture in a separate plastic container and refrigerate.

As it is almost impossible to transport a whole salmon on a hike in a backpack, this dish is better served at a picnic where it can be taken on a large unbreakable platter. It is lovely to look at surrounded by lemon slices and parsley. Serve the mayonnaise in a bowl on the side.

PICNIC SALMON LOAF

Serves 6

1 *16-ounce can red salmon, drained and skin and bones removed*
1 *8-ounce package cream cheese at room temperature*
1 *tablespoon lemon juice*
2 *teaspoons grated onion*
1 *rounded teaspoon prepared horseradish*
¼ *teaspoon salt*
¼ *teaspoon liquid smoke seasoning, if available*
½ *cup coarsely chopped pecans*
3 *tablespoons finely chopped parsley*
  parsley sprigs
6 *cherry tomatoes*
6 *smoked oysters*

Mix the salmon, cream cheese, lemon juice, onion and seasonings together in a bowl, mixing and mashing with a fork. Chill for several hours in refrigerator, then shape into a small loaf.

Roll the loaf in a mixture of the pecans and chopped parsley.

Chill. Wrap in foil or plastic and put in a plastic container to carry to picnic. Garnish with parsley sprigs and cherry tomatoes stuffed with tiny smoked oysters which you have packed in a separate small container.

This is good served with stoned wheat crackers.

PICKLED TROUT

Serves 18–20

Make lots of this wonderful preserved food at one time, since it will keep for two months.

18–20 *fresh small trout 6–8 inches long, cleaned*
   1 *teaspoon finely chopped fresh chives*
   1 *tablespoon paprika*
   1 *tablespoon finely chopped parsley*
   2 *tablespoons finely chopped fresh basil* OR *fennel*
     OR
   1 *teaspoon dried basil*
   1 *tablespoon monosodium glutamate*
   1 *tablespoon salt*
   1 *tablespoon pickling spice*

2 *teaspoons black peppercorns*
5 *cups good white wine vinegar*
   (we prefer Japanese rice vinegar)
½ *cup vermouth* OR *any good dry white wine*
   (substitute red if you prefer)
½ *cup dry sherry*
2 *quarts water*
½ *cup vegetable oil*
6 *tablespoons butter*
6–8 *large white onions, peeled and sliced thinly*

Clean the trout and set aside.

Put chives, herbs, seasoning, vinegar, vermouth, sherry and water in a large pot and bring the mixture to a boil. Turn down the heat and keep the pot at a simmer for 30 minutes.

Heat half the oil and butter in a large frying pan over medium-high heat. Brown the trout on both sides quickly two or three at a time, cooking about 3–5 minutes each side, just until tender but still firm. Don't overcook. Add more oil and butter as necessary. Drain trout on paper towels.

Layer trout and onion slices in a glass dish such as a shallow Pyrex baking dish. Pour the hot marinade over the trout and onion slices, let cool, and place in the refrigerator.

Marinate the fish for at least 3 days before eating. Refrigerated, they will keep this way for two months. The trout are preserved whole, but they can be fileted and boned before serving.

The pickled fish should be transported in a flat plastic container with a bit of marinade to keep them moist. If they are to go in a pack, the container must have a tight-fitting lid and be taped all around once with thin strips of masking tape and set in the pack flatly. The fish can be served directly from the container if it is attractive; otherwise, place the fish on a paper plate on some romaine or watercress leaves. Bring these greens in a separate plastic bag or pick watercress or mint on the trail.

SEAFOOD STUFFED EGGPLANT

 1 *medium eggplant*
 ¾ *cup fresh whole-wheat bread crumbs*
 5 *tablespoons butter*
 ¼ *cup Gruyère* OR *Parmesan cheese*
 2 *large scallions, chopped*
 2 *teaspoons chopped parsley*
 ½ *pound fresh crabmeat* OR *diced raw shrimp*
 ¼ *teaspoon salt*
 ¼ *teaspoon pepper*
    parsley sprigs

Oven temperature: 400°

Boil the whole eggplant in water for about 20 minutes. Drain, cool and cut out a wide hole in the top. Remove the pulp carefully with a spoon, leaving a shell one-half inch thick. Chop the pulp and reserve. Sauté the fresh bread crumbs in 1 tablespoon butter in a small skillet over medium heat, and mix in the grated cheese.

Preheat oven. Melt the remaining 4 tablespoons of butter in another medium-sized skillet, add the chopped scallions and parsley, and sauté for 2 minutes over medium heat. Now add the seafood, stirring for about 5 more minutes. Add the eggplant pulp and season with salt and pepper. Mix and cover, cooking for another 5 minutes over medium heat.

Place the filling inside the eggplant shell. (Bake any leftover filling in a small buttered dish and save for another meal.) Sprinkle with the cheese and bread crumbs and dot with a little butter. Bake for about 15 minutes. Let the eggplant cool to room temperature. Serve cold for a picnic entrée. Put the eggplant into a deep hard-sided container to pack. Serve it sliced on a plate garnished with parsley sprigs.

Meat and Eggs

BRISKET OF BEEF WITH CAPER SAUCE

Serves 8–10

This can also be made with cold sliced leftover steak or roast beef. Arrange the slices of leftover beef overlapping on a platter and spoon the caper sauce on them down the center. Garnish with little sour gerkins and parsley and serve with rye or French bread.

> 3–4 *pounds brisket of beef*
> 3 *tablespoons hot oil*
> *salt and pepper to taste*
> 1 *whole onion, prebaked in 350° oven 30–50 minutes*
> 1 *cup beef stock*
> 1 *cup dry red wine*

Braise a 3-to-4-pound brisket of beef by browning it quickly in hot oil in a deep iron or enamel pot. Add salt and pepper, the prebaked whole onion in its skin. Add the beef stock and wine, and barely simmer 3 hours, adding a little boiling water if the liquid gets low. Let it cool in the sauce. Slice the brisket uniformly, then put it back together. Wrap it in foil, and put it in a closely fitting container to hold it together.

Caper Sauce I

> 1 *tablespoon arrowroot*
> ⅓ *cup cold water*
> 1 *cup sour cream*
> 1 *tablespoon vinegar*
> ¼ *cup capers*
> 1 *tablespoon paprika*

Degrease the pan sauce and remove the onion. Thicken the sauce with arrowroot mixed with cold water; add sour cream, vinegar, capers, and paprika. Let the sauce cool and pour it into a container.

Caper Sauce II

> 1 *cup basic sauce*
> OR *blender mayonnaise (page 177)*
> ¼ *cup capers*
> 1 *tablespoon white wine vinegar*

½ teaspoon sugar
¼ cup sour cream
1 teaspoon hot horseradish
¼ cup light cream
  paprika

Mix the mayonnaise, capers, vinegar, sugar, sour cream, and horseradish. Add cream by the tablespoon to thin sauce. Sprinkle paprika on top. Take the sauce in a separate container.

COLD BEEF WITH BASIL SAUCE or VINAIGRETTE

Serves 5–6

Use cold and sliced boiled beef, roast beef or steak.
  Overlap the slices and dab with basil sauce:

3 *cloves garlic, peeled and minced*
6 *sprigs of fresh basil*
¼ *cup pine nuts*
  OR
6 *chopped walnuts*
3 *tablespoons olive oil*

Mix garlic, basil and nuts in a blender for a few seconds at high speed. Pour olive oil in slowly, while mixing. Garnish with parsley or watercress.
  For cold beef vinaigrette, pour a vinaigrette sauce (page 178) over the beef slices and serve garnished with artichoke hearts.
  Both these recipes are especially good served with rice or potato salad, rye bread and red wine.

MARINATED BEEF SLICES

Serves 8

Leftover steak is put to good use in this summer lunch.

1 *pound sirloin steak*
  salt
  pepper
1 *onion, peeled and thinly sliced*
2 *tablespoons lemon juice*

1 *cup sour cream*
1 *teaspoon soy sauce*
   lettuce
   paprika

Broil or sauté the beef or use cold leftover steak. Slice into thin strips and
salt and pepper them to taste. Place onion over the strips and sprinkle with
1 tablespoon of the lemon juice, mixing it in well. Let this stand for 30
minutes to an hour. In a separate bowl mix the sour cream, soy sauce and
the reserved tablespoon of lemon juice. Mix together and chill. Spread it
over the rows of sliced steak and onion. Serve on plates of crisp lettuce with
bread and butter. To transport, bring the sour-cream sauce in a separate
container and pour over the beef when ready to serve.

MEATLOAF HILDEGARDE

Serves 6–8

1 *pound lean ground beef*
½ *pound ground pork*
½ *pound ground veal*
1 *pound potatoes, scrubbed, peeled and grated*
1 *medium-sized onion, peeled and grated*
1–2 *cloves garlic, peeled and minced*
¼ *teaspoon oregano*
¼ *teaspoon basil*
½ *cup tomato purée*
   salt and pepper to taste

Oven temperature: 350°

Preheat oven. Blend meats and grated potatoes. Stir in onion and garlic.
Add oregano and basil to tomato purée, pour over meat-potato mixture and
blend thoroughly. Add salt and pepper to taste. Shape mixture into loaf and
bake in greased baking pan in preheated oven about 1½ hours. Delicious
hot or cold.

SLICED BEEF IN ORANGE JUICE

Serves 6

An unusual and very appealing dish—especially when served with a selection of fresh fruit and cheese.

    3 *cloves garlic, peeled and put through a garlic press*
  ½ *teaspoon comino* OR *powdered cumin*
  ½ *teaspoon powdered cloves*
  ½ *teaspoon salt*
  ¼ *teaspoon white pepper*
    2 *pounds sirloin steak* OR *thick round*
    2 *tablespoons olive oil*
    1 *cup boiling water*
    1 *beef bouillon cube*
    1 *yellow onion, peeled*
    1 *bay leaf*
1½ *cups fresh orange juice*
      watercress OR *shredded lettuce*
  ⅓ *cup diced cooked ham*
    6 *orange slices*
    6 *red onion slices*

Make a paste by mixing the garlic, comino, cloves, salt and pepper with a little of the orange juice in a small bowl. Perforate the steak in several places with the point of a sharp knife. Stuff this paste into the holes with your fingers.

Salt and pepper the meat, and then brown it quickly in hot oil. Drain off the oil and add water and beef bouillon cube to the meat. Add onion and bay leaf and cook covered on top of the stove about 1½ hours, or until tender. Cool, slice and place in a container large enough to hold the meat in two layers. Pour the orange juice over the meat slices and let stand overnight or longer. Serve on a bed of watercress or shredded lettuce garnished with ham bits and alternate orange slices and thinly sliced rings of red onion. You will need forks for this dish.

SAVORY MEAT ROLLS

    Serves 5–6

    1 *recipe pâte brisée (page 152)*
    1 *egg, lightly beaten*
  ½ *cup grated Gruyère* OR *Swiss cheese*
  ¾ *pound ground beef*
    1 *tablespoon finely chopped parsley*
      freshly grated nutmeg
      salt
      freshly ground black pepper

pinch of cumin and ground cloves
1 *egg yolk, beaten with 2 teaspoons water*

Oven temperature: 450°

Preheat the oven and lightly butter 2 large baking sheets. Roll out the dough very thinly and cut it into 5-inch squares. In a small bowl, beat the egg into the grated cheese and ground beef with the parsley and season to taste with nutmeg, salt and pepper, cumin and cloves.

Spread a portion of the meat-cheese mixture in the center of each dough square. Dampen the edges lightly with water. Roll the square with the edges overlapping and the ends tucked in (like a blintz). Prick each roll with a fork and decorate with a little design made from the pastry scraps.

Arrange the rolls on the prepared baking sheets. Brush the tops with the beaten egg yolk. Bake for 15 minutes or until crisp and golden. Let cool and pack in a small box or plastic container.

TENDERLOIN OF BEEF STUFFED WITH PÂTÉ, BAKED IN BRIOCHE

Serves 8–10

This dish, worthy of the most elegant picnic, is not difficult to make, but it does require some advance preparation. You can make the brioche dough a day ahead of time, and it's also advisable to make the pâté well in advance so that it has plenty of time to set well.

Brioche

This recipe makes a very light pastry.

½ *cup warm water*
1 *package active dry yeast*
2 *tablespoons sugar*
1 *tablespoon salt*
1 *cup butter, softened*
6 *eggs, at room temperature*
4½ *cups all-purpose flour, sifted before measuring*

Put the water in the large bowl of an electric mixer, sprinkle on the yeast and stir it in. Add sugar, salt, butter, eggs and 3 cups of the flour. Beat at medium speed for 4 minutes, scraping the sides with a rubber scraper during the mixing. Add the remaining flour and beat at low speed for about 2 minutes, or until smooth.

Cover bowl with waxed paper, and then with a damp towel. Let the dough rise in a warm place (85° F), free from drafts. (An oven with only a gas pilot light burning is a good spot.) After the dough has doubled in bulk (about 2 hours), refrigerate covered with a damp towel and a plate for several hours or overnight.

Pâté

1 *5–6-pound beef tenderloin*
   salt and pepper
2 *bay leaves*
¼ *cup Madeira*

1 *cup chicken liver pâté (follow recipe on page 159,*
       but eliminate the gelée)
   OR
1 *can liver pâté*

1 *egg*
1 *teaspoon cream*
   watercress

Oven temperature: 450°

Preheat oven. Tuck the small end of the roast under, to make it as uniform as possible in shape. Sprinkle with salt and pepper and place the bay leaves on top. Put the roast in a shallow, open roasting pan and sprinkle the Madeira wine over it. Roast until rare, or about 60 minutes for a 6-pound roast.

Let the roast cool, and then slit it down the center. Fill it with pâté, pushing it in with your fingers. There should be a strip of pâté about ¾″ thick down the center—don't try to put in too much. Gently push the roast together again and place seam side down. Grease a cookie sheet. Roll out the brioche dough on a lightly floured board into a rectangle about 15 or 16 inches long and about ⅛ inch thick. It should never be more than ¼ inch thick. Trim the dough evenly, reserving the scraps to make cut-outs for decorating.

Lay the filet, seam side up, on the dough. Fold the dough over lengthwise, one side at a time, pressing the edges together to seal. Fold the ends in and pinch together to seal. Transfer the filet, seam side down, to the cookie sheet.

Roll out the dough trimmings and cut out small shapes, using a cookie cutter or a fluted pastry cutter. Decorate in any design you wish.

Cover with a towel and let rise in a warm place (85° F), free from drafts, until the dough doubles in bulk, or about 1 hour.

Preheat oven to 400°. Beat egg with 1 teaspoon cream, and gently brush over the pastry with a pastry brush. Bake for 30 minutes, until deep golden brown. Cover with foil if it is getting too brown.

Let stand at room temperature until cool. Using 2 spatulas, carefully transfer loaf to an unbreakable serving platter and cover loosely with foil or a plastic oblong cover. Place it in a box or basket to take to a picnic by car.

For a backpacking picnic, cut off as much of the loaf as you'll need, put it in your pack in a hard-sided container, and slice at the site. (Don't forget to take along a good slicing knife.) Serve each person a slice, or overlap the slices on a serving plate garnished with watercress or wild mint.

Serve with a good French mustard or homemade mayonnaise.

Cold Mustard Sauce

Make vinaigrette sauce (page 178), but add 1 egg yolk, 2 tablespoons (instead of the 1 tablespoon) Dijon mustard, and 2 tablespoons water to the other ingredients before you start mixing in the oil.

Caper Mayonnaise

Make sauce mayonnaise pistou (page 178) and add 1 tablespoon capers, drained. Chill.

COLD ROAST PORK ROLL

Serves 8–10

A small picnic version of a festive Italian roast pig called "Porchetta," this cold pork roast, stuffed with liver and nuts, is delicious and great for picnicking.

2 *cloves garlic, peeled and pressed*
1 *teaspoon salt*
  freshly ground black pepper
1 *teaspoon brown sugar*
1 *teaspoon fresh sage leaves, crumbled*
1 *teaspoon fennel seed, crushed in a mortar*
1 *teaspoon vegetable oil*
3 *pound pork loin, boned**
½ *pound veal liver, cut into strips ½ inch × 3–4 inch*

* Have your butcher bone the loin roast.

⅓ *cup shelled pistachio nuts*
2 *tablespoons bourbon*
    watercress OR *parsley*

Oven temperature: 375°

Preheat oven. Mix the garlic, salt and pepper, brown sugar, sage, fennel and oil together in a small bowl to make a paste.

Lay the meat flat and rub it with half the mixture. Then lay the liver strips on the pork, and spread the nuts on top of all. Roll up the pork from the narrowest end. Tie it at 1-inch intervals lengthwise and crosswise. Rub the rest of the paste on the top (the fat side) of the meat roll. Dribble the bourbon over it.

Roast on a rack until a meat thermometer registers 170° (about 2 hours).

Cool the meat and slice neatly into slices about ⅓-inch thick, being careful to keep the liver pieces in place. Put the slices back together and wrap the roast carefully and tightly in foil.

When you are ready to serve, arrange the pork slices on a plate garnished with watercress or parsley.

Serve with chutney or hot mustard and rye bread.

CRÉPINETTES

Serves 8

Crépinettes are fresh country "sausage" made with pork. You can vary the ingredients by adding ½ cup of chopped chestnuts or pistachio nuts. You may want to change the seasonings by trying other herbs, such as sage or fresh coriander. Crépinettes are fun to make, delicious, and very nourishing, and are a good alternative to a pâté for a picnic. If your butcher can't provide caul fat, you can use the meat mixture as a filling for meat pies, using *pâte brisée* (page 152).

½ *pound lean pork, shoulder* OR *neck*
½ *pound veal* OR *poultry, skin removed and boned*
½ *pound hard salt pork*
½ *teaspoon allspice*
2 *tablespoons salt*
    freshly ground pepper
1 *clove garlic, peeled and crushed*
½ *teaspoon cumin seeds*
½ *teaspoon thyme*
    large sheet of caul fat, cut into 4–5 inch squares

2 *tablespoons vinegar*

½ *cup vegetable* OR *corn oil*
OR
2 *tablespoons melted butter*

½ *cup bread crumbs*

Put your meats through a grinder twice* and season, or place all ingredients in a Cuisinart food processor and grind. You can have your butcher grind the meats at the time you buy them.

Caul fat is a special pure fat used to envelop the sausage. Ask your butcher for it. Soak it in water with vinegar until it is soft and pliable. Cut it into squares, put 2 heaping tablespoons of sausage meat in the middle of each square. Tucking the ends in, fold the sides over so that they overlap. The fat seals during cooking. Fry the crépinettes in hot oil over medium heat, or bake them with melted butter brushed on top 45 minutes at 350°; then roll them in bread crumbs while still warm.

Crépinettes will keep for weeks if placed in a dish and covered with ½ inch of melted lard.

* Salt pork is easy to grind when frozen.

FAGGOTS

Serves 8

2 *tablespoons butter*
1 *large onion, peeled and finely chopped*
1 *clove garlic, peeled and crushed*
1 *pound pork liver,* OR *beef liver and kidney*
¼ *pound lean pork*
¼ *pound salt pork*
2 *teaspoons fresh sage leaves, crumbled*
    salt
    freshly ground black pepper
½ *teaspoon mace*
OR
¼ *each nutmeg and cinnamon*

2 *eggs, slightly beaten*
2 *cups fresh bread crumbs (white or whole wheat)*
    large sheet of caul fat
2 *tablespoons vinegar*

a little beef stock OR *gravy drippings from the pan*
2 *tablespoons brandy*

Oven temperature: 350°

Melt the butter in a small skillet; sauté the onions and garlic in the skillet until transparent (10 minutes). Grind the meats and salt pork and sauté the mixture in a large skillet over medium heat with sage, salt and pepper about 5 minutes. Cover and cook over low heat, stirring occasionally, for a half-hour. Add onions and garlic.

Preheat oven. Drain the juices from the sauté pan and set aside in a small bowl. Mix the meat with the mace, eggs and bread crumbs. Taste for seasonings.

Place the caul fat (see previous recipe) in a bowl of warm water and vinegar for 15 minutes or more until pliable, then cut into 5-inch squares. Put a dumpling-size piece of the meat mixture on each square and roll up into a cigarlike shape. Arrange the faggots in a buttered shallow baking dish. Add the juices reserved from the sauté pan mixed with the two tablespoons of brandy. Bake 1 hour. Serve tepid or cold, sliced.

You can preserve the faggots for up to 2 weeks by covering them with melted lard and refrigerating.

GALETTES WITH SPINACH AND SORREL

Serves 6

1 *pound fresh spinach*
butter or shortening
⅓ *cup loosely packed sorrel leaves**
½ *cup flour*
½ *pound sausage meat (half lean salt pork, half ground fatback)*
1 *tablespoon bourbon* OR *rye*
salt and freshly ground pepper to taste
½ *teaspoon mace, cinnamon* OR *nutmeg*
large piece of caul fat

Oven temperature: 350°

Preheat oven. Wash the spinach well, shake off the excess water and place in a pan with a little butter over low heat, to wilt. Drain and chop with the uncooked sorrel. Put the spinach and sorrel in a mixing bowl, add the flour, sausage, liquor and seasonings to taste.

* If sorrel is not available, add one teaspoon of fresh lemon juice.

Wrap the sausage mixture in 4-inch squares of caul fat previously soaked in water and vinegar (as described in the recipe for Crépinettes, page 142). Shape them into small round dumplings by folding all the corners inward, pinching them together at the center and forming a ball-like shape with your hands. Brush with melted butter and bake 45 minutes. Halfway through the baking turn them over to brown the other side. Wrap in three layers of foil to keep warm for the picnic. These are also good served tepid or cold.

HAM ROLLS STUFFED WITH CHICKEN MOUSSE

> **Serves 8**
>
> 8 *thin slices of baked or boiled ham*

Chicken mousse mixture

1 *cup finely minced cooked chicken*
½ *cup homemade mayonnaise*
¼ *cup sour cream*
2 *tablespoons sliced black olives*
2 *teaspoons capers*
1 *teaspoon minced pimento*
2 *tablespoons minced green pepper*

1 *teaspoon minced fresh lemon verbena*
   OR *minced fresh summer savory*
   OR
¼ *teaspoon dried savory*

   salt and pepper to taste

Combine ingredients in mousse mixture, stirring lightly with a fork.

Place the ham on a plate, top each slice with a large dollop of the mousse mixture, and roll. Secure with a toothpick and arrange them evenly in a picnic container surrounded by parsley sprigs and celery sticks.

MOUSSAKA

Serves 6–8

    2 *medium-size eggplants*
    3 *tablespoons vegetable oil*
 1½ *pounds ground lamb*
    1 *small onion, peeled and chopped*
    ¼ *teaspoon* each *thyme and oregano*
    2 *teaspoons salt*
    1 *cup tomato purée*
    5 *tablespoons tomato paste*
    3 *cloves garlic, peeled and pressed*
    3 *eggs, beaten*
    6 *ounces Muenster cheese, shredded*

Oven temperature: 400°

Preheat oven. Cut the eggplants into quarters lengthwise. Brush with 2 tablespoons of the oil. Bake 20 minutes. Scoop out the flesh, being careful not to damage the skins.

Reduce oven heat to 350°.

Line a round 1½-quart charlotte mold (3½–4 inches deep) with the 8 sections of eggplant skin. The outsides should be against the dish, with points meeting and overlapping a little at center of the dish.

Sauté the lamb and onion together in 1 tablespoon of oil until cooked; add the eggplant pulp, thyme, oregano, salt and tomato purée, tomato paste and garlic. Simmer this mixture a few minutes.

Take off the heat and stir in the eggs.

Pour some of the mixture into the lined dish, and sprinkle on some of the shredded cheese. Layer the eggplant mixture and cheese until it is used up. Fold the skins over the top. Cover the casserole with a lid or two thicknesses of foil.

Bake at 350° for 30 minutes. Cool in the dish and wrap securely for a picnic. Moussaka is good tepid or cold and is a specially attractive sight on a picnic table.

Unmold onto a plate to serve.

SPICED MEAT TURNOVERS

Serves 12

    1 *cup chopped fresh mushrooms*
    4 *tablespoons butter*

    1 *teaspoon lemon juice*
       salt and pepper to taste
    1 *tablespoon all-purpose flour*
  ½ *cup milk*
    1 *cup minced onions*
 1¼ *cups ground lamb (shoulder OR leg)*
  ¾ *cup ground sausage*
       dash nutmeg
  ½ *teaspoon allspice*
  ½ *teaspoon chervil*
    1 *egg, beaten*
    1 *recipe pâte brisée (page 152), rolled out and cut into 4-inch rounds*

   Oven temperature: 375°

Preheat oven. Sauté the mushrooms until tender (about 10 minutes) in 2 tablespoons of butter with the lemon juice and salt and pepper. Sprinkle on the flour and stir in the milk. In another pan, sauté the onions in 2 tablespoons butter until transparent, or about 10 minutes. Remove onions and sauté together ground lamb and sausage meat, cooking slowly and stirring and breaking up the meat with a wooden spoon. Season with salt and pepper, grated nutmeg, allspice and chervil. Add sautéed onion to the mixture and combine well.

   Top each pastry round with a portion of meat mixture and a teaspoon of mushroom mixture. Fold over and crimp the edges. Brush with beaten egg and pierce with a fork. Bake on a buttered cookie sheet 30 minutes or until golden brown.

VITELLO TONNATO

Cold Roast Veal with Tuna Sauce

   Serves 8–10

    1 *3½–4-pound boneless veal roast*
       salt
       freshly ground pepper
    2 *tablespoons olive oil*
    1 *cup dry white wine*

    1 *sprig thyme*
       OR
    1 *teaspoon dried thyme*

    1 *bay leaf*

1 *small onion, peeled and coarsely chopped*
1 *carrot, scrubbed, pared and coarsely chopped*
1 *stalk celery, with leaves, scrubbed and chopped*

Oven temperature: 350°

Preheat oven. Have your butcher bone, roll and tie a piece of veal shoulder or leg to make a rolled roast, 3½–4 pounds. Salt and pepper it, then brown it lightly on all sides in olive oil in the roasting pan. Add all the other ingredients above, and cover the pan.

Place the roasting pan in the preheated oven and braise for 2 hours.

Remove the veal roast from the pan and let it cool, then refrigerate.

Strain the sauce into a bowl and degrease it by running paper towels on top of it, leaving the pure sauce underneath. Add this sauce to the following tuna sauce:

1 *can water- or oil-packed tuna, thoroughly drained*
2 *cloves garlic, peeled and sliced*
½ *cup olive oil*
1 *tablespoon white wine vinegar (*OR *cider vinegar)*
  juice of half a lemon
¼ *cup cream*
  dash of white pepper
4 *tablespoons capers*
  sauce the veal roast was cooked in
12 *anchovy filets, drained well on paper towels*

Combine all the ingredients, including the roasting juice, except for the capers and anchovies, in a blender and blend for one minute at high speed. Stir in 2 tablespoons capers and 6 mashed anchovy filets.

Place the sauce in a container with a secure lid. Take the veal roast from the refrigerator and slice it uniformly into thin slices. Take along a bunch of parsley or watercress (or pick it on the trip).

Wrap the extra anchovies and capers in plastic wrap. When ready to serve, arrange overlapping slices of veal on a bed of parsley or watercress on a large unbreakable platter. Cover with the sauce and decorate with anchovies and capers. Don't forget utensils.

SUMMER OPEN-FACED SANDWICHES

It's creative and fun to make sandwiches at the picnic site. Offer a large basket of various sorts of thinly sliced homemade breads, a crock of un-salted fresh butter, a dish of mayonnaise, a crock of imported mustard and an assortment of condiments.

Roast beef, onion and bacon   Cover a piece of buttered bread with a slice of rare roast beef and a slice of crisp bacon crumbled over a very thin slice of onion.

Smoked salmon and asparagus   On buttered white toast, place a strip of smoked salmon; spread with creamed horseradish and asparagus tips, shaped into a flower.

Shrimp with fennel and capers   Crush ½ teaspoon of fennel seed in a mortar, and mix in with 1 package cream cheese. Onto a slice of but-tered bread, thinly spread a little cream cheese with fennel, and top with baby shrimp. Press down and sprinkle 8 or 10 capers and chopped onion among the shrimp.

Ham and cucumber with cheese   Spread a thin slice of black bread with mustard, mayonnaise, a slice of ham and a slice of Swiss cheese. Top with four thin slices of marinated cucumber.

Liverwurst, cheese and mayonnaise   Top buttered rye bread with 3 nar-row strips of Swiss cheese alternating with thin slices of liver-wurst, and dot with mayonnaise and a sprig of parsley.

Ham and avocado   Combine 1 teaspoon lemon juice, 1 teaspoon horse-radish, ¼ teaspoon salt and a dash of Tabasco sauce. Fold this into ⅓ cup homemade mayonnaise for the dressing. On sliced and but-tered pieces of rye bread, assemble layers of Swiss cheese, boiled ham slices, sliced ripe avocado, tomato slices and lettuce. Drizzle with the dressing.

LES OMELETTES FROIDES

Serves 4

8 *fresh eggs**
4 *tablespoons fresh butter*
 salt
 cayenne pepper
1 *teaspoon sunflower seeds*

* Buy fresh country or fertile eggs at a health-food store if you can.

Filling

>   1   *8-ounce package Neufchâtel*
>   OR *cream cheese*
>   1   *tablespoon fresh minced parsley*
>   1   *teaspoon chopped chives*
>   1   *tablespoon fresh minced tarragon*
>   OR *a little pinch of dried tarragon*
>   1   *small clove garlic, peeled and minced*
>   2   *scallions with some green parts, finely chopped*

Make the filling by stirring the cheese in a bowl until soft, and mix in the other ingredients.

To cook the omelette, preheat a burner at medium high heat. Beat 2 eggs slightly in a separate bowl. Add a pinch of salt and cayenne pepper to the mixture. Melt a tablespoon of the butter in the pan and pour in 2 eggs. Cook the omelette lightly until almost firm. Place 3 tablespoons of the herb cheese filling in the center. Fold the sides over to the center, cook a bit longer until sealed. Gently remove the omelette from pan onto a serving platter. Sprinkle sunflower seeds on top and chill in the refrigerator. Continue making the next three omelettes in this manner.

Just prior to departure *les omelettes froids* should be taken out of the refrigerator and securely placed in an airtight container. They make a superb entrée for picnicking, and are very good served with wild asparagus vinaigrette or salad as a complementary vegetable course.

SCOTCH EGGS

Serves 5–6

>   6   *small eggs*
>   1   *pound pork sausage*
>   1   *tablespoon bread crumbs*
>   3   *tablespoons finely chopped parsley*
>   1   *medium onion, peeled and minced*
>   1   *tablespoon chervil*
>   2   *tablespoons tarragon*
>   ½   *teaspoon salt*
>   *freshly ground pepper to taste*
>   *all-purpose flour*
>   1   *cup vegetable or peanut oil*
>   *capers*

Boil eggs 10 minutes and then immerse in cold water, for easy peeling. Set the eggs aside as you prepare the sausage mixture.

In a mixing bowl or Cuisinart food processor, mix the sausage, bread crumbs (whole-wheat or wheat-germ bread crumbs may be substituted), parsley, onion, chervil, tarragon, salt and pepper. Cover the boiled eggs with sausage mixture, about half an inch thick. Roll the sausage balls lightly in flour and deep-fry in hot oil, turning them to brown on all sides. Let them cool and slice in half. Garnish with a few capers and wrap them individually in plastic wrap. Arrange in a picnic container lined with lettuce leaves or watercress, and serve with a variation of the basic sauce mayonnaise, accompanied by carrot sticks, radishes and small cherry tomatoes.

Pâtés and Mousses

PASTRIES FOR PÂTÉS

Pâté Pastry (or Pâte à Pâté)

To cover a 4-cup pâté

Not as delicate as the short crust, this dough works better for covering a pâté because it's a bit more elastic.

3½ cups all-purpose flour
½ teaspoon salt
¼ pound (1 stick) chilled butter, cut into small pieces
½ cup lard, chilled and cut into small pieces
4 egg yolks
⅓ cup ice water

In a large bowl combine the flour and salt with the butter and lard and the egg yolks. Blend with a pastry blender or 2 knives until it is a mealy mixture; add just enough of the ice water 1 tablespoon at a time to make the dough hold together in a ball. Form the dough in two balls and knead each on a floured board, pushing a little section of the dough at a time with the ball of your hand against the board to thoroughly mix in the fats. Form into one ball. Wrap the dough in waxed paper and chill for two hours.

Take the dough out of the refrigerator half an hour before you want to use it. Roll it out in whatever shape required to line your pâté pan or to cover a pâté that is to be baked *en croûte* on a flat pan.

Pâte Brisée

2 8-to-9-inch pastry shells or to cover a good-sized pâté

1 egg
½ cup ice water or dry white wine such as vermouth or a Chablis
¼ cup oil
½ pound (2 sticks) chilled butter
3½ cups all-purpose flour
½ teaspoon salt

Beat the egg with the water or wine and oil in a small bowl.

Cut the butter into little pieces and put into a bowl in which you have put the flour mixed with salt. Use a pastry blender or a fork to combine these ingredients until they have a mealy texture, like oatmeal.

Make a well in this flour-butter mixture and add the liquid mixture of egg, water and oil and mix with a fork until you can form the mixture into a ball with your hands. Form the dough into two balls, and wrap in waxed paper and refrigerate until firm—at least half an hour. Use it within three days or freeze it for up to two months.

Take the dough out of the refrigerator about one hour before using to soften. Roll it out on a floured board with a floured rolling pin to a circle 1 inch larger than your pan for a pie or tart. Fold the dough in half and lay it in the pan. Prick the bottom with a fork and crimp the edges if using a pie tin or press into a French tart pan.

Variation: Use 1 cup whole-wheat pastry flour in place of 1 cup of the white.

COUNTRY PÂTÉ

Serves 10–12

This recipe is marvelously good, like a real French country pâté, particularly when served with homemade French bread.

2½ *pounds pork shoulder* OR *other pork*
 1 *pound veal*
 1 *pound chicken livers*
 2 *cups of any of the following, in any combination: cooked ham, cubed;*
      blanched salt pork, cubed; unsalted pistachio nuts; cooked tongue,
      cubed; cooked sweetbreads, chopped; truffles, sliced; cooked
      chicken, cubed; cooked rabbit, cubed
 ½ *pound thinly sliced salt pork, boiled 10 minutes and drained*
    fresh thyme sprig OR *pinch dried thyme*
 1 *bay leaf*
 ¼ *cup flour*
    radish roses, gherkins, 3 hard-boiled eggs, OR *cornichons to garnish*

Marinade

 2 *ounces cognac* OR *good brandy*
 2 *ounces olive oil*
    pinch of thyme
    pinch of poultry seasoning
 6 *peppercorns*
 ½ *teaspoon salt*
    bay leaf
 ½ *cup dry white wine*

1 *onion, peeled and chopped*
1 *carrot, scrubbed, pared and chopped*
2 *shallots, chopped*
1 *clove garlic, peeled and crushed*
4 *sprigs parsley, chopped*

Seasoning mix

½ *teaspoon salt*
⅓ *cup Madeira*
2 *pinches poultry seasoning*
4 *eggs, beaten with the other ingredients*

Oven temperature: 400°

Trim the pork and veal and reserve one-third of the best meat. Cut this third into cubes and place it in a bowl with half the chicken livers and the marinade. Leave six hours or overnight.

When the meat has marinated long enough, grind the rest of the pork, veal and chicken livers two times through the finest blade of a meat grinder or Cuisinart food processor. Remove the meat chunks and liver from the marinade and strain the marinade into the ground meat. Add the seasoning mix and stir thoroughly. Mix the ground meat and the marinated meat, and add two cups of any of the following in any combination: ham, blanched salt pork, unsalted pistachio nuts, tongue, sweetbreads, truffles, chicken, or rabbit.

Preheat the oven. Line a 2-to-3-quart terrine with one layer of thin slices of the salt pork. Pour in the pâté mixture and cover with the rest of the salt pork. Place fresh or dried thyme leaves and a bay leaf on top. Place the terrine lid on and seal the edges with a mixture of flour and water. Place enough water in a larger pan to come one-half to two-thirds of the way up the sides of the terrine. Bring to a boil, and then place the terrine in it. Bring to a boil again, and then carefully transfer both dishes to the preheated oven. Cook for 2–2½ hours. The flour/water mixture should turn a deep brown, but it shouldn't burn, and the fat bubbling through should be clear. Remove from the oven and let cool. Refrigerate for at least 24 hours, and preferably for 3 or 4 days.

If you're traveling by car, wrap the pâté well in foil or heavy plastic wrap. Take a large platter on which to serve it, radish roses, hard-boiled eggs, gherkins or cornichons for garnish, and a sharp carving knife to slice it very thinly. Unmold and remove most of the salt pork before slicing.

For a pack, unmold at home, and take just what you'll need in a hard-sided container.

CANARD FARCIE EN CROÛTE
(STUFFED DUCK PÂTÉ IN A CRUST)

Serves 8–10

   1 *boned, large domestic duck, bones and giblets reserved**
      dash Madeira
      salt and freshly ground black pepper to taste
   1 *recipe pâte brisée (page 152)*
   ½ *pound pork fat (salt pork or bacon), cut into thin slices*
   ⅓ *cup butter*
 1⅓ *cups chopped mushrooms*
   ¼ *pound foie gras* OR *chicken livers*
   1 *duck liver*
   ¼ *pound boned rabbit, cut into pieces†*
   ¾ *pound boned pork flank, diced*
   ¼ *pound lean pork, cut into pieces*
   1 *truffle, minced*
   ½ *cup brandy*
      jellied stock
   ½ *cup Madeira*
   2 *medium eggs*
      salt and freshly ground black pepper
      thyme
   1 *bay leaf, crumbled*
   1 *egg, slightly beaten*

   Oven temperature: 375°

First make a jellied stock. Put the duck bones and giblets and any pork skin left from trimming the pork required later in the recipe into a large pan. Cover with water and bring to a boil. Cover the pan and cook at a rolling boil for about one hour. Remove the pan from the heat and strain the liquid into a clean pan. Boil the strained liquid down to 1¼ cups. It should have a good strong flavor. Add a dash of Madeira and seasoning to taste. Put the stock into the refrigerator, and if it does not set into a good jelly, return it to the heat and reduce further. Set aside.

Season the duck inside and out with salt and pepper. Set aside. Line a large terrine with two-thirds of the dough. Boil the pork fat in water for 10 minutes. Drain and arrange the fat around the sides.

For the stuffing, first melt one-third of the butter in a small pan. Add the

---

*Your butcher will bone the duck for you.
† Substitute chicken or game birds if rabbit is unavailable.

mushrooms and cook them until the juices have evaporated. In another pan, melt the remaining butter. Add the foie gras or chicken livers, the duck liver, rabbit and both pork meats and brown well. When the mixture is almost done add the truffle. Pour in half the brandy and ignite. Remove the pan from the heat and set aside to cool. When cool, grind the meats finely or purée in a blender. Put the mixture into a bowl and beat in the remaining brandy, the Madeira, ½ cup jellied stock and eggs. Season with salt and pepper and thyme and crumbled bay leaf to taste. Preheat oven.

Spread one-fourth of the meat mixture on the bottom of the dough-lined terrine. Stuff the duck with half the mixture and fold it into shape. Put the duck into the terrine and spread the remaining quarter of stuffing mixture on top. Roll out the remaining dough to make a lid and seal it in place. Make a hole in the center and brush over with the beaten egg. Bake for 1½ hours. If the crust browns too quickly, protect it with foil.

Reheat the remaining jellied stock and while the pâté is still warm, pour it through a funnel placed in the central hole of the pastry lid. Pour it slowly so the stock can sink in. Stop when the pâté is full.

Leave the pâté in a cold place or in the refrigerator for at least 12 hours, or preferably 24, before serving.

For a large group of picnickers, you will want to present the whole duck *en croûte*, so unmold it and wrap in two or three thicknesses of aluminum foil. You may take a portion of the pâté in the same manner.

EASTER PIE

Serves 6–8

¾ *pound lean veal*
¾ *pound lean pork*
½ *cup dry white wine*
 2 *teaspoons Madeira*
    salt
    freshly ground pepper
 1 *tablespoon chopped parsley*

1   *medium onion, peeled and chopped*
½   *cup butter*
2   *mushrooms, washed and sliced*
    grated nutmeg
    ground cloves
1   *recipe pâte brisée (page 152)*
6   *hard-boiled eggs, peeled and cut in half lengthwise*
1   *egg, beaten with a little water*
    watercress
    several colored Easter eggs

Oven temperature: 350°

To make the filling, cut the veal and pork into small pieces, and put in bowl with wine and Madeira. Marinate overnight. The next day, grind the meat and add salt, pepper and parsley.

In a small frying pan over medium heat, cook the onion in the butter until it is soft, but not brown. Add the mushrooms and cook 5 minutes. Season with nutmeg, cloves, salt and pepper to taste. Preheat the oven.

Roll out two-thirds of the dough into a large rectangle and place it on a cookie sheet. Leaving a two or three-inch margin all around, spread half the meat mixture in the middle. Cover the meat with half the onion and mushroom mixture, and then cover this with the remaining meat mixture. Arrange the egg halves in a double row on top and cover with the remaining onion-mushroom mixture.

Cut out a square shape at each corner of the dough rectangle. Brush the edges with the beaten egg and bend them up, pinching the edges together so that the pastry forms a little box around the filling.

Roll out the remaining dough to the shape of a lid. Lay it on top of the pie and pinch the edges together to make a close seal. Slash the top, decorate with two lines of pastry leaves cut from the pastry scraps, and brush all over with beaten egg.

Bake for 1½ hours, until brown. Serve at room temperature with a green salad. To carry the pie, put it on a platter and cover with plastic wrap. Take watercress and Easter eggs separately for garnish.

LEBER KÄSE (GERMAN LIVER PÂTÉ)

Serves 8–10

This is a popular German pâté, not so fine and smooth in texture as that available from butcher shops in Germany, but a hearty, rich loaf for a picnic in any case.

1¼ *pounds lean pork, ground twice by your butcher*
  1 *pound pork liver, chopped*
  1 *clove garlic, peeled and minced*
  1 *onion, peeled and chopped*
  1 *small piece of ginger, chopped to make ¼ teaspoon*
  1 *cup heavy cream*
  ½ *cup ice water*
  2 *eggs, lightly beaten*
  ¼ *pound slab bacon, diced*
  2 *teaspoons salt*
  ½ *teaspoon sugar*
     a pinch of ground cloves
  ½ *teaspoon crushed peppercorns*
     parsley
     watercress
     sour gherkins

Oven temperature: 350°

Preheat oven. Grease a regular-sized loaf pan or two smaller ones with lard.

Put the liver through the medium blade of a meat grinder with the garlic, onion, and ginger two times. Mix this in a bowl with the pork; add the cream and then the water, ¼ cup at a time, mixing well with your hands after each addition and letting the meat absorb each addition of liquid before adding more. Mix in the eggs, bacon, salt, sugar, ground cloves and peppercorns, mixing well with your hands. Put the mixture into the loaf pan and cover with three layers of foil. Bake it in another pan, filled with enough boiling water to reach two-thirds of the way up the pâté loaf pan. Bake 2 hours or until the sides have shrunk from the pan and the juices run clear.

Let the loaf sit 15 minutes and lay a 2-to-3-pound weight on top of the foil inside the edges of the pan. Leave the weight on 10–12 hours or overnight. Then refrigerate the pâté. To transport, carry it in the pan in which it was cooked wrapped in leakproof plastic bags. When ready to serve, unmold it onto a platter and garnish with parsley, watercress and little sour gherkins. Slice it and serve with rye bread and butter.

If you want to take the pâté in a pack, make it in the two small loaf pans. Take one and save the other for another meal. It keeps well for several days or a week.

MILLIE'S CHICKEN LIVER PÂTÉ EN GELÉE

Serves 6–8

2 cups chopped chicken livers
2 large green onions, minced
5 tablespoons butter, melted
1 tablespoon vegetable oil
⅓ Madeira or brandy
¼ cup heavy cream
½ teaspoon salt
⅛ teaspoon allspice
⅛ teaspoon freshly ground white pepper
pinch of thyme
½ package unflavored gelatin
¾ cup hot beef bouillon
1 bay leaf or a sprig of thyme
watercress to garnish

Sauté the chicken liver and onion in 1 tablespoon butter and the oil in a medium-size skillet over medium heat for a few minutes, until cooked but still pink inside. Blend them in an electric blender and add the Madeira, cream, the remaining butter, salt, allspice, white pepper and thyme. Taste for seasoning. Mix gelatin dissolved in ½ cup cold water into the hot beef bouillon. Put a bay leaf or a sprig of thyme in the bottom of the mold and pour in enough of the gelatin mixture to coat the mold about ¼ inch. Chill the mold until the gelatin thickens somewhat so that you can then turn the mold to coat the sides.

Pack the liver mixture into the mold and chill several hours.

Wrap the entire mold in foil and carry it right side up inside a leakproof container or plastic bag.

If it is warm, chill the mold in a cold stream or in snow, then unmold it by leaving it upside down over a paper plate in the sun. Take some watercress in a little plastic bag to garnish.

PASTELÓN PARA COMIDA CAMPESTRE

Spanish-Style Picnic Pie with Ham and Tomatoes

Serves 12

You can make this with homemade short crust or puff paste, or you can buy an equal amount of puff paste from your baker.

    4 *tomatoes*
    ½ *cup olive oil*
    2 *onions, peeled and finely chopped*
    3 *cloves garlic, peeled and minced*
    1½ *teaspoons salt*
    1 *teaspoon freshly ground pepper*
    1 *cup boiled ham, cut in strips*
    1¾ *cups cooked shrimp (see "To Boil Shrimp," page 288), with*
        ¼ *cup reserved for garnish*
    ½ *cup chopped parsley*
    2 *tablespoons Madeira*
    1 *pimento, chopped*
    1 *recipe pâte brisée (page 152)*
    ½ *cup sliced black olives*
        parsley
    1 *egg*
    1 *tablespoon cream*
    10 *whole black olives to garnish*

Oven temperature: 450°

Preheat oven. Blanch the tomatoes in boiling water. Cool them enough to handle, then peel, squeeze gently to remove seeds, and chop them. Reserve.

In a skillet, heat half the olive oil and sauté the onions and garlic slowly, until translucent (about 10 minutes).

Add the tomatoes, salt, and pepper and cook over moderate heat until the mixture is quite thick, 15 to 20 minutes. Let cool.

In another skillet, toss the ham and shrimp in the rest of the olive oil with the parsley, Madeira and pimento until heated through, about 10 minutes. Divide the pastry into two parts, one slightly larger than the other. Roll out the smaller to a 12-by-5-inch rectangle and put it on a baking sheet. Spread this with half the tomato-onion mixture. Next, spread on all the ham mixture, then sprinkle on the sliced olives, then add another layer of tomato-onion mixture.

Lay the larger piece of pastry over the filling and seal the edges with a fork, dampening to seal. Brush the edges and entire "pie" with an egg beaten with cream. Cut three short slashes in top of the pie or make a little pipe of foil and put it in a round hole one-fourth inch in diameter made in the center top.

Bake for 20 minutes. Reduce heat to 350° and bake 30 minutes or more until nicely brown. Cool and pack the pastelón carefully in a bread pan or a box, so it won't break in transit.

For a backpack, take about one-third of the pastelón wrapped in plastic wrap or foil inside a hard-sided plastic container. Take whole olives, ¼ cup shrimp and parsley in separate plastic bags to garnish.

PÂTÉ D'ARTICHAUTS EN CROÛTE

Serves 8–10

1 *recipe pâte brisée (page 152)*

Purée

6 *tablespoons butter*
pinch saffron
3 *large onions, peeled and minced*
salt and pepper to taste

Mushroom-Rice Mixture

½ *pound mushrooms, stems included, chopped*
2 *tablespoons butter*
salt and pepper to taste
1 *tablespoon chopped parsley*
1 *tablespoon chopped fresh thyme and chervil combined*
OR
1 *teaspoon each dried thyme and chervil*
1 *teaspoon lemon juice*
1½ *cups cooked brown rice (see "To Boil Rice," page 288)*

Artichoke filling

12–14 *frozen or canned artichoke hearts*
2 *tablespoons butter*
1 *tablespoon all-purpose flour*
¼ *cup cream*
½ *teaspoon dill*
white pepper
salt
1 *teaspoon vinegar*
½ *pound baked ham, diced*

Oven temperature: 375°

Make the pastry dough and put it in the refrigerator to chill.

To make the onion purée: first heat the butter in a large deep skillet. Cook the onion and saffron slowly until the onion is soft, transparent and slightly browned (about 15 minutes). Season to taste with salt and pepper. Purée this mixture in a blender and reserve.

To make the mushroom-rice mixture: cook the mushrooms in a separate skillet in the butter with salt and pepper, herbs and lemon juice until tender (5–10 minutes).

Combine the rice and mushrooms in a bowl and set aside.

To make the artichoke filling: cook the frozen artichoke hearts until tender, drain and coarsely chop them (or use canned hearts, which are already cooked). Melt the butter in a saucepan, add the artichoke hearts, sprinkle with flour and cook on low heat for 5 minutes. Slowly add the cream, stirring constantly until smooth. Stir in the seasonings, vinegar and ham, and let the mixture cool slightly.

Roll out the pastry into 2 rectangles about 6 inches by 14 inches. Put one of them on a greased baking sheet.* Spread half the mushroom-rice mixture on the pastry, leaving a ¾ -inch border all around.

Cover the rice with the artichoke mixture, then the onion purée, and the rest of the rice. Cover all with the other rectangle of pastry and crimp the two rectangles together, dampening the edges. Make two slashes on the top, decorating with fanciful shapes cut from the pastry scraps. Refrigerate for at least 20 minutes before baking. Preheat oven.

Bake for 30–40 minutes, or until nicely browned. Let cool at room temperature, and then place the pâté on a piece of foil. Lift it carefully into a hard-sided protective container, or wrap half of it if you're using a backpack. Be sure to serve the pâté at room temperature.

Make a small pie or tart with any ingredients left over. You'll probably have enough for a 6-inch pan.

* You can also bake this in an 8" × 4" × 2½" tube pan with collapsible sides, available in specialty gourmet utility shops. Line the pan with the pastry and layer it the same way.

HAM MOUSSE MADRILÈNE

Serves 6–8

1 *tablespoon butter*
1 *tablespoon all-purpose flour*

½ *cup cream*
   salt and white pepper
   tiny grating of nutmeg
½ *pound cooked ham*
¾ *cup aspic or madrilène jelly (canned)*
 1 *cup heavy cream, whipped*
   salt
   cayenne pepper
 2 *egg whites*
   watercress and whole cherry tomatoes to garnish

Make ½ cup béchamel by melting the butter in a small saucepan over medium heat. Add and stir in the flour, cooking a few minutes. Take the pan from the heat and add the cream slowly, stirring steadily. Return to low heat and cook for 3–4 minutes. Season with salt, white pepper and nutmeg. Grind the ham twice. With an electric beater or a blender, combine it with the béchamel. Put the ham mixture into a bowl, stir in the aspic and fold in the whipped cream. Season strongly with salt and cayenne. Beat the egg whites until they are very stiff. Fold a little of the ham mixture into them. Then add the whites to the rest of the ham mixture, folding gently but thoroughly from the bottom to the center and down. Oil a 4-cup mold and pile in the ham mousse lightly. Refrigerate until chilled. Serve with fresh bread and butter. Chicken can be substituted nicely here for the ham, if desired.

To transport, wrap the mousse in a plastic leakproof bag secured with rubber bands. Set right side up to carry. Take a serving plate and invert the mousse onto it 15–30 minutes before serving. If set in the sun for this length of time, it should unmold, but don't leave it there too long, as the heat could spoil it. Take the tomatoes in a little plastic container and the watercress in a plastic bag for garnish. Everything will fit nicely into a pack or a picnic basket.

PHEASANT MOUSSE

   Serves 8–10

 1 *tablespoon butter*
 3 *tablespoons shallots, minced*
 2 *cups chicken stock*
 2 *envelopes unflavored gelatin, softened in* ¼ *cup dry white wine*
 2 *cups chopped pheasant meat*
      (OR *other game such as rabbit* OR *sage hen*)

⅓ *cup canned foie gras*
3 *tablespoons cognac*
   pinch of allspice
   salt and pepper to taste
⅔ *cup heavy cream, whipped*
   parsley sprigs OR *watercress to garnish*

In a heavy-bottomed 2-quart saucepan, sauté the shallots in the butter over moderately high heat until soft and transparent. Add the chicken stock and dissolved gelatin. Cook for two more minutes and remove from the heat.

Add the chopped pheasant meat and the foie gras. Blend the mixture in a blender until smooth. Add the cognac, allspice, salt and pepper, and blend again. Place in a bowl.

Fold the whipped cream into the pheasant mixture. Taste for seasoning. Place in a mold and chill two hours till set.

The mousse travels very well except in very hot weather. Wrap the mousse, mold and all, in foil and put it in a leakproof plastic bag secured with a rubber band. Sit it squarely in a pack, held in place by other items in the pack. Look at the mousse when you arrive. If it looks too soft, put it in snow or cold stream water, if available, while you lay out the picnic. It should unmold nicely if you place it upside down on a platter in the sun for a few minutes and then tap the bottom. Garnish with watercress or parsley.

SALMON-AVOCADO MOUSSE

Serves 4

This colorful seafood salad, "frosted" with its own dressing, is delicious.

1 *envelope unflavored gelatin*
¼ *cup cold water*
¾ *cup boiling water*
2 *tablespoons sugar*
1 *tablespoon lemon juice*
1 *tablespoon vinegar*
2 *teaspoons grated onion*
½ *teaspoon salt*
½ *teaspoon horseradish*
1 *1-pound can salmon, drained and flaked with a fork*
½ *cup mayonnaise*
⅓ *cup sliced pitted ripe olives*
¼ *cup finely chopped celery*

Soften gelatin in cold water. Add boiling water and stir until the gelatin has dissolved. Add sugar, lemon juice, vinegar, onion, salt and horseradish; chill until partially set. Stir in salmon, mayonnaise, olives and celery. Spoon into an oiled 3-cup mold and chill five hours or overnight.

Avocado Dressing

　1　*large, ripe avocado*
　½　*cup sour cream*
　½　*teaspoon salt*

Seed, peel and mash the avocado to make about ⅔ cup. Mix in sour cream and salt. Blend thoroughly, chill.

To transport, wrap the mold well in foil, secure it inside a leakproof plastic bag, and place it squarely in a pack. Let the mold sit briefly in the sun upside down on a plate to unmold it, then spread with the avocado dressing. Garnish with a lemon twist.

Beware of taking a gelatin-base mousse in very hot weather. If you find it's softened too much on a warm day, set it in the shallow waters of a cold stream or a snowfield for a while. Then invert it over a plate to unmold.

Quiches and Stuffed Breads

BREAD STUFFED WITH COLD MEAT SALAD, SWISS STYLE

Serves 10

2 cups ground cold meat
 (cooked ham, pork, veal, chicken OR rare roast beef)*
2 hard-boiled eggs, peeled and chopped
3 tablespoons minced onions
2 dill pickles, chopped
4 tablespoons finely chopped fresh green herbs (including parsley
 and scallions OR chives)
 dash of Tabasco
1 tablespoon Worcestershire sauce
 mayonnaise
 butter
1 loaf French bread,
 homemade if possible (page 208)

Mix the meat with the other ingredients with enough mayonnaise to make a smooth but stiff mixture.

Cut the ends off the bread and remove the inside with a fork, leaving a shell ¾ inch thick.

Brush the interior with soft butter and fill it firmly with the meat mixture so that there are no air holes.

Wrap the loaf in foil and put it in the refrigerator for several hours before slicing.

You can slice the loaf, put it back together and rewrap it so that it's ready to serve for your picnic; or place it on a board or platter and slice it as you serve it for a delightful surprise.

* If you don't have a meat grinder, finely chop the meat with a knife.

BREAD STUFFED WITH WILD MUSHROOMS

Serves 10–12

You can vary this unusual picnic sandwich by trying different kinds of mushrooms in the stuffing—all wild edible mushrooms such as morels, boletes, or oyster mushrooms are wonderful. It's worth doing with domestic mushrooms as well.

  1 *large onion, peeled and chopped*
½ *clove garlic, peeled and minced*
  4 *tablespoons (½ stick) butter*
  2 *pounds wild* OR *domestic mushrooms*
      wiped with a damp cloth and sliced
½ *cup chopped fresh parsley*

½ *teaspoon dried thyme*
    OR
  1 *sprig of fresh thyme*

    salt and pepper to taste
  1 *cup dry white wine*
  1 *round loaf French* OR *Italian bread*
    olive oil
    several slices of bacon

Oven temperature: 375°

Preheat oven. In a large frying pan, sauté the onion and garlic in the butter over low heat until transparent (15 minutes). Add the mushrooms, parsley, thyme, salt and pepper. Cook 5 minutes, add wine, and cook 10 minutes over medium heat to reduce liquid.

Slice the top off the loaf of bread and remove the bread inside, leaving an inch and a half thickness of bread inside the loaf all around. Fill the loaf with the mushroom and onion mixture. Replace the top of the bread and rub the whole loaf lightly with olive oil.

Bake for 20 minutes on a bed of several slices of bacon. Baste with bacon drippings during cooking. Serve hot (wrapped in layers of foil to retain heat) or at room temperature. Cut into pie-shaped wedges when serving.

CLAM PIE WITH WILD OYSTER MUSHROOMS

    2 6-inch pies or 1 10-inch pie

This pie keeps well in the refrigerator for up to two days. It is at its best when served at room temperature, which, of course, makes it perfect picnic fare. Oyster mushrooms have a strong flavor that blends nicely with the clams, but you can use any species of edible wild or cultivated mushrooms in their place.

  2 *recipes pâte brisée (page 152)*
  3 *dozen fresh clams, littleneck* OR *any small variety*
  1 *pound wild oyster mushrooms (*OR *any other variety),*
      wiped with a damp cloth and chopped coarsely

2 *tablespoons butter*
1 *tablespoon lemon juice*
   pinch each thyme and marjoram

Clam Stock for Filling

   strained juice from cooking clams
1 *carrot, scrubbed, pared and cut in chunks*
1 *stalk celery, washed and chopped*
1 *medium onion, peeled and cut in chunks*
1 *bay leaf*
6 *peppercorns*
1 *cup dry white wine*
2 *sprigs parsley*

Velouté Sauce for Filling

4 *tablespoons butter*
4 *tablespoons all-purpose flour*
2 *cups clam stock*
2 *eggs, separated (2 whites reserved in one bowl and the*
   yolks in 2 separate bowls)
2 *tablespoons brandy*
2 *teaspoons Dijon mustard*
1 *tablespoon Worcestershire sauce*
1 *tablespoon lemon juice*
   salt and white pepper
1 *tablespoon milk*

Oven temperature: 450°

Make the pâte brisée and store in the refrigerator. Butter two 6", or one 10" pie plate.

Wash and scrub the clams thoroughly. Bring about 1½ quarts water to a boil in a large pot and put the clams in. Boil until they open slightly (about 15 minutes), discarding the ones that don't open. Take the clams out and let the liquid in the pot cool so the sand from the clams will sink to the bottom. When the pot liquor is cool, pour the liquid through a strainer lined with cheesecloth into a large saucepan. Boil the clam juice down to make about 2 cups, then add the carrot, celery, onion, bay leaf, peppercorns, wine and parsley and let the mixture simmer for at least half an hour.

Meanwhile, take the clams out of their shells, chop them coarsely and reserve.

Sauté the mushrooms in a medium-sized skillet in which you have melted the butter. Add lemon juice, thyme and marjoram. Cook over medium heat, stirring with a wooden spoon until just cooked through, about 5 minutes for most mushrooms. Smaller, tender varieties cook more quickly; large, older oyster mushrooms should be cooked over lower heat about 10 minutes. Set aside.

Roll out a little more than half the pastry into 2 rounds to fit the bottoms of the buttered pie tins, with about a ½-inch overhang all around. If you're using a 10-inch tin, roll the pastry to the appropriate size.

Strain the clam stock. Preheat oven.

In another 2-quart heavy-bottomed saucepan, melt the butter and stir in the flour to make the base for the velouté sauce. Take off the heat and stir in the clam stock. Return to the heat, stirring vigorously until smooth and thick. Add 1 beaten egg yolk, the brandy, mustard, Worcestershire sauce, lemon juice, chopped clams and salt and white pepper to taste. Leave the sauce over low heat while you roll out the top crusts. Do not let it come to a boil.

Roll out the remaining dough ¼ inch thick in two pieces slightly larger than the pie plates, or in one large round to fit over a 10-inch pie.

Beat the egg whites stiff and lightly fold them into the velouté. Spoon the filling into the bottom crusts. Fill almost to the edge and heap the filling a bit in the center. Lightly place the top crusts on the pies, moisten the edges and flute. Prick the tops in several places.

Mix the milk with the remaining egg yolk and paint the crusts with a pastry brush.

Bake for 15 minutes and then lower heat to 350° and continue baking until nicely browned, about half an hour.

Let the pies cool. Refrigerate to chill.

Wrap the pies well in heavy plastic or foil to go in a backpack or basket.

These pies can serve as a main course or, if cut in small wedges, as an hors d'oeuvre. It's best eaten at medium temperature, not chilled, so don't put it in a cooler and set in a sunny spot prior to serving.

FRUIT-STUFFED BREAD FROM NORMANDY

Yield: 2 round loaves

Bread

   1 *package active dry yeast*
  ½ *cup plus 2 tablespoons warm water*
   2 *cups all-purpose flour*
   1 *egg*

2   *tablespoons butter, softened (not melted)*
1   *tablespoon oil*
½   *teaspoon sugar*
¾   *cup heavy cream*
    pinch of salt

Filling

3   *small quinces, quartered**
4   *apples, peeled and quartered*
10 *tablespoons (1¼ sticks) butter*
    pinch of cinnamon
3   *tablespoons sugar*
¼   *cup Calvados* OR *brandy*
4   *ripe medium-sized pears, cored and quartered*
¼   *teaspoon vanilla extract*
1   *egg, beaten with a little water*

Oven temperature: 375°

Dissolve the yeast with the 2 tablespoons water in a large bowl. Stir in the other ½ cup warm water. Sift in the flour, mixing it with your fingers until the mixture becomes the consistency of meal. Add a bit more water if too dry. Sift a layer of flour over this mixture and let it rest for about an hour until doubled in bulk.

Add the egg, butter, oil, sugar, cream, vanilla and salt to the flour mixture. Mix well and knead for about 5–7 minutes. Form it into a ball and place it in a buttered bowl, covered. Let rise again in a warm place until doubled in bulk (1–2 hours). While the bread is rising prepare the filling.

Preheat oven. In a large frying pan cook the quinces and apples in the butter and cinnamon over medium heat. As they begin to soften, lower the heat and sprinkle them with sugar and Calvados (substitute plain brandy if you wish); then at the last minute add the pears. Stir the fruits together, take them off the heat and let the mixure cool.

Divide the dough in half. Roll out two-thirds of each portion to a thin 9-inch round, no more than ⅛ to ¼ inch thick.

Lay these rounds into 2 1-quart casseroles or 6-inch soufflé dishes.

Fill to the top with fruit, heaping it up very full. Roll out the remaining dough into an 8-inch round. Lay over the top and pinch the sides together, using cold water to seal the edges. Let rise again until double in bulk, 30 minutes to one hour. Brush with egg.

Bake 50 minutes until golden brown.

* Substitute 6 apricots, pitted and quartered, OR 2 peeled and pitted peaches OR 3 pineapple slices, quartered, when quinces aren't available.

Cool in the pans half an hour, then remove to a rack. When the loaves are cool, wrap them in foil to take on a picnic. Wrap also in a leakproof plastic bag for a pack.

SPINACH QUICHE

Yield: 9-inch quiche
Serves 6

½   *recipe pâte brisée (page 152)*
 2   *teaspoons chopped shallots*
 2   *tablespoons butter*

 2   *pounds fresh spinach*
     OR
 1   *package frozen*

½   *teaspoon salt*
⅛   *teaspoon freshly grated pepper*
     nutmeg
     cayenne
 3   *eggs*
1½ *cups light cream*
¼   *cup Swiss cheese*

Oven temperature: 350°

Preheat oven.

Prepare ½ recipe *pâte brisée*. Roll out and place in a pie tin. Prick the pastry with a fork on the sides and bottom and bake 10 minutes. Cook frozen or fresh spinach in boiling water a few minutes, place it in a colander to drain, and rinse with cold water. Drain on paper towels and pat dry, then chop finely. Raise the oven temperature to 375°.

Sauté the shallots in 1 tablespoon butter for a few minutes. Add the spinach, the salt, pepper, a large dash each of nutmeg and cayenne. Beat the eggs with the cream. Stir in the spinach. Check seasonings and then pour the mixture into the partially baked pie shell, sprinkle with cheese and dot with the remaining tablespoon of butter.

Bake for about ½ hour.

This is great cold and as a leftover. Individual slices can be wrapped for hiking.

STUFFED SYRIAN PITA BREAD

Serves 4–6

Use the recipe for Syrian bread (page 217). Make the rounds only 4 inches in diameter. Slice the bread rounds in half after they have been baked and cooled. Pack each half with some of the following filling:

1 *large can water-packed tuna fish, drained*
1 *tablespoon freshly chopped parsley*
1 *tablespoon finely chopped pimento*
1 *tablespoon good olive oil*
  salt and freshly ground pepper to taste
  a few drops fresh lemon juice
1 *shallot* OR *scallion, minced*
  dash Tabasco

Mix all the above ingredients thoroughly with a fork. Taste for seasoning. Stuff each halved pita and garnish each with the following:

1 *small hard-boiled egg*
    quartered and arranged in a pinwheel on top
1 *Mediterranean Greek olive, placed in the center*
4 *thin strips of green or red pepper*
    placed between each egg section

Wrap each stuffed Syrian pita bread in plastic wrap and pack side by side in a plastic picnic container.

TORTA RUSTICA

Serves 10–12

Both of us have spent a little time in Milan, and both of us love a particular delicatessen called Salamario. Staring in the window, you can see an incredibly beautiful food display even before you enter. And as soon as you step inside the door, you see, on a middle island filled with wonders, the torta rustica—a delight to the eye in layers of pink, green and yellow, with highlights of bright orange. Here is our version of that wonderful treat.

4 *tablespoons butter*
2 *cups spinach, washed, well-drained and chopped*
  salt and pepper
  a grating of fresh nutmeg
4 *eggs*

1   *recipe brioche dough, made the day ahead*
        (see Tenderloin of Beef Stuffed with Pâté, page 139)
2   *pounds Mozzarella cheese, thinly sliced*
1   *cup Ricotta cheese*
2   *pounds prosciutto, thinly sliced*
2   *2½-ounce cans pimentos, drained*
1   *egg, mixed with water*
        homemade mayonnaise

Oven temperature: 400°

Heat 2 tablespoons of the butter in a medium-sized frying pan, add the spinach, and sauté over low heat until all the moisture has cooked out (about 30 minutes). Season with salt and freshly ground black pepper and a grating of fresh nutmeg. Meanwhile, make two 2-egg omelettes, one at a time, in an 8-inch frying pan, using the remaining butter. Set aside.

Roll out half of the brioche dough on a lightly floured pastry cloth to a 10-inch round about 1 inch thick. Line an 8-inch spring-form pan with the dough. There should be about a 1 inch overlap of dough at the top rim.

Line the dough bottom and sides with Mozzarella. Lay in one omelette. Cover with ½ cup of the spinach spread and smooth with the back of a tablespoon. Do the same with ½ cup of Ricotta cheese. Cover with a 1-inch layer of thinly sliced ham, putting big chunks of pimento between slices at several points. Cover with a ½-inch layer of Mozzarella and the remaining Ricotta. Repeat ham and cheese layers to top, ending with an omelette covered with a spinach layer and a 1-slice-thick layer of Mozzarella.

The layering should fill the pan completely so that it heaps up in the middle above the rim. Preheat oven.

Roll out the rest of the brioche dough to a 9-inch circle.

Place on top and pinch the 2 pieces of dough together all around. Make a nicely fluted edge by pinching. Put three short sharp gashes in the top with a razor blade.

Make decorative cut-outs with the dough scraps to decorate the top.

Brush the torta with the egg and water mixture and bake for 30 minutes. After 20 minutes check to see if it is getting too brown; if so, cover with foil for the last 10 minutes. Let cool in the pan. Wrap it all in foil to carry to a picnic.

Undo the spring-form pan at the site, leaving the torta on the base. Place it on a larger platter. Garnish all around it with radish roses, cornichons (or tiny domestic pickles), pickled mushrooms and parsley sprigs. Cut it in cakelike wedges and serve with homemade mayonnaise made with 2 extra tablespoons of Dijon mustard.

WILD MUSHROOM QUICHE

Serves 6–8

Edible wild mushrooms make a delicious and unique quiche, but you can combine wild mushrooms with domestic mushrooms for an almost equally good flavor.

½ *recipe pâte brisée (page 152)*
3 *tablespoons butter*
2 *green onions* OR *shallots, minced*
1 *teaspoon lemon juice*
1 *pound wild mushrooms, washed, patted dry and sliced about ¼ to ½ inch wide*
¼ *teaspoon salt*
3 *egg yolks*
¾ *cup light cream*
½ *teaspoon salt*
⅛ *teaspoon cayenne*
1 *teaspoon freshly ground black pepper*
¼ *cup grated Swiss cheese*

Oven temperature: 375°

Roll out the pastry dough into a circle 10 inches in diameter and fit it into a pie pan, fluting the edges. Prick the sides and bottom of the pastry with a fork. Bake in the preheated oven 10 minutes. Let cool.

In a large saucepan melt the butter, add the onions or shallots and cook about 1 minute. Add the fresh lemon juice, mushrooms and ¼ teaspoon salt. Cover the pan and simmer the mushrooms for about 10 minutes. Reserve.

Preheat oven. In a small mixing bowl beat the egg yolks; then add cream and ½ teaspoon salt, freshly ground pepper and the cayenne pepper. Stir this into the mushroom mixture while stirring over low heat. Turn off heat.

Sprinkle the grated Swiss cheese on the bottom of the pastry shell. Gradually pour the mushroom mixture into the pastry shell, and bake for 30 minutes. Let the quiche cool to room temperature. To pack the quiche for the picnic you may want to cut it into serving slices before wrapping it in aluminum foil or plastic wrap. Whichever way, make sure the quiche is placed securely in the top of the backpack to avoid tilting or squishing it. Serve individual slices as wonderful hors d'oeuvres.

If you're going to the picnic by car, take the quiche whole, covered with the plastic wrap or foil, and cut it just before serving.

SALADS

One day last summer, we and a group of friends gathered up our picnic packs, filled with food and wine, and started on a hike. There had been no communication concerning the picnic menu for the day, so each hiker knew only what she herself had brought, but we all knew that any food would be a welcome treat after the long uphill climb to Twin Lakes. It was hot when we arrived at noon. There was only one tent pitched on the opposite shore from us and no sign of inhabitants, so we took the opportunity to take a refreshing dip in the lake before lunch.

We had chosen a picnic site on a grassy bar of land which divides the two lakes, where the wildflowers are like a solid carpet. It was a comfortable place to sunbathe for a time after our swim before laying out our lunch. We chatted and opened our bottle of white wine before lunch. As the food and serving pieces came out of the packs, we realized that there were six salads!

Each one, remarkably different from the others, was a treat: a cold curried chicken salad with pecans and fresh grapes; a Middle Eastern cucumber and potato salad dressed with a mixture of fresh chopped cilantro, parsley leaves and rice vinegar; a tomato and Mozzarella salad with lots of fresh basil; a rice salad garnished with green peas and hard-boiled eggs, and a dish of cold beets in mustard sauce. Luckily we also had a loaf of French bread and three bottles of wine. It was a delightful picnic.

Salad Dressings

BASIC SAUCE MAYONNAISE

Yield: 3 cups

Mayonnaise, the base for various sauces and dips, adds a special touch to any picnic when made by hand.

2 *egg yolks*
½ *teaspoon Dijon mustard*
½ *teaspoon salt*
½ *teaspoon wine vinegar*
¼ *teaspoon confectioners' sugar*
olive oil, about 2½ cups
wine vinegar
lemon juice

It is essential to begin with all ingredients at room temperature. Using a wire whisk or a fork, beat egg yolks in a wide-bottomed bowl. Beat in mustard, salt, wine vinegar and powdered sugar. When the mixture is smooth, begin pouring in a constant thread of olive oil (the better the quality of the oil, the better the taste). Stir vigorously as the oil is added. When about ⅓ of a cup of oil has been poured, the mixture should begin to emulsify. Continue, adding a sprinkling of vinegar every so often. After several additions of vinegar, switch to lemon juice. It is possible to use as much as 2½ cups of oil, adding lemon juice when necessary to ensure the proper consistency.

BASIC BLENDER MAYONNAISE

Yield: 1½ cups

1 *egg*
½ *teaspoon dry mustard*
½ *teaspoon salt*
2 *tablespoons vinegar*
1 *cup vegetable* OR *olive oil*

Place egg in container of electric blender. Add mustard, salt and vinegar, and ¼ cup of the oil, cover, and turn motor to low speed. Immediately uncover and, with motor still running, pour in remainder of oil in a thin steady stream. Leave blender on about a minute after the last of the oil has been added. Mayonnaise may be stored in tightly covered container in refrigerator for up to three days.

The mayonnaise may spoil in very hot weather. Make it immediately before going on a picnic, allowing just enough time to chill it in the refrigerator.

Variations

Creamy Rich Mayonnaise:

Add ½ cup whipped cream just before serving.

Mayonnaise Pistou:

Add ¼ cup minced fresh basil, 2 tablespoons chopped pine nuts and 2 cloves garlic put through a press.

Mayonnaise Vert or Sorrel Mayonnaise:

Add 4 tablespoons blanched green fresh herbs or sorrel, finely minced. (Blanch the herbs quickly in boiling water, and drain on a paper towel before mincing them.) Add a drop of green food coloring if the mayonnaise is too pale.

Mayonnaise with Capers:

Add 3 tablespoons capers to plain mayonnaise or any of the above. This is particularly nice with cold fish and meats.

VINAIGRETTE SAUCE

Yield: 2½ cups

1½ *cups olive oil* (OR ¾ *cup olive oil,* ¾ *cup corn* OR *safflower oil*)
 ⅓ *cup good wine vinegar* OR *Japanese rice vinegar (a favorite of ours)*
 1 *tablespoon dry wine*
 1 *tablespoon Dijon mustard* OR *1 teaspoon dry mustard*
    few grindings pepper
    salt to taste
 2 *tablespoons chopped mixed herbs—parsley, chervil, chives*
 1 *teaspoon chopped capers (optional)*

Mix the above ingredients except the oil together in a bowl with a fork or whisk, beating vigorously, then taste for seasoning. Add the oil slowly while beating with a whisk to make the sauce creamy. Pour into a jar and refrigerate.

Variations

Vinaigrette Sauce with Minced Eggs:

Rub 3 hard-boiled eggs through a food mill or fine chopper and add to the sauce.

Chicken, Cheese and Meat Salads

CHICKEN-APRICOT SALAD

Serves 10–12

¼ cup mayonnaise
¼ cup sour cream
1 cup yogurt
⅓ cup milk
2 tablespoons lemon juice
2 teaspoons Dijon mustard
1 teaspoon salt
1 cup diced dried apricots
3 cups diced cooked chicken (see "To Cook Chicken," page 287)
1 cup chopped celery
⅓ cup finely chopped scallions
crisp lettuce leaves (optional)

Blend mayonnaise, sour cream, yogurt, milk, lemon juice, mustard, and salt in large bowl. Add apricots, chicken, celery and scallions. Toss lightly, combining well. Chill. Spoon in a picnic container. If desired, sprinkle salad with additional chopped apricots when serving. Serve from the container if attractive, or spoon out into a plastic bowl or platter lined with lettuce leaves. Take the lettuce separately in a plastic bag, chilled and sprinkled with water.

CHICKEN AND TONGUE SALAD

Serves 8–10

2 cups diced cooked chicken (see "To Cook Chicken," page 287)
1 cup diced cooked or smoked tongue
3 hard-boiled eggs, peeled and chopped
½ cup chopped pecans
½ cup minced celery
2 tablespoons minced parsley
1 tablespoon minced fresh tarragon
OR
½ teaspoon dried tarragon

salt and pepper to taste

> 1 *cup mayonnaise (homemade* OR *blender, page 177,*
>   OR *commercial)*
> 1 *sliced tomato*
>   *watercress (optional)*

Combine all ingredients except tomato and watercress in a large bowl, mixing lightly. Put in a plastic container. Pack the tomato and watercress in separate containers. Slice the tomato for a garnish when ready to serve, alternating watercress sprigs and sliced tomato over the salad served from the container it was carried in, if attractive, or in a plastic bowl or platter brought along for this purpose. Bring salad servers.

COLD BEEF SALAD PARISIENNE

Serves 10–12

This dish is complemented especially well by sourdough rye (page 214) and sweet butter. The sauce is outstanding alone and can be used on other cold meats or salads.

Sauce Gribiche

> 3 *hard-boiled eggs*
> 1 *tablespoon minced parsley, chervil, tarragon and chives,*
>   *mixed together*
> 1 *teaspoon Dijon mustard*
> ½ *teaspoon salt*
>   *pepper to taste*
> 1½ *cups olive oil*
> ½ *cup vinegar*
> ½ *cup sour pickles, chopped*

Salad

> 1 *pound cold boiled beef, sliced*
> 1 *large potato, boiled and peeled (see "To Boil Potatoes," page 287)*
> 1 *large tomato, quartered*
> 1 *pound cooked fresh green beans*
> 1 *large carrot, scrubbed, pared and cut in julienne strips*
> 2 *hard-boiled eggs, peeled and quartered*
>   *several romaine leaves for a bed*

Remove yolks from the eggs and mash them in a bowl. Add herbs, mustard, salt and pepper. Alternately add oil and vinegar, a little of each at a time, beating vigorously after each addition, adding the vinegar whenever the mixture begins to get too thick. After the oil and vinegar are mixed in, add the whites of the eggs, finely chopped, and the chopped sour pickles.

Take the cold beef, vegetables and eggs in a plastic container. Arrange them on a large paper plate or plastic platter lined with romaine lettuce taken in a separate plastic bag. Take the sauce in another container and spoon it over the vegetables and meat when you are ready to serve.

CURRIED CHICKEN SALAD

Serves 8–10

This lovely cool chicken salad has a rather unique flavor, which comes from the combination of fresh herbs and apples.

    2 *medium-sized tart apples*
    3 *teaspoons lemon juice*
    2 *cups diced chicken (see "To Cook Chicken," page 287)*
    2 *cups sliced celery with leaves*
  ½ *cup pecan halves*
    2 *teaspoons minced onion*
    1 *cup creamy rich mayonnaise (page 178)*
       pepper to taste
    1 *teaspoon salt*
    2 *teaspoons good curry powder (more if you wish)*
       romaine leaves for a bed
    4 *hard-boiled eggs, peeled and sliced*

Peel and core, then dice the apples, placing them in cold water to which 1 teaspoon lemon juice has been added.

Combine the chicken with the celery and pecans (saving a few for garnish). Add the drained apples and onion. Mix the mayonnaise, pepper, salt, remaining 2 teaspoons lemon juice and curry powder. Pour over the salad and toss lightly but thoroughly. Taste for seasoning. Pack in a plastic container and chill. Take the eggs whole and quarter them for garnish when ready to serve. Present the salad at your picnic site on a bed of lettuce garnished with sliced egg and pecan halves.

DEVILED BEEF TOSS

Serves 8–10

Mustard-Horseradish Dressing

½ tablespoon sugar
1 teaspoon salt
1 teaspoon dry mustard
¼ teaspoon white pepper
   dash paprika
1 tablespoon horseradish
½ teaspoon grated onion
⅔ cup olive oil
¼ cup white wine vinegar

Deviled Beef Toss

1 head of romaine, washed, dried and torn in pieces
½ small head iceberg lettuce, washed, dried and torn in bite-size pieces
1½ cups cooked rare roast beef strips
1 cup cherry tomatoes, halved
½ medium onion, peeled, sliced and separated into rings
1 1-to-2-ounce can rolled anchovy filets, drained on paper towels

In a bowl combine all the ingredients for the dressing except the oil and vinegar. Beat the mixture with an electric beater while slowly adding the oil and vinegar alternately. Put in a container to travel.

Put the pieces of lettuce in a plastic bag. Sprinkle a little water over them before closing. Chill until ready to pack.

Toss the beef strips, tomatoes, onion rings and anchovies lightly together in a bowl and chill before packing in a plastic container.

Take the dressing separately. Arrange the meat and vegetables over the greens on a platter or in a bowl at the picnic. Spoon dressing over all.

SAUERWURST SALAT

Serves 4–6

1 pound bologna, cubed, to make about 3 cups
   (ring bologna is good for this)*
4 sour gherkins, sliced

---

* You can use cold cooked pork or any sort of cooked cold sausage in this dish.

1 *small sweet onion, peeled, sliced thinly and separated into rings*
1 *2½-ounce can chopped pimentos, drained*
½ *teaspoon sugar*
½ *cup basic vinaigrette sauce (page 178)*
  salt and freshly ground pepper
  lettuce leaves

Toss the bologna, gherkins, onion and pimento together in a large mixing bowl with the sugar and vinaigrette. Salt and pepper to taste.

Pack the mixture in a plastic container and serve in a bowl lined with lettuce leaves. Take the lettuce leaves in another plastic bag.

This is delicious served with rye bread and sweet butter on the side.

SPANISH MEAT SALAD

Serves 6

4 *cups cubed cold cooked meat (beef, ham, pork, veal or lamb;*
   a combination of any of the above is best)
1 *small red Spanish onion, peeled and minced*
4 *tablespoons finely chopped watercress*
2 *tablespoons finely chopped parsley*
⅓ *cup olive oil*
3 *tablespoons red wine vinegar*
  salt and pepper
1 *large canned pimento, chopped and drained*

Toss all the above together lightly and serve on a bed of lettuce, taking the lettuce leaves separately in a plastic bag, and arranging the salad attractively on a plastic platter or large paper plate just before serving.

SWISS SALAD

Serves 6

This is a hearty salad, whose taste depends on the type and quality of cheese used. Our first choice is Appenzeller, the most flavorful and nutty of Swiss cheeses, but you can use a good Gruyère or Emmenthaler (the one with large holes that we call Swiss).

Dressing

- ½ cup yogurt
- ½ teaspoon hot horseradish
- 1 teaspoon dry mustard
- ½ teaspoon powdered cumin **or** caraway seed
- 1 teaspoon grated lemon rind

  salt and pepper to taste

Salad

- 1 bunch leaf lettuce
- ½ pound "Swiss" cheese, cubed
- 4 hard-boiled eggs, peeled and coarsely chopped
- 1 small red Spanish onion, peeled and minced

  salt and pepper

Mix the dressing ingredients with a fork in a small bowl. Wash and dry about 8 small-to-medium lettuce leaves, and put in a plastic bag in the refrigerator to chill. Mix the cheese, eggs, onion, salt and pepper, toss lightly with the dressing, and put into a plastic container and chill.

To serve at the picnic site, spoon the salad out onto lettuce leaves on a plastic or paper plate or into a bowl lined with lettuce.

Fish Salads

HERRING SALAD

Serves 12–16

This nourishing version of a Scandinavian main dish makes a large amount. You can save part of it for another meal, since it keeps well for several days refrigerated. Serve with plenty of black bread and sweet butter.

- 2 *cups cooked and diced beets*
- ½ *cup cooked and chopped fresh green beans*
- 1 *large jar of creamed pickled herring*
- 2 *cups (2 medium) boiled, peeled and diced potatoes (see "To Boil Potatoes," page 287)*
- 2 *cups diced ham, veal or roast beef*
- 1 *dill pickle, chopped*
- 2 *crisp green apples, peeled, cored and diced*
- ½ *onion, peeled and finely chopped*
- 1 *teaspoon sugar*
- 5 *tablespoons wine vinegar*
  salt and freshly ground pepper
- 2 *teaspoons capers*
- 2 *hard-boiled eggs*

Toss all ingredients except the eggs together lightly with a fork in a large bowl. Cover and refrigerate. Pack the amount you want to use for the picnic in an appropriate plastic container. Take unpeeled hard-boiled eggs separately to garnish. Peel and slice them at the site right before serving, and lay them decoratively on the salad.

MUSSEL SALAD

Serves 10

- 4½ *quarts fresh mussels, scrubbed and washed with a stiff brush*
- ½ *cup dry white wine*
- 4 *shallots, chopped*
- 1 *sprig of thyme*
- 6 *parsley sprigs*
- 1 *tablespoon freshly ground black pepper*
- 2 *pounds (3–4 large) potatoes, boiled, peeled, cooled and thinly sliced (see "To Boil Potatoes," page 287)*

½ *cup vinaigrette sauce (page 178)*
1 *tablespoon each of chopped parsley and chopped chives*

Put the mussels, wine, shallots, thyme, parsley and pepper into a large pot. Add water to cover. Boil rapidly, uncovered, over high heat for about 7–10 minutes or until the mussels open. Take the mussels out of the water with a slotted spoon as they open, throwing away any that don't open. Remove them from their shells. Set the mussels aside and discard shells.

Put the potato slices in a large bowl. Strain the boiling mussel liquor through two thicknesses of cheesecloth, pour over the potatoes and set aside to cool. Drain the potato slices in a colander and put them in a plastic container. Scatter the mussels over them and pour the vinaigrette sauce over all. Chill until ready to pack for a picnic.

Serve the salad in a bowl or on a platter at the picnic. Sprinkle chopped parsley and chives over the salad just before serving.

SHRIMP AND CELERY VINAIGRETTE

Serves 6

1 *pound baby shrimp, fresh or frozen, cooked*
   (see "To Boil Shrimp," page 288)
2 *cups very thinly sliced celery*
   (or put through the fine blade of a food chopper)
¼ *cup minced parsley*
½ *cup vinaigrette sauce with minced eggs*
   (page 179)
1 *teaspoon ground fennel*

Combine the shrimp, celery and parsley with the vinaigrette sauce to which you have added the fennel. Chill and store in tight container to take on a picnic. Serve with buttered Finn Crisp or Norwegian flat bread.

SHRIMP STUFFED TOMATOES

Serves 6

This is an easy picnic salad. Although tomatoes are difficult to transport on a long hike, there's no reason not to serve them on preplanned picnics, when you bring foods in coolers by car to a designated spot. Fix everything ahead, and then spoon the cool refreshing shrimp salad into a tomato rosette for each person just before serving.

Shrimp-Rice Salad Stuffing

     6 large tomatoes
     2 cups cooked shrimp, cut in pieces and chilled
            (see "To Boil Shrimp," page 288, OR use canned)
  1½ cups cooked rice, chilled (see "To Cook Rice," page 288)
     ⅓ cup chopped celery
     ¼ cup sliced pitted black olives
     1 tablespoon chopped parsley
         salt and pepper to taste

Dressing

     ¼ cup salad oil
     2 tablespoons red wine vinegar
     ½ teaspoon dry mustard
     ¼ teaspoon paprika
     1 small clove garlic, peeled and minced

With stem end down, cut each tomato into 6 wedges, cutting to but not
through base of tomato. Spread wedges apart slightly; carefully scoop out
pulp. Salt lightly inside and set tomato shells in a colander cut side down
to drain. Dice and drain tomato pulp. Combine diced tomato, shrimp, rice,
celery, olives and parsley. Toss gently with dressing, sprinkle with salt and
pepper, and chill. Place tomato shells in the refrigerator to chill after they
have drained 30 minutes or more.

   For dressing, blend salad oil, vinegar, dry mustard, paprika, and garlic.

   Pack the tomatoes and the shrimp salad filling in separate plastic containers. Put them in a cooler to transport.

   To serve, spoon the shrimp salad into tomato shells. If desired, garnish
with watercress and additional cooked shrimp.

SUMMER SALAD WITH SMOKED SALMON

         Serves 6–8

     2 teaspoons butter
     4 slices smoked salmon, drained on paper towels
            and cut in strips
     8 mushrooms, washed, patted dry and chopped
     1 head Boston lettuce, washed, dried
            and torn in small pieces
     2 tomatoes, sliced

½ cup sliced radishes

1 tablespoon each *chopped fresh chervil, fresh parsley, and fresh dill*

1 teaspoon *chopped fresh chives*

Sour Cream Dressing

1 cup *sour cream*

2 teaspoons *tarragon vinegar*

1 tablespoon *white vinegar*

1 teaspoon *horseradish*

½ teaspoon *salt*

Melt butter in a medium-sized skillet, and sauté the salmon and mushrooms together over medium heat for about 5 minutes, stirring often. Set aside off heat. Put the lettuce in a large bowl. Add the tomatoes, radishes, chervil, parsley, dill and chives. Mix the cold vegetables and herbs with the salmon and mushrooms. Place in a plastic container and chill.

Make the dressing by beating all the ingredients together, and put it in a separate container to chill in the refrigerator. If you will be traveling by car, carry the salad and the dressing separately and toss at the picnic.

If you want to serve it on a hike, pack the prepared vegetables and the salmon-mushroom mixture in plastic containers, the lettuce in a plastic bag, and the dressing in a little jar with a screw-on lid. Toss the salad in a plastic bowl at the picnic.

Don't forget salad servers.

Potato and Grain Salads

CURRIED RICE SALAD

Serves 4–6

2 cups cooked rice (see "To Cook Rice," page 288)
¼ cup coarsely diced fennel root OR celery
1 canned pimento, drained and diced (approximately ⅓ of a cup)
½ cup cooked shrimp OR drained and flaked tuna
 (see "To Boil Shrimp," page 288)
4 pitted black olives, halved
4 mushroom caps, washed and chunked
1 tablespoon finely chopped parsley
1 tablespoon finely chopped chives
2 teaspoons curry powder
 tiny pinch cinnamon
1 teaspoon Pernod
⅓ cup vinaigrette sauce (page 178)

Toss all the ingredients lightly with the vinaigrette in a large plastic container.

A variation of this salad can be made by stuffing 8 ripe tomatoes with the curried rice mixture. Slice the tops off the tomatoes. Remove and discard the pulp. Fill tomatoes with the curried rice salad and cover with the tomato "lids." Dribble olive oil over tomatoes and bake 15 minutes at 350°. Place closely together in a hard-sided plastic container for hiking, and serve at room temperature.

POTATO AND BEET SALAD

Serves 8

When beets and potatoes are marinated in a vinaigrette sauce, the combination turns an exotic red color. An attractive picnic provision, it can be served as either a main course or a side dish.

2 cups diced fresh cooked OR canned beets
 (3 medium-sized beets OR 1 medium can, drained)
2 cups warm boiled potatoes, peeled and sliced
 (see "To Boil Potatoes," page 287)
4 tablespoons minced shallots OR green onions
¾ cup vinaigrette sauce (page 178)

1½ *cups green mayonnaise (page 178)*
     salt and freshly ground pepper
1 *cup cooked and diced green beans**

Scrub beets and boil until tender, about 20 minutes. Rinse and dice. Toss the potatoes, beets, and onions in a large bowl with vinaigrette and let them marinate several hours. Add any of the other vegetables. Take and serve the mayonnaise separately. Garnish with any or several of the following: green or black olives, anchovies, sliced hard-boiled eggs, watercress or parsley sprigs. Take the garnishes packed separately in a small plastic container.

* If you wish, you may substitute an equal amount of cooked peas, cauliflower, broccoli, carrots, turnips or asparagus; diced beef, pork, poultry or fish; tuna or salmon.

RED POTATO SALAD

Serves 6

½ *cup finely chopped red cabbage*
1 *pound (3–4) new potatoes, boiled, peeled and thinly sliced*
     (see "To Boil Potatoes," page 287)
½ *cup vinaigrette sauce with minced eggs (page 179)*
1 *anchovy filet, minced* OR *a pinch of tarragon*
4 *hard-boiled eggs, peeled and cut into quarter wedges*

Mix the red cabbage with the potatoes, and pour the dressing, to which you have added the anchovy or tarragon, over all and toss thoroughly. Put in a plastic container and chill before transporting. Garnish with quartered eggs at picnic site. Carry these in a separate plastic container.

SPIRITED POTATO SALAD

Serves 6–8

2 *tablespoons vinegar*
1 *teaspoon celery seed*
1 *teaspoon mustard seed*
3 *medium-large potatoes, boiled, peeled and diced*
     (see "To Boil Potatoes," page 287)
2 *teaspoons sugar*
1 *teaspoon salt*
2 *cups finely shredded cabbage*
¾ *pound corned beef (*OR *1 12-ounce can corned beef),*
     chilled and cubed

   ¼ *cup finely chopped dill pickle*
   ¼ *cup sliced green onion, including some of the green part*
   1 *cup homemade mayonnaise*
   ¼ *cup milk*

Combine vinegar, celery seed, and mustard seed; set aside.

While potato cubes are still warm, drizzle with the vinegar mixture. Sprinkle with sugar and ½ teaspoon salt; chill thoroughly.

Before serving, add cabbage, corned beef, pickle and green onion.

Combine mayonnaise, milk and the remaining ½ teaspoon salt. Pour over the entire mixture, and toss lightly. Chill before the picnic and serve on plates. Don't forget a large serving spoon and forks.

Vegetable Salads

ASPERGES À LA MAYONNAISE

Serves 6–8

Asparagus-hunting trips in spring are great fun. The vegetable found at the roadside on the banks of ditches is an incomparable taste treat, but fresh asparagus from the market is good too, of course.

24 *good-sized spears of wild or domestic asparagus*

1½ *cups homemade mayonnaise (page 177), using lemon juice*
   in place of vinegar
   OR
1½ *cups of vinaigrette sauce (page 178), using lemon juice in*
   place of vinegar

Steam the asparagus in an asparagus cooking pot or in a very deep sauce-pan, tied in bunches of 4 or 5 spears. The bunches must stand upright in a pot deep enough for a lid to be placed on top. Cook only until tender, or about 10 minutes for medium-sized stalks, testing with a fork.

When the asparagus is done, rinse it quickly under cold water and drain it well. Pack it in a container long enough or deep enough to hold the spears without bending. Take the sauce separately in another container.

Serve each person several spears topped with sauce and pass more sauce around. Eat with your fingers.

AUTUMN SALAD

Serves 8–10

The red, brown, yellow and pale-green colors of this salad make a rich seasonal design.

½ *head of romaine lettuce, washed and patted dry*
8 *slices bacon, cooked, drained and crumbled*
¼ *pound Swiss cheese, sliced into small strips*
3 *medium tomatoes, peeled, seeded and diced*
2 *avocados, peeled, seeded and diced*
½ *cup vinaigrette sauce (page 178)*

Tear the lettuce into bite-size pieces. Pack in a plastic bag with a sprinkle of water, and chill. Put the bacon and cheese in separate plastic bags. Take the tomatoes and avocados in separate plastic containers. At the picnic, arrange

the bacon, cheese, tomatoes and avocados on top of the lettuce in separate sections in a plastic bowl or on a platter. When ready to serve, sprinkle the salad with the vinaigrette, and pass the rest of the vinaigrette with a serving spoon. Take forks or chopsticks for each person.

CAULIFLOWER BLUE CHEESE SALAD

Serves 4–6

1 *medium onion, peeled, thinly sliced and separated into rings*
½ *small head cauliflower, rinsed and broken into about*
    3 cups of flowerets
½ *cup sliced radishes*
¾ *cup vinaigrette sauce (page 178)*
    several romaine leaves, torn up
1 *small head iceberg lettuce, washed, patted dry and*
    torn into small pieces
½ *cup crumbled blue cheese OR Roquefort*

Mix and marinate the onion, cauliflower, and radishes in the vinaigrette for at least half an hour. Put this mixture in a plastic container. Take the lettuce in a plastic bag sprinkled with a little cold water. Take the cheese in another plastic bag.

When ready to serve, turn the vegetable mixture out onto a platter or into a bowl lined with the lettuce. Sprinkle the cheese over all. Take forks or chopsticks for each person.

CAULIFLOWER SALAD WITH ANCHOVY DRESSING

Serves 8

1 *head of cauliflower, rinsed and broken into flowerets*
½ *onion, peeled and finely minced*
1 *tablespoon chopped green pepper*
8 *tablespoons olive oil*
1 *teaspoon dried marjoram*
1 *teaspoon chopped canned pimento*
    salt and pepper
6 *anchovy filets, drained and finely chopped*
½ *cup white wine vinegar OR cider vinegar*
¼ *cup white wine*
6 *green pimento-stuffed olives, sliced*

Parboil the cauliflower ten minutes in boiling salted water in a large sauce-pan. Drain and rinse in cold water. Put in a large plastic container.

In a small frying pan, sauté the onion and green pepper over low heat in 2 tablespoons of the olive oil for five minutes. To this pan, add the remaining olive oil and all the other ingredients except the olives; bring to a boil. Turn off heat.

Pour this mixture over the cauliflower and chill the mixture in the refrigerator until ready to pack. Serve garnished with the green olives.

CELERIAC SALAD

Serves 8–10

2 *pounds celery root* OR *knobs*
1 *medium cucumber, scrubbed and peeled*
¾ *cup thinly sliced radishes*
2 *small dill pickles, finely minced*
⅓ *cup vinaigrette sauce (page 178), substituting lemon juice for vinegar*
2 *teaspoons chopped shallots*
1 *teaspoon sugar*
  parsley sprigs
2 *hard-boiled eggs, peeled and sliced*
6 *black olives*

Place the celery knobs in a large saucepan and cover with cold salted water. Bring them to a boil and cook until tender, about 30 minutes. Drain, rinse and cube. Cut the cucumber in half, remove the seeds with a spoon and slice it thin. Add it to the celery together with the sliced radishes. Pour the vinaigrette, to which you have added the shallots and sugar, over the salad and toss. Pack the salad into a plastic container. It will keep, improving over several days. To serve, garnish with parsley, hard-boiled egg slices and olives. Take the garnishes separately and put the salad together at the picnic.

CREAMY COLESLAW WITH CARAWAY

Serves 4–6

1 *head of cabbage, washed and shredded in a food mill or*
   on a grater to make 4 cups
2 *teaspoons sugar*
1 *tablespoon caraway seeds*
¼ *cup white wine vinegar* OR *Japanese rice vinegar*
¼ *cup heavy cream*
2 *tablespoons yogurt*
   salt and freshly ground pepper

Toss the cabbage with sugar and caraway seeds and vinegar. Let the slaw marinate in this dressing several hours or overnight. Add the cream, yogurt, salt and pepper. Taste for seasoning. Mix well, place in a medium-sized container, and refrigerate before transporting to the picnic.

GOURMET BEAN SALAD

Serves 20

1 *16-ounce can* OR *1½ cups cooked kidney beans*
1 *16-ounce can* OR *1½ cups cooked wax beans*
1 *16-ounce can* OR *1½ cups cooked garbanzo beans*
1 *16-ounce can* OR *1½ cups cooked whole Blue Lake green beans*
4 *hard-boiled eggs, peeled and quartered*
¾ *cup sliced crisp radishes*
1½ *cups black Greek olives*
1 *cup ripe tomatoes, cut into wedges*
1 *cup sliced artichoke bottoms*
   (use canned OR *fresh frozen ones cooked—not pickled or marinated)*
1 *cup drained marinated artichoke hearts*
3 *tablespoons minced anchovy (drained on paper towels)*

Fresh Basil Dressing

¼ *cup minced fresh basil*
4 *tablespoons minced fresh garlic*
4 *ounces capers, with their liquid*
2½ *cups olive oil*
¾ *cup good red wine vinegar*
   salt and pepper to taste

1 *tablespoon chopped fresh parsley*
8 *tablespoons finely chopped fresh shallots*
4 *tablespoons fresh lemon juice*
2 *tablespoons Worcestershire sauce*
2 *tablespoons dry mustard*
1 *tablespoon sugar*

Rinse the beans under cold water and drain them well in a large colander.

Mix and toss them together with remaining ingredients and the basil dressing.

After tossing, let the salad chill for at least 2 hours before serving. It will keep several days.

This makes a large portion. Pack what you need in a plastic container and use the rest for another meal.

LAIT DE CONCOMBRE À LA MENTHE

Serves 6

This salad, refreshing and cool, contrasts well with any heavier dish on your picnic menu.

2 *unpeeled cucumbers*
2 *teaspoons salt*
6 *green onions, finely sliced*
2 *cups yogurt*
½ *teaspoon freshly ground black pepper*
⅓ *cup finely chopped fresh mint*
 fresh mint leaves

Wash and score the cucumbers with the tines of a fork before slicing. Slice the cucumbers and place in a colander. Sprinkle with 1 teaspoon of salt. Put a plate on top to help press the water out, and leave for half an hour. Rinse the cucumber slices and pat dry. Toss the cucumbers with the remaining teaspoon of salt, onions, yogurt, pepper and mint in a medium-sized bowl. Refrigerate for at least two hours before placing in a container to pack for a picnic.

MARINATED TOMATOES

Serves 6–8

6 *tomatoes, sliced*
1 *cup pitted ripe olives*

2 *cups chopped onion*
¼ *cup minced fresh parsley*

Curry Dressing

1 *teaspoon salt*
2 *teaspoons sugar*
⅛ *teaspoon turmeric*
¾ *teaspoon cumin*
¼ *teaspoon pepper*
6 *tablespoons olive oil*
2 *tablespoons lemon juice*

Combine the dressing ingredients. Mix the tomato slices with the olives, onion and parsley. Marinate the tomato mixture for at least two hours. Take the tomatoes in a shallow, hard leakproof plastic container and serve them directly from it.

MOZZARELLA AND TOMATO SALAD

Serves 6–8

3 *large ripe tomatoes, thinly sliced*
4 *tablespoons olive oil*
1 *garlic clove, peeled and crushed*
  salt and freshly ground pepper to taste
2 *teaspoons lemon juice*
¼ *pound Mozzarella cheese*
2 *cups fresh basil leaves, whole if small or chopped coarsely if large*

Quarter each tomato slice. Mix oil, garlic, salt, pepper and lemon juice in a small bowl. Slice the Mozarella into fairly thin pieces, approximately the same size as the tomato slices. Season both the cheese and tomato pieces with salt and pepper. Arrange in a picnic container. Dribble half the dressing over the tomato-cheese mixture and put half in another container to take. Take the basil leaves, washed and dried, in a separate plastic bag with a sprinkle of water. At the picnic site toss the cheese and tomato mixture with the basil and dressing (saving a small portion of dressing to top each serving). Take salad servers or a large serving spoon, and forks or chopsticks for each person.

RED BEAN BOWL

Serves 6–8

1 *16-ounce can kidney beans, drained and rinsed*
½ *cup chopped celery*
¼ *cup chopped onion*
  salt and pepper to taste
1 *unpeeled tart apple, cored and diced*
⅓ *cup diced aged Swiss cheese*
4 *slices bacon, fried crisp, drained well and crumbled*
¼ *cup vinaigrette sauce (page 178)*

Combine all the ingredients in a large bowl and toss with the vinaigrette.
Put in a plastic container and chill one hour before packing for a picnic.

Take a plastic bowl or plate on which to serve the salad, as well as a serving spoon and forks.

SALADE JEAN-CLAUDE

Serves 4–6

This wonderful recipe comes from Jean-Claude, one of the head chefs at the Plaza Hotel in New York City.

1 *small cucumber, peeled and thinly sliced*
1 *cup diced boiled potatoes (1 medium-sized potato)*
2 *tomatoes, diced*
½ *cup shredded red cabbage*
2 *carrots, scrubbed, pared and thinly sliced*
1 *green pepper, washed, cored and sliced*
8 *Mediterranean-style black olives*
4 *anchovy filets*
4 *jumbo shrimp, cooked*
8 *French sardines packed in olive oil, drained well on paper towels*
2 *hard-boiled eggs, peeled and cut lengthwise into 4 sections*
1 *teaspoon chopped parsley*

Dill Dressing

3 *tablespoons mayonnaise*
2 *tablespoons sour cream*
¼ *cup olive oil*
1 *teaspoon dried dill weed*

2 *tablespoons fresh lemon juice* OR *white vinegar*
   salt
   grated pepper
   dash of nutmeg

Toss cucumber, potatoes, tomato, cabbage, carrots, and green pepper. Put into a plastic container. Pack the olives, anchovies, shrimp, sardines and eggs in another container. Take the chopped parsley wrapped in plastic wrap. Chill everything.

Combine mayonnaise with sour cream. Add oil drop by drop while stirring. Then add rest of ingredients and mix well. Pour into a small plastic container to take to the picnic.

To serve, put the vegetables in a bowl, arrange the fish, eggs and olives over them; dribble the dressing over all. Sprinkle with parsley. Take a serving bowl plus a salad server and fork for each person.

TURKISH CUCUMBER SALAD

Serves 6–8

2 *large cucumbers, peeled and sliced thinly*
1 *medium-sized potato, boiled, peeled and sliced thinly*
     (see "To Boil Potatoes," page 287)

1 *teaspoon chopped fresh cilantro leaves*
   OR
1 *teaspoon dried coriander leaf*

1 *tablespoon chopped parsley and chives*
⅓ *cup Japanese rice vinegar* OR *white wine vinegar*
1 *tablespoon vegetable oil*
   salt and white pepper to taste

Put the cucumber slices in a colander; salt them and let them sit 20 minutes. Rinse them quickly in cold water, and pat dry on paper towels. Toss the cucumber slices with the potato, cilantro, parsley, chives, vinegar and oil in a medium-sized mixing bowl.

Chill and take the salad in an attractive plastic container to serve from— or take along a wooden or plastic bowl. In addition to a serving spoon, take forks or chopsticks for each picnicker.

WATERCRESS SALAD

Serves 8–10

If you think you'll find fresh watercress near unpolluted streams, or dandelion greens, make this dressing ahead of time and carry it with you on your hike. Otherwise, carry the watercress from home in a separate plastic bag.

2 *bunches fresh watercress,*
   trimmed and washed

Dressing

4 *slices of bacon*
2 *teaspoons white wine vinegar*
3 *teaspoons lemon juice*
1 *teaspoon Dijon mustard*
½ *teaspoon sugar*
   salt and freshly ground black pepper
1 *egg yolk*
¾ *cup salad oil*

Place the washed watercress in a plastic bag or container, and refrigerate before hiking time. In a skillet, fry the bacon strips. When very crisp, remove them and drain on paper towels. When cool, crumble and reserve.

Combine the vinegar, lemon juice, mustard, sugar, salt, pepper and egg. Whisk until creamy. Add the salad oil, slowly whisking all the time. Add the bacon bits to the dressing and place in a container. Refrigerate.

To serve, spoon the dressing generously over the watercress and toss gently.

ZUCCHINI-TOMATO SALAD

Serves 6

4 *small zucchini, scrubbed and thinly sliced*
2 *tablespoons peanut* OR *olive oil*
2 *large ripe tomatoes, sliced thinly*
1 *tablespoon chopped fresh thyme*
   OR
1 *teaspoon dried thyme*
   salt and pepper
½ *cup vinaigrette sauce (page 178)*

In a medium-sized skillet fry the zucchini in hot oil until nicely browned on each side. Remove and drain on paper towels. Cut the tomatoes into slices, then quarter each slice. Season the tomato and zucchini slices lightly with thyme, salt and pepper, and arrange in an attractive shallow plastic container. Pour the vinaigrette over them. Refrigerate about an hour before placing in a backpack or basket for the picnic. Take a serving spoon and forks for each person.

BREAD

Breaking bread and sharing food are age-old symbols of friendship. Bread, the most basic of foods, enriches any meal and lies at the heart of every picnic. One imagines a crusty loaf of French bread with a good cheese and a nice red wine. This combination is an elegant and complete picnic in itself.

We like the tradition of serving sweet butter and fruit jams with bread, but we would also like to say a word here about cheese, as cheese is certainly an important item in almost every picnic. A picnic is a good place to experiment with different kinds, and you should search your delicatessen for interesting varieties of quality cheese.

Once, while looking for an unusual cheese to take on a hiking picnic, we sampled a Greek Kasseri. It tasted a little harsh and curiously salty, but still appealing, so we took a chance. After a full morning's walk in the mountains, we stopped for lunch. The Kasseri had mellowed to "room" temperature and the true flavors of the cheese had emerged, mellow but assertively sharp. It was a different cheese than the one we had tasted earlier, and a fantastic treat!

Good cheeses do not have to be imported. Try such American and Canadian cheeses as Canadian Black Diamond, Colorado Mountain Blackie, Oregon Tillamook, Wisconsin Longhorn, Star Valley Swiss and Ile de France (an American Camembert).

Buy your cheese cut from a wheel, and try to avoid all the prepackaged varieties. Always taste the cheese, consider its appearance, and then make your choice.

Cheese may be eaten as an hors d'oeuvre, as the body of a meal, as a complement for the last of your wine, or as dessert. It's really the most versatile of foods.

Basic Breads

ANADAMA BREAD

Yield: 2 loaves (9¼" × 5¼" × 3")
4 small loaves (6" × 3" × 2")

1 *package active dry yeast*
¼ *cup lukewarm water*
2½ *cups boiling water*
½ *cup corn meal*
1 *tablespoon butter*
1 *tablespoon salt*
½ *cup molasses*
3 *cups whole-wheat flour*
2½ *cups sifted all-purpose flour*
vegetable oil

Oven temperature: 400°

Dissolve yeast in lukewarm water in a cup. Pour the boiling water over the corn meal in a large bowl. Add the butter and the salt, stirring well.

When the corn-meal mixture has cooled to lukewarm, add the molasses and yeast water. Mix thoroughly, stir in the whole-wheat flour and add enough white flour, about 2½ cups, to make a stiff nonsticky dough.

Turn the dough out onto a floured board and knead it until smooth and elastic (about 5 minutes). Put it in a greased bowl, brush the top with oil, cover with a towel and let rise in a warm place one hour or until doubled in bulk.

Punch it down, knead it again lightly, and then shape into loaves—two large or four small ones. Place into greased loaf pans and brush with oil. Cover and let rise again until double in bulk. Preheat oven. Bake for 15 minutes, then reduce heat to 350° and bake 35 minutes longer (45 minutes longer at high altitudes). Let cool to room temperature before packing. You can store and transport the bread in plastic bags.

BAGELS

Yield: one dozen

1 *tablespoon* OR *package active dry yeast*
1½ *cups warm water*

    3 teaspoons salt
2½ tablespoons sugar
    6 cups all-purpose flour

Oven temperature: 350°

In a large bowl dissolve the yeast in the warm water. Add salt and 1½ tablespoons sugar, then stir well to dissolve. Sift the flour, then add it to bowl and stir well. Knead the dough on a lightly floured surface for about 10 minutes. Let the dough rise in a greased bowl for 15 minutes. Punch it down and form a square with the dough with a thickness of about one inch. With a sharp knife cut the square into twelve equal strips. Roll each one between your fingers to form a rope about ½ inch in diameter. Join the ends to form a circle, or doughnut shape. Cover with a towel and let rise in a warm place about 20 minutes. In a deep pot, bring a gallon of water mixed with the remaining 1 tablespoon sugar to a boil. Carefully drop in 3 bagels at a time, or as many as the pot will hold comfortably. Simmer the bagels 7 minutes, then transfer with a slotted spoon to a towel to cool. Bake on an ungreased sheet for 30 to 35 minutes or until golden brown.

Let cool, then store in plastic bags to keep fresh until picnic time.

BLACK RUSSIAN RYE BREAD

Yield: 2 medium loaves

    3 packages active dry yeast
    2 cups lukewarm water
½ cup plus 1 teaspoon sugar
    3 tablespoons very soft butter
    2 tablespoons unsulfured molasses
    4 teaspoons salt
    1 teaspoon caraway seeds
    3 tablespoons caramel coloring (see below)
3⅓ cups rye flour
1⅓ cups all-purpose flour (approximately)
       melted butter
       milk

Oven temperature: 375°

Grease a large baking sheet. Dissolve the yeast in ¾ cup of lukewarm water with 1 teaspoon of sugar in a large bowl; set aside for 10 minutes.

Meanwhile, make the caramel coloring: Dissolve ½ cup of sugar in a small saucepan over moderate heat, stirring until all the sugar dissolves.

The sugar crystals which form at the sides of the pan may be brushed back into the pot with a small basting brush dipped in cold water.

When the sugar is dissolved, turn the heat to high and rotate the pan until the syrup is a dark black-brown. (Be careful to watch the syrup, as it turns dark very quickly. It should be quite dark, but not burned.) Remove from heat and cool. This makes about 6 tablespoons of syrup, and you only use 3 tablespoons in the bread, so save the rest for another batch. You may even double the proportions, as caramel syrup keeps well in a jar when stored at room temperature.

To the yeast, add 1¼ cups of lukewarm water, the softened butter, molasses, salt, caraway seeds, and caramel coloring. Beat in the rye flour and then the all-purpose flour, ½ cup at a time, to make a stiff dough.

Turn the dough out onto a floured surface and let it rest, covered with the bowl, for 10 minutes. Knead the dough for 10 minutes until it is smooth and satiny, and form it into a ball. Put it into a large buttered bowl and brush the top with melted butter. Cover with a towel, and let it rise in a warm place for 1½ to 2 hours, or until it is almost double in bulk.

Punch the dough down, knead it a few times on a floured surface and form it into two balls. Put each ball in a medium-sized mixing bowl lined with a towel. Make sure the balls are smooth side down. Cover with another towel and let rise in a warm place one hour more or until almost double in bulk. Turn on the oven some time during the last half-hour the bread is rising.

Invert the dough onto the baking sheet, placing the loaves at least 4 inches apart. Remove the towels, and brush the loaves with milk. Pierce each loaf four or five times with a floured skewer to prevent cracking. Place them in the preheated oven and bake 40–50 minutes, or until the loaves are well-browned.

Immediately take the loaves off the baking sheet by inverting them over a wire rack. If done, the loaves should sound hollow when tapped with your finger on the bottom. You can put them back on the baking sheet and return them to the oven if they seem undercooked.

Take a whole loaf or very thin slices, and serve with many, many picnic menus. Carry the loaf in a pack or basket, wrapped in foil or heavy plastic.

CUBAN BREAD

Yield: 2 loaves

This bread, a Latin version of French bread, is the daily staple in Cuba. When the Hemingway family lived in Havana, the housekeeper would make this recipe.

1 *package active dry yeast*
2 *teaspoons sugar*
1 *cup lukewarm water*
½ *teaspoon salt*
6–7 *cups sifted all-purpose flour*
½ *cup corn meal*

Oven temperature: 400°

Dissolve the yeast and sugar in the warm water and let sit for 5 minutes. Stir in the salt and flour 1 cup at a time, beating well after each addition with a dough hook or a wooden spoon.

Shape the dough into a round ball, place it in an oiled bowl and let it rise in a warm place until double, about one hour. Turn the dough out onto a floured surface and shape it into a round loaf.

Generously sprinkle corn meal on a baking sheet. Put the loaf on the sheet and let it rise 10 minutes more. Slash the top with a sharp knife or razor blade. Spray the top with water and set the loaf in a cold oven. Now turn the oven to 400° F. Bake the bread about 50 minutes or until crusty and golden.

Let cool on a wire rack. If baked the day of the picnic, wrap in foil to keep warm. Otherwise pack in plastic bags until time to eat it.

FRENCH BREAD

Yield: 3 loaves

Making the French baguette becomes easy after a few tries, and the home-made version is absolutely superb—often better than those from Parisian bakeries. This recipe includes simple instructions for simulating a French baker's steaming oven, creating the wonderful crustiness of real French bread. Though it requires patience in the rising, it is worth waiting for. And if shortcuts are attempted, you may have a chewier Italian type of bread, which is excellent also. You may also want to try the new "french bread pans," available in specialty food stores.

1 *package active dry yeast*
⅓ *cup lukewarm water*
4 *cups unbleached all-purpose flour*
2½ *teaspoons salt*
1½ *cups lukewarm water*
Oven temperature: 425°

In a mixing bowl dissolve the yeast in ⅓ cup of lukewarm water. After about 10 minutes, add the flour, salt and the remaining water, stirring well. Put the dough onto a floured board and begin to knead it until smooth and flexible. Add a bit of flour if the dough is sticky, until it feels like a large soft marshmallow in the hands. Knead gently for about 10 minutes. Place the dough in a large, well-oiled bowl, cover with a cloth and let it rise at medium room temperature (70° F., not too warm) for a total of three hours. Punch it down and let it rise again slowly, another two hours. Knead again slightly, and let rise again, about one to one and a half hours.

Now punch down the dough. Divide it with a sharp knife into three equal portions and roll each out into a long slim loaf. If you'd prefer one large round picnic loaf, don't divide the dough. If using French bread pans, place the shaped pieces of dough in them for the final rise; otherwise, place them 3 inches apart on a floured cloth. Let rise two hours. Preheat oven. Gently but quickly roll each delicate loaf, one at a time, onto a baking sheet or (preferably) a piece of asbestos sprinkled with a little corn meal to give the bottom crust an authentic texture. Using a very sharp knife or razor blade, slash the top of each loaf with three or four diagonal cuts.

To prepare your oven, first heat a brick right on top of the stove burner until it is very hot, and then place it in a pan of water. Put it on the bottom of the preheated oven. Immediately insert the loaves in the upper third part of the oven. The steam will produce the texture you want. If you don't have a brick, spray the unbaked loaves with cold water from an atomizer just once when you put them in the oven. The bread is not like a soufflé, so it will not fall if the oven is opened, but it does need the intense heat for baking and for the golden-brown crust. Bake for 30 minutes or until golden brown.

This is the best bread with cheese. Always store in airtight plastic bags (the bread freezes well this way too). Transport in plastic bags, and try to make the bread as close to picnic time as possible.

ITALIAN TORTANO BREAD

Yield: 2 loaves

⅓ *pound salt pork*
1 *tablespoon*
   OR *package of active dry yeast*
¼ *teaspoon salt*
4 *cups all-purpose flour*

grease (from frying salt pork)
3 *tablespoons cracked peppercorns*

Oven temperature: 375°

Remove the skin from the salt pork and cut the meat into very small cubes.
Fry cubes over high heat until they are browned. Drain and reserve the
grease from the crisp salt pork cracklings. Let it stand at room temperature
before using it in the bread recipe.

Dissolve the yeast in the water in a large bowl. Let stand 5 minutes, then
add the salt, 2 cups flour and 4 tablespoons of the grease. Stir in 1 more cup
of flour and mix well. Knead the dough on a floured surface for 10 minutes,
adding flour as needed, up to 1 cup, for a smooth elastic consistency. Let
dough rise in a warm place in a greased bowl until double—about 1½
hours.

Punch it down and as you do, make a little well in the center of the bread.
In it put 2 more tablespoons of the grease, the pepper and the fried pork
rind. The dough will be sticky. Turn it out onto a floured surface and knead
it again until the ingredients are evenly distributed.

Divide the dough into four equal parts. Shape them with the palms of
your hands into long ropes. Seal together the ends of two of the pieces and
twist them together to make a twisted shaped loaf. Do the same with the
other two pieces. Place them on a greased baking sheet, cover them with a
floured towel and let the two loaves rise for 45 minutes in a warm place.
Preheat the oven to 375° F. Brush the loaves with melted grease left from
frying the pork, and bake for 35 minutes or until golden brown. Let them
cool on racks. This bread is especially good with sausages or cold sliced
meats served with homemade mayonnaise and hot mustard.

MOUNTAIN BREAD

Yield: 2 loaves (9¼" × 5¼" × 3")

Mountain bread is extremely nutritious, yet because of the long kneading
and many risings, it is unusually light. Serve it with English Cheddar to
complement its wonderfully nutty flavor, or as sandwich toast.

½ *cup wheat berries, soaked*
1½ *tablespoons active dry yeast*
2½ *cups lukewarm water*
1 *cup scalded milk*
1½ *tablespoons sea salt*
3 *teaspoons honey*

  3 *teaspoons molasses*
  6 *tablespoons butter* or *soya or sunflower margarine*
  1 *egg*
  1 *tablespoon corn meal*
  1 *tablespoon sesame seeds*
  1 *tablespoon powdered lecithin*
4½ *cups whole-wheat flour*
  1 *cup soy flour*
  ¼ *cup wheat germ*
  1 *cup bran*

Oven temperature: 350°

Pour boiling water over the wheat berries and let them soak in a small bowl for 1 hour or more. In a large bowl, dissolve yeast in ½ cup warm water. Meanwhile, scald the milk and stir in the salt, honey, molasses and butter or margarine cut into pieces. Add a slightly beaten egg to the mixture. Add the corn meal, sesame seeds and lecithin to this mixture and add it to the dissolved yeast in the large bowl. Add 2 cups of warm water, and gradually add 4 cups of wheat flour and all the soy flour, wheat germ, bran and softened wheat berries. Mix thoroughly, beating about 100 strokes with a wooden spoon. Mix in remaining ½ cup of wheat flour to make the dough smooth and easy to handle. Let this mixture rest for 20 minutes to relax the gluten.

Turn dough onto a lightly floured board and knead till smooth and elastic, a good 20–25 minutes. Place in a greased bowl and cover with a towel. Let it rise in a warm place for 2½ hours. Punch down dough and let rise again for 1½ hours. Divide the risen dough into 2 individual loaf shapes and place them in well-greased loaf pans. Cover and let rise until double in bulk, about 1 hour.

Preheat oven. Brush the loaves with cold milk and place in the middle of the oven. Bake 50 minutes or until deep golden brown. Remove from pans. Brush loaves with soft butter and cool on wire rack.

OATMEAL BREAD

Yield: 2 small (6″ × 3″ × 2″) loaves or
1 large (9¼″ × 5¼″ × 3″) loaf

This very, very light bread has a nutlike flavor. Though wonderful for sandwiches or with any cheese, it is best of all with unsalted butter and a wildberry jam.

         1 *cup oatmeal*
         2 *cups boiling water*
         2 *tablespoons melted butter*
         2 *teaspoons salt*
         3 *tablespoons honey* OR *molasses*
         1 *package active dry yeast (dissolved in ¼ cup warm water)*
      1½ *cups whole-wheat flour*
  2½–3 *cups all-purpose flour*

         Oven temperature: 350°

Put oatmeal in a large bowl. Pour the boiling water over the oatmeal and let stand until cool. Add butter, salt, honey or molasses and yeast. Add enough whole-wheat flour to make a wet spongy dough. Let rise about 30 minutes to an hour, then add the all-purpose flour and knead 10 minutes. Let rise in warm place until double in bulk. Punch down and divide dough to place in loaf pans. Let rise again an hour or more. Preheat oven. Bake for 45 minutes (slightly longer in high altitudes). Let cool before storing in plastic bags for easy transport to the picnic site.

PARMESAN OR CARAWAY TWISTS

These little twists, made from puff paste, are light as air. They are wonderful at picnics as an accompaniment for soup, Trout Ceviche (page 234) or for any of the "Sauces, Spreads and Dips," pages 225–228.

We don't give the recipe for puff pastry here, but you can buy it frozen or from a baker or you can make your own following the instructions in a good French cookbook.

         1 *pound puff paste*
             salt
       ½ *cup Parmesan (freshly grated)*
             Hungarian paprika

         Oven temperature: 350°

Preheat oven and butter a cookie sheet. On a floured board roll out the paste to about ⅛ inch thick in a long rectangle about 12 inches by 24 inches. Sprinkle lightly with salt, then with the Parmesan, and finally sprinkle paprika over all.

Fold the entire length of the dough from the bottom up to about the middle of the rectangle.

Then fold the top half back down over the first fold so that you have three thicknesses of folded pastry. Slice this roll of folded pastry in ½-inch slices and then, holding each slice by its ends, twist each slice several times. Lay on a buttered cookie sheet and bake 15–20 minutes or until lightly browned.

Variation: Instead of sprinkling the pastry with paprika and Parmesan, use caraway seeds.

RYE BREAD

Yield: 1 large
(9¼" × 5¼" × 3") loaf

    3 *cups all-purpose flour*
    1 *cup rye flour*
    1 *tablespoon cocoa*
    1 *tablespoon caraway seeds*
    ½ *teaspoon salt*
    4 *tablespoons sugar*
    1 *package active dry yeast*
 1½ *cups warm water*
    1 *egg, at room temperature*

Oven temperature: 425°

Sift the white flour and rye flour together into a medium-sized bowl. Add the cocoa, caraway seeds, salt and sugar. Stir in the yeast, dissolved in ½ cup warm water. Add the egg and up to 1 cup of warm water. When you've mixed the ingredients well, the mixture should be of a sticky consistency and hard to stir. Knead the mixture for a few minutes or until dough is resilient and pliant. Then put it in a well-greased loaf pan to rise in a warm place for 45 minutes. Preheat oven. Bake for one hour. Brush the top with milk halfway through baking. After baking, remove from pan immediately and cool. Other combinations of flours will work well, with or without cocoa and caraway seeds. Store in plastic bags for the picnic.

SOURDOUGH RYE BREAD

Yield: 3 loaves

1 *cup starter**
1½ *quarts lukewarm water* OR *potato water if you have it*
½ *cup blackstrap molasses* OR *honey*
10 *cups rye flour*
2 *teaspoons salt*
2 *tablespoons butter* OR *margarine*

Oven temperature: 350°

Mix the starter, lukewarm water, molasses and 6 cups of the flour and let it "work" for about 3 hours in a warm place (or overnight). Stir it well and then take out 1 cup starter to save for the next batch.

Stir in the salt and the butter or margarine. Mix in 4 more cups of flour. Knead for about 10 minutes. Shape into 3 round loaves. Put into pie tins or other round pans and let rise 2–3 hours or until dough has expanded by one-third. Preheat oven. Bake 1½ hours (10 to 15 minutes longer at high altitudes).

* To make a sourdough starter, combine 1 tablespoon of dry yeast, 2½ cups warm water, 2 teaspoons sugar or honey, and 2½ cups flour. Let it ferment for 5 days, *stirring daily*. The starter can be kept indefinitely in the refrigerator. If it turns watery, stir it again. It should be thick like mud. The starter should be used periodically, maybe once a week. To make bread or pancakes, the starter is mixed with flour and water to make a "sponge." This sponge, after 3 hours or overnight, becomes sour. A new starter is taken from this mixture for future use, before the other ingredients are mixed in.

SPIRAL HERB BREAD

Yield: 1 loaf (9¼" × 5¼" × 3")

Herb Filling

2 *fresh shallots, minced*
1 *cup minced fresh parsley*

  1 *clove garlic, peeled and mashed*
  3 *sprigs fresh thyme, minced*
15 *leaves basil, minced*
  2 *tablespoons softened butter*
  1 *egg, lightly beaten*
 ¼ *teaspoon salt*
    pinch of cayenne pepper
    freshly ground black pepper to taste
    few drops of salsa verde OR *Tabasco sauce*

Bread

   1 *tablespoon active dry yeast*
  ½ *cup warm water*
  ½ *cup scalded milk*
   1 *tablespoon sugar*
   1 *tablespoon salt and a pinch*
   4 *tablespoons butter* OR *margarine*
3–4 *cups all-purpose flour**
   1 *egg, slightly beaten*

Oven temperature: 375°

In a skillet, sauté the shallots and herbs in half the butter over moderate heat for about 10 minutes. Put the mixture into a bowl. Stir in the egg and other seasonings and let cool and set aside to use in the bread recipe.

Dissolve the yeast in the water and let stand for 10 minutes in a large bowl. Add the scalded milk, sugar, salt and butter or margarine. Stir well; then add the flour, mixing well. Let this dough mixture stand for 10 minutes, then proceed to knead the dough on a floured surface for 15 minutes. Put it in an oiled bowl, oil the dough surface, and let it rise in a warm place, covered with a towel, for an hour or until double in volume. Punch the dough down, let stand another 15 minutes, then roll out the dough into a rectangle ¼ inch thick and about 10 inches long. Brush with half the beaten egg, then spread the herb mixture on it, almost to the edges. Roll it up carefully and seal the edges. Place in a greased loaf pan. Brush the top with the remaining beaten egg and let it rise in a warm place for another hour.

Preheat the oven and bake for 50 minutes to an hour, or until the top is golden. Cool on wire racks. Store in plastic bags. Slice at the picnic site and serve with butter and a selection of cheeses and cold cuts.

---

* You may use a combination of white and whole-wheat flours if you wish.

SWEDISH SAFFRON BREAD

Yield: 3–4 braided loaves

      2 *packages active dry yeast*
      3 *cups lukewarm milk*
      1 *teaspoon saffron*
  1½ *cups sugar*
      ¼ *teaspoon salt*
      2 *eggs*
      1 *cup melted butter*
      8 *cups all-purpose flour*
      1 *cup seedless raisins*
      2 *tablespoons sugar*
    30 *almonds, ground*
      4 *bitter almonds, ground (optional)*
          almond paste (optional)

Oven temperature: 375°

In a small bowl, dissolve yeast in ½ cup lukewarm milk. In a large bowl, mix 2½ cups milk, saffron, sugar, salt, 1 egg, butter and a small amount of flour. Add yeast and remaining flour. Now add the raisins. Beat with wooden spoon until smooth and firm. Sprinkle with flour. Cover with a towel (or cheesecloth). Let rise in warm place until doubled in bulk—about 2 hours. Turn out on floured board and knead until smooth. Divide into 9 equal portions. Roll each piece out with your hands to 14 inches long. Make braided loaves by braiding three pieces and tucking ends under. Place each loaf on a buttered baking sheet. You can divide the dough into 12 smaller pieces for 4 small loaves or make buns if you prefer. Cover and let rise. Pre-heat oven. Brush with slightly beaten egg. Sprinkle with sugar and ground almonds. If you'd like, you can put some almond paste in the crevices. Bake loaves 15 to 20 minutes. For buns, place in hot oven (425°) for 5 to 10 minutes. Baking times for both forms will be a little longer in high altitudes.

Cornish Saffron Bread

To the Swedish dough add (at the point raisins are added above):

  ⅓ *cup chopped candied lemon peel*
  ⅓ *cup citron*
  ⅓ *cup walnuts*
  1 *cup currants*
  1 *cup raisins*

Let the breads cool before placing in airtight plastic bags. You may serve this bread with apricot jam as a dessert.

SYRIAN PITA BREAD

Yield: one dozen

2 *cups warm water*
1 *package active dry yeast*
2 *teaspoons salt*
5 *cups unsifted all-purpose flour*
1 *cup whole-wheat flour*
2 *tablespoons oil*
½ *cup corn meal*

Oven temperature: 500°

Measure the water into a large bowl. Sprinkle in yeast. Stir until dissolved. Stir in salt and 3 cups of the white flour until smooth. Mix in up to 2½ cups more flour, using the 2 remaining cups of white and ½ cup of the wheat, to make a soft dough.

Turn it out on a board and knead until smooth and elastic, about 10 minutes. Place in an oiled bowl and brush the top with oil as well. Cover with a towel and let it rise until double in bulk.

Punch down and invert the bowl over the ball of dough, letting it rest 30 minutes.

Preheat oven. Mix corn meal with ½ cup of remaining wheat flour on a board. Divide the dough into 12 pieces and shape into circles about 6 inches in diameter. Coat both sides of the dough rounds with the corn meal/wheat flour mixture. Place on an ungreased cookie sheet, two at a time. Bake for 5 minutes; cool on racks and store in plastic bags. The bread can also be frozen.

Since these breads are large, flat and round, make sure to transport them on top of the pack or basket, or else put them in a plastic container for safer carrying. This will be necessary if you stuff the pita as described in the stuffed pita bread recipe, page 172.

Sweet Breads

APRICOT NUT BREAD

Yield: one large (9¼″ × 5¼″ × 3″) loaf or
two small (6″ × 3″ × 2″)

1–1½ *cups sifted all-purpose* OR *whole-wheat flour*
  2 *teaspoons baking powder*
  ½ *teaspoon salt*
  ¼ *teaspoon baking soda*
  ½ *cup white* OR *firmly packed brown sugar*
    OR
  ⅓ *cup of honey*
  ½ *cup chopped dried apricots*
  ½ *cup chopped walnuts* OR *pecans*
  1 *teaspoon grated orange peel*
  1 *egg*
  ¾ *cup milk*
  ¼ *cup salad oil*

Oven temperature: 350°

Preheat oven. Sift together the flour, baking powder, salt and soda into a
large mixing bowl. Mix in the sugar, apricots and nuts. Add the orange peel,
egg, milk and oil. Stir until blended and pour into a greased loaf pan (or 2
small loaf pans). Bake for 45 minutes. Cool 10 minutes; remove from pan
and cool on rack before storing in plastic bags to transport to the picnic.

BANANA BREAD

Yield: 1 large (9¼″ × 5¼″ × 3″) loaf

This is an excellent banana bread recipe!

  ½ *cup butter, softened*
  1 *cup sugar*
    OR
  ⅔ *cup honey*
  2 *whole eggs*
  ½ *cup chopped nuts*
  3 *very ripe bananas*

2½ cups all-purpose flour
½ teaspoon salt
2 teaspoons baking powder
½ teaspoon baking soda
1 teaspoon vanilla extract

Oven temperature: 375°

Preheat oven. In a large mixing bowl, cream together the butter and sugar or honey.

Add eggs to this mixture and beat well. Add the nuts. In a separate bowl, mash the bananas well with a bit of water and mix in with the butter mixture.

Sift the flour with the salt, baking powder and soda and add it to this mixture. Stir in vanilla.

Bake for 30–35 minutes. For high-altitude baking, add a bit more water with the bananas and bake 50–55 minutes. Store in a plastic bag for easy transport to the picnic site.

CARROT BREAD

Yield: one medium (8″ × 4″ × 2½″) loaf or
two small (6″ × 3″ × 2″) ones

2 cups all-purpose flour
1¼ cups sugar
2 teaspoons cinnamon
2 teaspoons baking soda
½ teaspoon salt
½ cup grated coconut
½ cup currants
½ cup chopped pecans
2 cups grated carrot
1 cup bland vegetable oil
3 eggs
2 teaspoons vanilla extract

Oven temperature: 350°

Preheat oven. In a large bowl, combine the flour, sugar, cinnamon, baking soda and salt. Add the coconut, currants and pecans and mix together well. Add the grated carrot, oil, eggs and vanilla. Mix together with a wooden spoon and bake in either a loaf pan or in a one-pound round tin.

The bread is done when it shrinks slightly from the sides and is firm to a gentle pressure and when a wooden toothpick inserted in the center comes out dry. Cool in the pan for 10 minutes, turn out and cool thoroughly on a rack. Wrap and store in the refrigerator. It slices best if aged one day.

The bread is easy to take along in a pack if wrapped in foil, or you can leave it in the pan or can it's baked in. If you've used cans, be sure to take along a can opener to open the closed end of the can so the bread can be gently pushed out.

FRUIT DATE NUT BREAD

Yield: 1 large (9¼″ × 5¼″ × 3″) loaf or
2 small (6″ × 3″ × 2″)

⅓ *cup butter* OR *margarine*
¼ *cup firmly packed brown sugar*
1 *large egg, slightly beaten*
¼ *cup honey*
1½ *cups whole-wheat flour*
1 *large ripe banana, mashed (*OR *1 cup grated apples*
    OR *1 cup chopped apricots, etc.)*
1 *teaspoon baking powder*
½ *teaspoon soda*
½ *teaspoon salt*
½ *cup chopped walnuts*
¼ *cup raisins*
¼ *cup chopped pitted dates*
3 *tablespoons yogurt, eggnog* OR *whole milk (optional)*

Oven temperature: 350°

Preheat oven. Combine all ingredients well, by first creaming together butter or margarine and sugar. Then stir in egg and honey; add flour, banana or other fruit, baking powder, soda, salt, walnuts, raisins and dates. Pour batter into large greased loaf pan or two small ones. Bake for 40 minutes (45 minutes at higher altitudes). Remove from pan; cool on rack. Store in plastic bags to keep the bread fresh.

These quick breads are really easy and fun, so you can vary and add ingredients. For a moister cakelike bread, add more banana and more nuts. We like to add yogurt for a softer batter, or add more flour if it gets too runny. Substitute a grated apple or other chopped fruits and nuts for the ingredients listed here, if you like. You can create your own sweet breads with little risk of failure.

PRUNE BREAD

Yield: 1 large (9¼″ × 5¼″ × 3″) loaf or
2 small (6″ × 3″ × 2″)

1 *cup all-purpose flour*
½ *cup whole-wheat flour*
2 *teaspoons cinnamon*
1 *teaspoon baking powder*
1 *teaspoon baking soda*
¼ *teaspoon salt*
6 *tablespoons butter, softened*
¼ *cup honey*
¼ *cup firmly packed brown sugar*
2 *eggs, slightly beaten*
grated rind of ½ lemon
1 *teaspoon vanilla extract*
¾ *cup sour cream*
¾ *cup chopped cooked prunes**

Oven temperature: 325°

Preheat oven. Sift the flours with the cinnamon, baking powder, soda and salt into a bowl. In another bowl, cream the butter with the honey, brown sugar and eggs. Add the lemon rind and vanilla. Fold in the sour cream and prune bits. Bake in 2 small greased loaf pans for an hour.

Let the bread cool in the pan 10 minutes or so before removing. Wrap in foil to take in a pack or cover the pan with foil and take the loaf in the pan in which it was cooked.

* You can use canned prunes for this recipe. Drain them in a colander, pit them, and chop them coarsely. Dried prunes, stewed, then treated the same way, give more flavor to the bread, however.

WALNUT SWIRL BREAD

Yield: 2 medium (7½″ × 3½″ × 2¼″) loaves

This is a nice tea bread, or it can serve as a dessert with jam and fruit.

Walnut Swirl Filling

2 *tablespoons butter, softened*
1 *cup firmly packed brown sugar*
½ *cup honey*

3 *cups chopped walnuts*
2 *eggs*
2 *teaspoons cinnamon*
2 *teaspoons ground cardamom*
1 *tablespoon vanilla extract*

Bread

2 *packages active dry yeast*
1 *cup lukewarm water*
¼ *cup honey*
⅓ *cup instant nonfat dry milk*
1 *tablespoon salt*
¼ *cup softened butter*
4 *cups all-purpose flour*
1 *egg white*

Oven temperature: 350°

To make the walnut filling, first melt the butter in a saucepan over medium-high heat. Stir in the brown sugar and honey. Remove from heat after about a minute and stir in the walnuts, eggs, cinnamon, cardamom and vanilla. Let the mixture cool. Refrigerate before using in the bread recipe.

Dissolve the yeast in warm water for 10 minutes; add the honey, dry milk, salt, butter and half the flour. Stir and beat until smooth. Stir in 1½ cups of the remaining flour, mixing well. Knead the dough on a floured surface for about 5 minutes, adding the remaining flour if necessary, until the dough is smooth and elastic, yet soft. Put it in a greased bowl, cover and let rise one hour until double. Punch down the dough, turn it out on a floured board and divide it in half. Let each piece rest for about 10 minutes. Roll out one piece of dough to form a rectangle ⅛ inch thick. Spread half the walnut filling on it evenly and roll it up. Place it in a greased loaf pan. Repeat this process with the remaining dough and filling. Cover both loaves and let them rise about a half-hour in a warm place. Preheat the oven. Brush the top of each loaf with a slightly beaten egg white and bake for 35–40 minutes or until the crust is golden. Let the bread cool for about 10 minutes before removing from the pan. Wrap it in foil to take for either pack or basket-style picnic.

SIDE DISHES
AND
CONDIMENTS

A picnic just isn't a picnic without things like pickles, relishes and deviled eggs. And though such side dishes are usually thought of as optional in a menu in a dining room, they are as much a part of the picnic menu as the main dish. In fact, side dishes often are the entire picnic. This was certainly true when the tradition of picnicking began in the early 1800's in England. The Picnic Society of London would gather for theatrical events, and each guest would contribute a dish to an elaborate indoor buffet. The meal was a potluck affair and the menu would fall in place according to the sorts of dishes contributed. The same is true today. If no dish is noticeably more important than another, the picnic is a smorgasbord of delights—all "side dishes" according to our classification.

Many recipes in this section could be served as the main dish of a picnic, but we have included them here because we have usually used them as accompaniments to a more substantial or "important" dish. We have found that dishes from various cultures mix happily on a picnic menu. For instance, our Swiss meatloaf Ticino is enhanced equally by an Italian caponata or a Middle Eastern wheat salad. Experiment.

Condiments contribute the spice, the perfume, the bite and the zest to a menu. Enjoy the recipes here and try to include a condiment in every picnic.

Sauces, Spreads and Dips

CREAM CHEESE WITH HERBS

Serves 8–10

8 *ounces cream cheese* OR *pot cheese (if available)*
1 *shallot, finely chopped*
1 *tablespoon finely chopped parsley*
1 *tablespoon chopped chervil*
1 *tablespoon chopped chives*
1 *cup heavy cream, whipped*
3 *tablespoons oil*
3 *tablespoons wine vinegar*
 salt
 freshly ground black pepper

Let the cheese soften at room temperature for about an hour. Using a wooden spoon or electric mixer, blend the cheese, shallot and herbs together in a bowl. Fold in the whipped cream, and then the oil and vinegar. Season to taste. Line a pierced mold or colander with muslin and put cheese into it to drain for two to three hours or longer.

Turn out the cheese into a plastic container or little mold to travel. Take some salad vegetables—radishes, carrot sticks and celery, raw cucumbers, peppers, etc.—to serve with the cheese. Also serve with rye bread and butter.

If you use a mold cover, secure the covering well with a rubber band or string.

HUMUS LEBANESE STYLE

Serves 8–10

A good spread for French bread or crackers.

1 *cup cooked garbanzos*
2 *tablespoons tahini (ground sesame) paste*
2 *tablespoons liquid from garbanzos*
2 *garlic cloves, peeled and crushed*
¼ *cup lemon juice*
 salt and pepper to taste
1 *tablespoon minced parsley*
2 *tablespoons olive oil*

Mash the garbanzos with a fork in a small bowl and mix in the sesame tahini, the liquid from the garbanzos, garlic and lemon juice. Salt and pepper to taste.

Put in a small plastic container and sprinkle the parsley and oil over the top. Secure the lid tightly before transporting.

KIRSCH CHEESE AMANDINE

Serves 6–8

      1 *8-ounce package cream cheese* OR *pot cheese (if available)*
      2 *teaspoons honey*
      1 *tablespoon kirsch*
      2 *teaspoons lemon juice*
  1½ *teaspoons finely grated lemon peel*
      ⅛ *teaspoon almond extract*
          slivered almonds

Soften the cheese at room temperature for about an hour, and mix in all the other ingredients, reserving the almonds. Form into a wedge shape and refrigerate 15 to 20 minutes. Now decorate the cheese with slivered almonds, inserted vertically and evenly all over the cheese, so that they stand up. This is lovely served with saffron bread and apricot jam, plus small crisp slices of apple or pieces of ripe pear. Refrigerate before packing.

Pack the cheese carefully in a plastic container. You may find it's easier to bring the slivered almonds in a separate piece of plastic wrap, and decorate the kirsch cheese right before serving.

NUT AND GARLIC MAYONNAISE

Serves 10

This is a good dip for shrimp or raw vegetables.

  ½ *cup shelled hazelnuts*
  ½ *cup shelled walnuts*
    3 *cloves garlic, peeled*
    1 *egg yolk*
    1 *cup olive oil*
        lemon juice
        salt
        pepper

Oven temperature: 375°

First, soak the hazelnuts in hot water until skins can be removed easily. Put the hazelnuts on a cookie sheet in a hot oven until they brown lightly (5 to 10 minutes). Watch carefully. Pulverize the walnuts and hazelnuts together with the garlic, either with a mortar or in a blender. Add the egg yolk, then beat in the oil very slowly and add a little lemon juice. Season with salt and pepper to taste.

Refrigerate well ahead of packing time. Transport in a plastic container and in a cooler for a car or basket picnic. If you're hiking, try to chill the mayonnaise in a stream if it's a very hot day, before serving.

PEPPER CHEESE

Commercial pepper cheese is so expensive that we decided to try to duplicate it—even improve it. Here is our version:

8 *ounces cream cheese* OR *pot cheese (if available)*
2 *ounces dry white wine*
¼ *pint heavy cream, whipped*
1 *clove garlic, peeled and crushed*
1 *teaspoon finely minced fresh fennel* OR *chervil* OR *summer savory*
4 *tablespoons peppercorns, crushed*

Let the cheese come to room temperature for about an hour. Mix everything together except peppercorns in a medium-sized mixing bowl. Mash and mix with a fork or use an electric beater. Chill for several hours, then form the mixture into a flattened round shape (or any shape you wish). Spread the crushed pepper on a flat surface and roll the cheese in it, pressing down slightly so that the pieces of pepper are pushed into the surface of the cheese. Roll the cheese around several times so that there is a lot of pepper coating it. Wrap in plastic wrap and chill.

Put in a plastic container only a little larger than the cheese if using a pack or take it as it is in a basket. Put on a plate and surround with thin slices of bread or crackers to serve.

ROQUEFORT SAUCE

Serves 8–10
Yield: 2 cups

2 *tablespoons lemon juice*
¾ *cup Roquefort, blue OR Gorgonzola cheese, crumbled*
1 *recipe basic mayonnaise (page 177)*
3 *tablespoons light cream*
½ *teaspoon Worcestershire sauce*
¼ *teaspoon cayenne pepper*
   salt to taste

Beat the lemon juice and cheese into the mayonnaise. (If you can get a really good Italian Gorgonzola cheese, try it instead of Roquefort. It is similar, and often better, than ordinary blue cheese or Roquefort, and makes for an interesting change.) Add the cream, Worcestershire sauce, cayenne and salt to taste. Mix well and chill. Serve the sauce with cold roast beef or as a dipping sauce for avocados or crudités.

Pack the sauce in a plastic container and refrigerate well. Transport it by cooler, if possible, or on a hiking picnic, cool in a stream before serving.

Meat, Fish and Eggs

CRABMEAT PÂTÉ WITH CELERY

Serves 8–10

- 1 8-ounce package of cream cheese
- 3 tablespoons grated onion
- 3 tablespoons chopped parsley
- 2 tablespoons chopped chives
- 1 tablespoon lemon juice
- 2–3 drops Tabasco sauce
- 1 4-ounce can of crabmeat, chopped finely and all shell removed
  freshly ground black pepper
- 1 bunch celery
  paprika

Let the cream cheese soften at room temperature about 1 hour. In a small bowl mix the cream cheese with the onion, parsley, chives, lemon juice and Tabasco. Drain the crabmeat well, then pat with paper towels to remove liquid. Add the crabmeat to the cream-cheese mixture and mix well. Pepper to taste. Discard the tough outer stalks of celery and peel off the strings from tender stalks. Remove the leaves, wash, and slice into 3-inch pieces. Fill each chunk with crabmeat pâté and dust with a little paprika. Put in a low, flat plastic container and refrigerate until time to leave for the picnic.

CRAB-STUFFED CUCUMBER ROLLS

Serves 10

- 1 cup cooked crabmeat
- 2 tablespoons vodka
- 4 medium-sized cucumbers
- 1 tablespoon salt

Egg Sauce

- yolks of 2 hard-boiled eggs
- 2 tablespoons vinegar
- 2 teaspoons sugar OR honey
- ½ teaspoon salt
- 2 tablespoons dry vermouth
- 1 tablespoon vodka

Shred the crabmeat and sprinkle with 2 tablespoons of the vodka. Peel cucumbers and cut into 1-inch lengths; then shave around and around into very thin curls, discarding the soft center and seeds. Sprinkle prepared cucumbers inside and out with 1 tablespoon salt. Next place a small dollop of crabmeat in each of the cucumber pieces and roll up. Arrange in a single layer between sheets of waxed paper in your container for transporting.

To make the egg sauce, mash the yolks and mix with vinegar, sugar, 1/2 teaspoon salt, vermouth and 1 tablespoon of vodka, then place in a jar until serving time. To serve, pour over the rolls and serve in small individual dishes.

MARINATED SHRIMP

Serves 6–8

1 1/2 cups tarragon wine vinegar
1 1/2 cups dry white wine
   1 cup cold water
1–2 cloves garlic, peeled and slivered
   2 bay leaves
2–3 stalks celery, washed and chopped
   1 tablespoon salt
      freshly ground black pepper
      cayenne pepper
1 1/2 pounds jumbo shrimp

In a 2-quart saucepan, put 1 cup *each* of the vinegar, wine and cold water. Add the garlic, bay leaves, celery with the leaves chopped fine, the salt, a generous grating of fresh pepper and a dash of cayenne. Boil this liquid for about a half hour to bring out all the tastes.

Wash the shrimp, but leave the shells on, and when the liquid is ready, drop in the shrimp and add more vinegar and wine if needed to cover. Boil for 5 minutes. Set pan off the flame and let the shrimp cool in the liquid. Refrigerate for about 24 hours so the shrimp can absorb all the marvelous flavors.

Remove shrimp from the marinade and serve cold on a bed of watercress or parsley with a homemade mayonnaise or fresh herb dipping sauce (page 15).

Pack the marinated shrimp in a secure container, the sauce and watercress in separate containers. Arrange the shrimp at the picnic site.

OEUFS VERTS

Deviled eggs covered with green gelled mayonnaise.

Serves 6–12

6 *hard-boiled eggs*
1 *tablespoon softened butter*
½ *teaspoon Dijon mustard*
salt to taste
white pepper
1 *cup green mayonnaise (page 178)*
½ *cup liquid gelatin*

Shell the eggs and split lengthwise. Using a fork, mash the yolks in a small bowl with the butter, mustard, salt and pepper until smooth. Fill the whites with this mixture, heaping it in with a teaspoon.

At the picnic, cover the egg halves with the green mayonnaise, which you have mixed with the liquid gelatin. (Make the gelatin according to package directions).

Chill the eggs and pack in a shallow, hard-sided container or egg holder to take in a backpack. Take the mayonnaise in a separate container. The eggs will be messy by the time you arrive at the site, but reconstruct them as well as possible. For a driving picnic you can put the mayonnaise on the eggs at home, place them on a bed of lettuce leaves on a serving platter, and hold them in your lap all the way (we have!).

PICKLED SHRIMP, SWEDISH STYLE

Serves 6–8

These are very nice appetizers served on toothpicks for a picnic.

2 *pounds shrimp*
3 *cups vinegar*
2 *onions, peeled and sliced*
2 *tablespoons pickling spice tied in a piece of cheesecloth*
2 *cups water*

Wash the shrimp and boil them in boiling salted water until tender, or about 3–5 minutes, depending on their size. Rinse and cool them, remove shells and veins. Bring all the other ingredients to a boil and pour over the shrimp. Leave the shrimp in the pickling mixture 12 hours or at least overnight, before serving.

Store in glass jars, taking out what you need for a picnic and carrying them in a plastic container.

SARDINES IN DILL SAUCE

Serves 8

4 *4-ounce cans sardines packaged in oil*
½ *cup fresh lemon juice*
½ *cup Dijon mustard*
½ *cup olive oil*
2 *tablespoons wine vinegar*
1 *tablespoon sugar*

6 *tablespoons chopped fresh dill*
OR
2 *tablespoons dried dill weed*

2 *tablespoons chopped parsley*
½ *teaspoon salt*
freshly ground pepper
½ *cup chopped radishes*
lettuce leaves

Drain the sardines on a paper towel. Place in a shallow dish and cover with ¼ cup of the lemon juice. Marinate for about two hours. Drain sardines on paper towels again. Spoon the mustard into a small bowl. Gradually add the oil, mixing with a fork until the mustard becomes creamy. With the exception of the radishes and lettuce, stir in the remaining ingredients, including the reserved ¼ cup of lemon juice. Arrange the sardines once again in the shallow dish. Pour the sauce over them. Cover and chill for at least two hours. Pack in a picnic container. Bring along some lettuce leaves and chopped radishes in a separate plastic bag. To serve, arrange sardines on lettuce with radishes.

SMOKED SALMON
WITH HORSERADISH CREAM

Serves 8–10

1½ teaspoons unflavored gelatin
  6 tablespoons cold water
  ½ cup heavy cream
  2 tablespoons prepared horesradish, drained
  1 teaspoon fresh lemon juice
  ¼ teaspoon sugar
  ¾ pound thinly sliced smoked salmon
     freshly ground black pepper
  6 thin slices pumpernickel
     lemon wedges
     watercress sprigs OR parsley

Sprinkle gelatin over the cold water in a small saucepan. Place the pan over low heat and stir until gelatin is completely dissolved. Let cool slightly, then chill 10 minutes. Whip the cream until stiff. Stir in the horseradish, lemon juice, sugar and gelatin mixture. Continue to beat until cream mixture is quite thick. Chill for a few minutes. Place a generous spoonful of the cream mixture down the center of each salmon piece. Gently fold the two sides over so they overlap just slightly. Sprinkle with the pepper. Place each cream-filled salmon roll seam side down in a rectangular plastic container, filling the container. Cover with plastic cap or foil and chill before packing. Serve with triangles of buttered pumpernickel, and garnish with lemon wedges and watercress on each plate.

STUFFED EGGS WITH RED CAVIAR,
CELERY STICKS AND OLIVES

Serves 12–24

  1 dozen hard-boiled eggs (page 287)
  ¼ pound (1 stick) butter, softened
  1 teaspoon Dijon mustard
     salt
     white pepper
  1 medium-sized jar red caviar
     small celery sticks
     black olives

Shell the eggs, split them lengthwise, and remove and mash the yolks until smooth with the softened butter, the Dijon mustard and salt and white pepper to taste. Stuff the whites with this mixture. Arrange the stuffed eggs in a plastic picnic container. Bring a medium-sized jar of not-too-expensive red caviar separately in your pack and put a little dollop on top of each egg just before serving outdoors. Decorate platters with small celery sticks and black olives.

TROUT CEVICHE

Serves 6

> 1 *medium-sized trout, washed, deboned and cut into chunks*
> *juice of 1 lime* OR *of half a lime and half a lemon*
> 2 *long, hot Hungarian wax chilis*
> OR
> 4 *small hot green chilis, chopped*
> 1 *large red* OR *white onion, peeled and grated*
> 1 *large tomato, peeled, cored, seeded and finely chopped*
> *salt and freshly ground white pepper*

Stir all the ingredients together and marinate them in a covered bowl for 24 hours in the refrigerator.

For a backpack, transfer the mixture to a tightly sealed container.

Serve ceviche with good French bread or little hard rolls.

Vegetables

ANTIPASTO

Serves 6

We use this delicious spicy combination either alone as a side dish or as a filling for other vegetables or pita bread.

- 1½ cups olive oil
- ½ cup white wine vinegar
- ¼ cup water
- 1 tablespoon salt
- 1 teaspoon sugar
  freshly ground black pepper
- 3 tablespoons minced fresh green herbs, including basil, oregano and chervil or chives,

  OR

- 3 teaspoons dried

- 1 large clove garlic, peeled and crushed
- ½ teaspoon dry mustard
- ½ pound carrots, scrubbed, pared and sliced finely
- ½ pound cauliflower, washed and broken in small flowerets
- ¼ pound small whole mushrooms, washed and patted dry
- ½ cup sliced black olives
- ½ cup Italian salami (⅛ pound good quality), cut in thin strips
- ½ cup (⅛ pound) good quality Fontina OR Muenster cheese, diced finely
- ¼ cup chopped pimento
- ¼ cup capers, drained
- 1 7-ounce can water-packed tuna, drained

Combine the first nine ingredients in a large saucepan. Boil the mixture gently, uncovered, 5 minutes.

Add the carrots and cauliflower and boil gently until tender but still crisp (about 15 minutes). Remove vegetables with a slotted spoon to a large mixing bowl. Add mushrooms to the marinade. Boil gently 5 minutes. Remove mushrooms with a slotted spoon to the bowl also. Chill and reserve cooking liquid.

Add the olives, salami, cheese, pimento, capers and tuna (in chunks) to the vegetables and mushrooms and toss lightly with a fork. Put in a plastic container and chill for a picnic. Take the cooking liquid in a separate small leakproof container as a dressing.

This antipasto is good with crackers, or take small tomato shells or artichoke hearts in another container and fill with the antipasto at the picnic.

ARTICHAUTS FARCIS

Serves 4

4 *artichokes*
1 *tablespoon oil (preferably olive oil)*
2 *teaspoons lemon juice* OR *white wine vinegar*

2 *cloves garlic, peeled and sliced*
OR
2 *scallions, minced*

¼ *cup butter, margarine* OR *good oil*
1 *cup dry bread crumbs,*
     made from a good white bread, one day old
¼ *cup finely minced parsley*
1 *teaspoon salt*
¼ *teaspoon freshly ground black pepper*
2 *tablespoons freshly grated Parmesan cheese*
¼ *cup liquid in which artichokes were cooked*
8 *tablespoons (1 stick) butter*

Oven temperature: 300°

Wash artichokes well between the leaves. Cut off the tops about 1 inch
down. Trim points off all leaves with scissors. Drop them into a large pot of
briskly boiling, unsalted water, to which the oil and 1 teaspoon of lemon
juice or vinegar have been added. Boil 20–30 minutes, or slightly longer at
higher altitudes, testing for tenderness with a sharp fork at the base. The
flesh at the base should be tender but firm, as the artichokes will be baked
in the oven. Drain upside down until cool enough to handle.

Sauté the garlic or scallions (wild, if in season) in a frying pan in the ¼
cup oil or butter until lightly brown. Pour over the bread crumbs in a
medium-sized bowl and mix well. Add parsley (Italian type, if available),
salt, pepper, and cheese and mix well. Drizzle the artichoke liquid over this
and mix gently with a fork, not allowing the dressing to compact.

Take the "choke" out of the artichoke by pulling out all the center leaves
which are attached to the central hairy base of the heart. Spread apart the
remaining leaves and fill the central cavity and between the leaves with the
stuffing. Place the artichokes in a baking pan, closely packed in to prevent
spreading, and bake, uncovered, for 30 minutes.

Melt the butter and add 1 teaspoon lemon juice. Take in a separate small jar or container to pour over the artichokes at serving time. Wrap the artichokes individually in foil and place in a leakproof plastic bag. Though these make an impressive display on an outdoor table, they have the disadvantage of being quite heavy, so have someone else carry the wine and the thermos on the hike.

BASQUE EGGPLANT

Serves 6

This dish was inspired by leftover hot eggplant, served for dinner the night before. It's a variation of Perla Meyers' Basque Eggplant from her book *The Seasonal Kitchen.*

      3 *anchovy filets, chopped*
    ¼ *cup milk*
      2 *medium eggplants*
        salt
  5–6 *tablespoons olive oil*
      2 *onions, peeled and finely sliced*
      3 *tomatoes, chopped*
        OR
      1 *medium-size can tomatoes*
      2 *small cloves garlic, peeled and mashed*
      1 *teaspoon fresh thyme*
      1 *tablespoon fresh basil*
        freshly ground white pepper
    ⅔ *cup Feta cheese, crumbled*
        chopped parsley
      1 *clove garlic, peeled and minced*

Put the anchovies to soak in a little bowl of milk. Slice eggplant into ½-inch pieces. Place in a colander, sprinkle with salt and let stand for one hour. Dry the eggplant slices well with paper towels to remove salt. Heat 3 to 4 tablespoons olive oil in a large skillet and sauté the eggplant over medium heat until lightly browned. Transfer them to plate.

Add 2 tablespoons of fresh olive oil to the skillet. Sauté the onions slowly until transparent. Add the tomatoes, garlic, thyme and basil. Cook until most of the liquid has evaporated and the mixture thickens. Add a large pinch of white pepper. Drain the anchovies, pat dry, and add them along with the Feta cheese. Spoon the tomato mixture over the eggplant slices and sprinkle with parsley and garlic. Arrange carefully in a close-fitting picnic container.

This dish is good served tepid or cold.

CAPONATA

Italian eggplant relish.

Serves 6–8

This refreshing mixture can be served as an appetizer with crackers, as a condiment, or as a vegetable side dish that would complement almost any meat or fish entrée.

1 *medium-to-large eggplant*

2 *large tomatoes*
   OR
1 *medium-size can (1½ cups) Italian plum tomatoes, drained*

½ *cup olive oil*
1 *large stalk of celery with leaves, scrubbed and finely chopped*
1 *small yellow onion, peeled and chopped (½ cup)*
⅓ *cup wine vinegar*
1 *teaspoon sugar*
2 *tablespoons chopped parsley*
6 *large green Spanish olives, pitted and sliced*
1 *tablespoon capers*
2 *teaspoons anchovy paste*
1 *tablespoon finely chopped pine nuts*
2 *tablespoons tomato paste, mixed with ½ cup of water*
   pepper
   salt

Parboil the eggplant whole for 10 minutes in a pot of boiling water large enough to cover it. Lift out of the water and cool. Peel and cube the eggplant, lightly salt it and put it in a colander to drain.

Blanch the tomatoes by immersing in boiling water for a minute, one at a time. Rinse in cold water and cut off ends, squeeze gently to remove seeds, then peel and chop them. Reserve.

In a large heavy skillet, heat ¼ cup olive oil, add the celery and cook 10 minutes on low heat. Now add the onion to the celery and cook 10 minutes more, stirring frequently until the onion is translucent. Remove vegetables from the pan with a slotted spoon and reserve. Add the other ¼ cup olive oil, increase heat and fry the eggplant cubes over medium-high heat, stirring almost constantly with a wooden spoon until lightly browned and tender (about 10 minutes).

Now return the cooked celery and onions to the skillet with the eggplant. Add the tomatoes and stir in the vinegar and sugar. Cook 5 minutes. Add the parsley, olives, capers, anchovy paste, pine nuts and tomato paste mixed with water and a few grindings of pepper. Taste for salt, but be careful, since the salted eggplant usually provides all the salt needed.

Cook the mixture uncovered until thick, or about 20 minutes, stirring from time to time. Taste for seasoning and let cool.

Chill until ready to pack in a plastic container.

CHAMPIGNONS À LA GRECQUE

Serves 8

A classic appetizer of the French cuisine, these mushrooms are a perfect way to begin a picnic while the wine is just being opened.

  1 *pound small, whole fresh mushrooms*
  1 *cup cold water*
  ½ *cup olive oil*
  ¼ *cup tarragon* OR *white wine vinegar*
  2 *whole bay leaves*
  1 *teaspoon fennel seed*
  ½ *teaspoon thyme*
3–4 *sprigs of parsley*
  1 *teaspoon salt*
 12 *whole black peppercorns*
    fresh parsley
    lemon slices

Remove the mushroom stems. Rinse and drain the whole mushroom caps in a colander. In a 2-quart enameled saucepan, mix the water, olive oil and vinegar. Bring to a boil and add the herbs. Then turn down heat and simmer, covered, for 10 minutes. Drop in the mushroom caps and simmer for 10 or 15 minutes more. Set the pan off the stove and let the mushrooms cool in the marinade. Bottle and refrigerate until needed. They will keep well for up to a week, or they can be eaten immediately.

The marinade can be reused for cooking more fresh mushrooms, or other vegetables. Serve on a bed of fresh parsley with lemon slices, taken in a separate plastic bag.

EGGPLANT UNDER OIL

Yield: 1 quart

The price of olive oil makes this rustic antipasto a gourmet delicacy; nevertheless, the recipe is worth passing on.

1 *large eggplant, peeled and sliced*
  salt
1 *quart of vinegar*
⅓ *cup dry red wine*
1 *large celery stalk with leaves, scrubbed and chopped*
3 *large cloves garlic, peeled and sliced thinly*
  olive oil to cover

Wash and sterilize a quart Mason jar and lid.

Slice eggplant into ¼-to-½-inch slices. Place the eggplant in a wooden box, generously salting between layers. A cigar box holds one large eggplant nicely. Cover with foil and pile on several bricks or other five-pound weights and leave one day.

Bring the vinegar and wine to a boil in a saucepan. Place eggplant in it, two or three slices at a time. Remove with tongs as soon as vinegar comes to a boil again. Rinse off excess salt with cold water. Drain on paper towels or dish towel.

Place in a hermetically sealed jar by rolling each eggplant slice to fit. Put some celery and garlic in between the slices. When filled, pour olive oil—unrefined cold pressed, if you can get it—over all, up to the rim of the jar. Make sure the oil has seeped down and thoroughly covered everything. Run a knife around the inside perimeter of the jar. Shake a little to remove air bubbles.

Screw the lid on tightly to seal. Once sealed, it will keep indefinitely, like any canned food, without refrigeration. We like to take the whole jar to a big picnic because it's so pretty. Take out several slices and arrange them on a plate with Greek olives and quartered eggs. For a backpack, put several slices in a plastic container. Refrigerate any remaining eggplant after the jar has been opened.

POIREAUX AU VIN ROUGE

Serves 6

This is a dish that looks beautiful, with the green of the leeks against the dark purple of the wine sauce.

1 *pound leeks*
3–4 *tablespoons olive oil*
   salt to taste
1 *glass red wine*
1 *tablespoon bouillon* OR *good meat stock*

Select small leeks, and cut them down almost to the white part of the vegetable. Clean thoroughly. Sauté them in the olive oil, turning as they take on color. Season with very little salt. Pour in the wine, simmer a minute, then add the stock and cook over moderate heat about 8 to 10 minutes, until tender. Place the leeks in a "picnic dish" and continue cooking the sauce a few more minutes until reduced by a third. Pour it over the leeks. Chill in an attractive oblong container which will hold the leeks laid in lengthwise. Serve outdoors on plates with forks.

RATATOUILLE

Serves 8–10

This aromatic vegetable casserole that comes from the south of France has many variations. The dish ages well, the flavors permeating one another.

2 *cups ½-inch cubes yellow summer squash*
   OR *zucchini*
1½ *teaspoons salt*
3 *cloves garlic, peeled and minced*
⅓ *cup olive oil*
⅓ *teaspoon cumin seeds*
2 *cups ½-inch cubes peeled eggplant*
½ *teaspoon oregano*
3 *medium-sized onions, peeled and sliced*
2 *green peppers, washed, cored and cut in strips*
½ *teaspoon marjoram*
3 *medium-sized tomatoes, sliced*
⅓ *teaspoon dill seeds*

Oven temperature: 350°

Preheat oven. Cover the bottom of a buttered 2½-quart casserole with zucchini cubes. Sprinkle with one-third of the salt, garlic and oil. Add cumin seeds. Make second layer with eggplant cubes. Sprinkle with one-third of the salt, garlic and oil. Add oregano. Make a third layer of the onion slices and a fourth of green pepper. Sprinkle with remaining one-third of the salt, garlic and oil and the marjoram. Cover casserole. Bake one hour. Add layer of sliced tomatoes and sprinkle with dill seeds. Bake uncovered for 15 more minutes.

Store it in the refrigerator until you are ready to pack it in an attractive shallow plastic container. It's very good served cold, but it's best tepid, so let the mixture come to room temperature for your picnic.

COURGETTES FARCIES

Serves 12

12–14 *small zucchini, washed and cut in half lengthwise*
 ¾ *cup olive oil*
  3 *cloves garlic, peeled and minced*
 ⅔ *cup bread crumbs or croutons*
 12 *black olives, pitted and chopped*
  2 *tablespoons capers*
 ¼ *cup finely chopped parsley*
12–14 *anchovy filets, coarsely chopped*
 ¼ *cup grated Swiss cheese*

Oven temperature: 375°

Scoop out and discard seeds and half the flesh from the zucchini. Boil them in salted water for 5 to 10 minutes and then sauté halves quickly in 4 tablespoons olive oil. Let cool. Preheat oven. Sauté the garlic and crumbs in 6 tablespoons of the oil for 2 minutes. Reserve two tablespoons of the crumbs for later. Add the chopped olives, capers, parsley and anchovies. Stuff the zucchini with this mixture, sprinkle with the cheese and reserved crumbs, and dribble with remaining oil. Bake in a dish for 20 minutes, brushing once with olive oil. Let them come to room temperature, then pack in a low, flat plastic container. Refrigerate until packing time.

STUFFED CUCUMBERS WITH CAVIAR

Serves 10

 6 *small cucumbers*
12 *anchovies*
 1 *tablespoon chopped fresh dill*
 1 *tablespoon chopped fresh chives*
 6 *ounces cream cheese, softened*
 2 *tablespoons sour cream*
   salt
   freshly ground pepper
   sour cream
   caviar
   lemon wedges
   parsley

Let the cream cheese come to room temperature for about an hour. Wash the cucumbers and scrape them lengthwise with a fork to make decorative grooves. Slice into 2-inch sections and scoop the seeds from the center with a corer or a spoon, leaving thick, firm cucumber rings.

Mash the anchovies in a medium-sized mixing bowl and mix them with the dill, chives, cream cheese and sour cream. Season to taste with salt and pepper. Fill the cucumber rings with this mixture and chill several hours. Arrange the rings in one or two layers in a shallow hard-plastic picnic container. Take a separate container of sour cream, a small jar of caviar, and lemon wedges and parsley wrapped in plastic wrap.

To serve, top each cucumber ring with a tablespoon of sour cream topped with a little caviar. Surround the dish with lemon wedges and parsley.

STUFFED MUSHROOMS

Serves 12

Rosalie Sorrels is a "traveling lady folksinger." She is an inspired cook and an enthusiastic picnicker. We asked her for her favorite picnic recipe and got this one, as well as the recipe for Chinook salmon (page 130). At one memorable picnic, an impromptu bidding contest took place for the last Stuffed Mushroom Rosalie. It was probably the most expensive mushroom in history!

24 *fresh whole mushrooms, 2 to 2½ inches in diameter; stems removed,*
    washed, patted dry and chopped
¾ *cup bread crumbs made with good-quality bread*

½ cup chopped fresh OR canned crabmeat
½ cup minced green herbs consisting of a mixture of parsley and chives
3 tablespoons finely chopped shallots
3 tablespoons minced scallions
8 tablespoons (1 stick) butter
⅓ cup cognac OR good brandy
½ cup grated Gruyère cheese

Oven temperature: 375°

Sauté the chopped stems, bread crumbs, crabmeat, herbs, shallots and scallions in 4 tablespoons of the butter in a large-size frying pan. Heat through, about 10 minutes, over medium heat, stirring occasionally with a wooden spoon. Set off heat to cool.

Melt the other 4 tablespoons of butter in a small saucepan. Wipe the mushroom caps off with a damp cloth. Don't wash them. Dunk each cap in the butter and set on a cookie sheet or in a shallow pan, hollow side up.

Preheat oven. Pour the stuffing mixture into a large mixing bowl and "rinse" the sauté pan with the brandy, scraping the bottom with a wooden spoon. Heating the brandy to boiling, boil a minute, scrape the liquid into the mixing bowl and stir it in lightly. Now add half of the grated cheese, tossing lightly. Stuff each mushroom cap with a heaping mound of this mixture. Sprinkle the tops with the rest of the cheese.

Arrange the stuffed mushrooms closely side by side and bake 15–20 minutes until lightly browned. Then turn the oven up to broil and place the mushrooms under the broiler to "bubble" the cheese.

You can cover them with foil to keep them warm to take to a picnic by car. Or let them sit at room temperature and then pack in a hard-sided plastic container for a pack or a basket. Arrange on a plate to serve at a picnic. They can be refrigerated a day or two before used.

Condiments

CUCUMBER RAITA

Serves 6–8

A very refreshing condiment to serve with any meat, fish or fowl. Though more like a relish if the cucumbers are chopped, it is also very good when made with sliced cucumbers.

2–3 *cucumbers, peeled and seeded*
1 *onion, peeled and minced*
1 *tablespoon of fresh chopped coriander leaves*
    OR
1 *tablespoon chopped parsley and 1 teaspoon cilantro*
    (dried coriander leaf)
1 *teaspoon ground cumin.*
1–2 *tablespoons salt and a dash of white pepper*
1½ *cups yogurt*

First peel, then seed the cucumbers by cutting them lengthwise and running a spoon down the center; then chop them coarsely or slice in quarter-inch pieces. Salt and drain the cucumbers in a sieve for 15 minutes, then squeeze out the excess liquid by hand. Toss all the ingredients together and taste for seasoning, adding salt and pepper if necessary. Pack in a plastic container and chill.

It tastes best very cold, so if possible put it in a cold stream or in the snow for a few minutes just before serving.

ENGLISH GREEN APPLE AND RIPE TOMATO CHUTNEY

Yield: 12 half pints

2 *pounds green cooking apples, peeled and chopped*
3½ *pounds fresh ripe garden tomatoes, cored and chopped*
2 *cups dried currants or dark raisins*
1 *large white onion*
2 *cups brown sugar*
⅓ *cup mustard seed*
¼ *cup coarse salt*
2½ *cups cider vinegar*
3 *cloves garlic, peeled and minced*
4 *tablespoons grated ginger root*
3 *crushed whole red chili peppers*

Place all ingredients in a large saucepan and simmer for 2½ hours. Wash and sterilize 12 ½-pint jars and their lids in a dishwasher or in boiling water for 10 minutes. Ladle the mixture into jars to within ½ inch of top, wiping off the rims of the jars with a clean damp cloth before screwing on lids as tightly as you can. Place the jars in a large pot, on a rack, with enough boiling water to come one inch over the tops of the jars. Boil for 5 minutes to insure the seal.

Take the desired amount, perhaps two jars, to your picnic.

ENGLISH PICKLED CARROTS

Yield: 4 pints

3–4 *pounds small garden carrots*
1 *teaspoon salt*
2 *cups white vinegar*
2 *cups malt vinegar*
1¼ *cups sugar*
4 *teaspoons whole mixed pickling spices*

If possible, use finger-sized carrots fresh from the garden, washed but unpeeled. If these are unavailable, wash, peel and slice larger carrots. Cover the carrots with boiling salted water and cook 8 minutes. Drain and rinse in cold water. Combine the vinegars, sugar and pickling spices and bring to a boil. Reduce heat and simmer 5 minutes. Sterilize 4 pint-sized canning jars and their two-piece lids in a dishwasher or in boiling water for 10 minutes. Pack the carrots into jars and cover with vinegar mixture to within ½ inch of top. Wipe the rims of the jars before screwing on the lids, as tightly as you can. Place the jars in a large pot, on a rack, with enough boiling water to come one inch over the tops of the jars. Leave ample room between jars for the boiling water to circulate. If your pot is not large enough for all the jars to fit comfortably, boil them in two batches. Boil for 5 minutes, covered. Take out the jars and set on a towel to cool.

Take the amount you need in a separate picnic container.

ENGLISH PICKLED ONIONS

Yield: 6 pints

5 *pounds small round onions, peeled*
10 *cups malt vinegar*
2 *teaspoons coarse salt*

  6 *small pieces fresh ginger root*
 60 *whole allspice*
 60 *peppercorns*

Wash and sterilize 6 pint canning jars and their lids in a dishwasher or in boiling water for 10 minutes. Bring the vinegar with the salt to a boil. Add the onions and boil for 3 minutes. Ladle the onions into the jars, adding 1 marble-sized lump of ginger, 10 allspice and 10 peppercorns to each jar. Pour the boiling vinegar over the onions, wiping off the rim of each jar with a clean damp cloth before screwing on the lids as tightly as you can. Place the jars on a rack in a large deep pot filled with water to come one inch above the tops of the jars. Cover and bring to a boil. Keep at a rolling boil for 20 minutes.

You should let the onions sit two or three weeks before serving, but you can keep them for a long time on a shelf. Take as much as you need for your picnic in a plastic container, and refrigerate the opened jar.

GARLIC OLIVES

Serves 8

   1 *9-ounce can green olives*
   2 *cloves garlic, peeled and sliced*
   4 *dried red chili peppers*
1½ *tablespoons wine vinegar*
   1 *teaspoon dried dill weed*

Drain the liquid from the olives into a small saucepan. Put the olives aside. Add garlic and chili peppers to the liquid. Simmer for 5 minutes. Add the vinegar and the dill. Pour over the olives and mix well. When cool, pack into a jar or plastic container to take picnicking. Chill.

TORSHI

Yield: 6 pints

Preserved pickled vegetables, Armenian style

   3 *small cloves garlic, peeled*
   1 *small head cauliflower, washed and broken in flowerets*
   1 *green or red bell pepper, washed, cored, seeded and cut into strips*
   1 *large yellow onion (a good sweet kind), peeled and cut into chunks*
   2 *large celery stalks, scrubbed and cut into pieces*

1 *cucumber, scrubbed, peeled and cut into 2-inch chunks*
½ *head cabbage, cut into 6-inch wedges (and then cut each of these wedges in half)*
6 *small dried hot chili peppers, seeded*
6 *teaspoons picking spice*
2 *cups cider vinegar*
5 *cups water*
2 *tablespoons plus 1 teaspoon salt*

Have 6 pint jars and lids well washed and sterilized. Pierce the garlic cloves with a sharp knife point in several places to release the flavor, and put one in each jar. Distribute the vegetables equally among the six jars. When the jars are half-full, put a chili pepper and 1 teaspoon of pickling spice in each jar. Finish filling with the vegetables.

Heat the vinegar with water and salt to boiling and pour over the vegetables in the jars.

Seal (see English Pickled Onions, page 246, for method) and store. Take a jar along for a picnic, or a smaller amount transferred to a plastic container with a tight lid.

WILD-FRUIT JAMS AND JELLIES

All the recipes included here for jams and jellies require crabapple pectin:

Crabapple Pectin

During apple harvest time, there are crabapples everywhere. In fact, they are usually free for picking, since they are not very good to eat. All varieties (and there are many) are exceedingly rich in pectin.

Put about 6 to 8 cups of crabapples in a large pot and cover with cold water to come just an inch or less above the level of the apples. Bring the pot to a boil. Reduce heat to maintain a gentle boil, just above simmer, and boil until the apples are soft. The skin should break so that the juices are released.

Some crabapples are very hard-skinned and require as long as an hour boiling time to soften, while others turn very soft, even mushy, in a few minutes. When they are soft, stir, mash and press the apples against the pot with a wooden spoon to break the skin, if necessary. (If the apples are very soft and the skin has broken on all of them, this step is not necessary.)

Put a square of a double thickness of cheesecloth in a colander over a bowl. Pour the cooked apples and their liquid into the colander. Gather up the cheesecloth around the apples and tie it with a string at the top, saving all the liquid which drains into the bowl. Hang the cheesecloth bag from a hook or a nail anywhere in your kitchen is convenient. Let the bag hang over a bowl until it is dry, usually 12 hours. The liquid in the bowl is pure pink, thick apple pectin. Reserve it in a jar for making all your jams and jellies.

Crabapple Jelly

Using a proportion of 2 to 3 (2 cups honey to 3 cups of apple pectin) gently boil crabapple pectin and honey, adding a little lemon juice to taste, until it seems ready to jell.

There is no rule that says how long you must boil the mixture in order for it to jell, since each variety of apple has different amounts of pectin. Watch the mixture and take out a teaspoonful when it looks thick. If you use a thermometer, the jelling point is 220° to 222°.

Pour the jelly into sterilized jars and seal with a thin layer of paraffin, adding another layer when the first is hard. Label and store.

You can flavor this basic jelly with a fresh herb for variety. A single mint leaf, a sprig of rosemary, or a few rose geranium petals will flavor several jars of jelly.

Rose-hip Jam

You can pick rose hips any time of the year, even during the winter, when they are shriveled and dried on the bush. Only avoid the black ones which have been frozen too often and have neither flavor nor nutrients left. Put the rose hips in a pan with twice the amount of water (1 cup water for 2 cups rose hips) and boil gently for half an hour. Let the mixture cool and put in a crock or a glass jar for 24 hours. Then blend it about 20 seconds. Strain this mixture. Combine equal amounts of crabapple pectin and rose-hip juice. Combine this mixture with an equal amount of honey, and then taste for sweetness, adding more honey as necessary. Boil the mixture perhaps 30 minutes to an hour, sometimes longer. Watch it carefully. Take out a teaspoonful and put it in a little dish to see if it will jell. Even a teaspoonful takes some time to jell, so your jam may be done before you realize it.

There is necessarily a lot of guessing. If the mixture does not jell, it's necessary to pour it back in the pot and boil longer. (Or you could call it syrup or even resort to using commercial pectin. Jams and jellies made with honey and crabapple pectin are much superior in flavor to the varieties made with sugar and commercial pectin.) If it's too thick or gummy, you can melt it down again by adding fruit juices to thin it.

When you think the mixture is thick enough, pour it into sterilized jars and seal with melted paraffin.

Red Currant Jam

Put freshly picked currants in a saucepan with about one-half as much water as currants and boil gently for about 30 minutes. Then strain them through a strainer, pushing down with a wooden spoon to extract all the juice.

You can put the currant mixture through a food mill for a more pulpy jam. You can also use cheesecloth in the strainer for a clearer jelly mixture. It's all a matter of preference. The flavor of wild currants will remain delicious.

Mix the currant juice with equal amounts of crabapple pectin and honey in the proportion 1 to 1 to 1. (These proportions can be varied to taste.) Boil the mixture gently until it's thick, 30 minutes to an hour sometimes. Then pour into sterilized jars and seal with a thin layer of melted paraffin, adding another layer after the first has hardened.

DESSERTS

Beside a fresh-water stream, in a grassy meadow or on a white sandy beach, the scene is set for a perfect picnic when a lovely dessert is planned.

Picnic desserts needn't be elaborate, but when they are, the occasion is even more delightful. You can certainly create an artful and appealing arrangement with something simple, like a sliced orange decorated with sections of Swiss hazelnut chocolate, and it will be welcomed and appreciated, but more sophisticated desserts like layer cakes are really wonderful. Whatever you decide to make, it is important to know how to pack the dessert dishes. (Refer to the notes on packing for instructions.)

If you are exerting yourself on a long day's hike, you can safely afford to treat yourself to those few extra calories with the hope of "walking it off." A little indulgence is one of the beauties of picnicking. Also, in many cases, we have adapted older recipes to substitute honey for sugar and whole-wheat flour for white. These healthier confections are just as successful and delicious as sweets made with sugar.

Eating out of doors in the fresh air and sunshine, food seems to taste better than ever, and just when you think you could never eat another morsel, your attention is turned to an irresistible dessert.

Cakes and Tortes

BANANA HONEY CAKE

Serves 8–10

1	cup honey
1	teaspoon soda
1	cup oats
¾	cup butter, softened
½	cup sugar
2	eggs
1	cup mashed bananas
1½	cups sifted all-purpose flour
¾	teaspoon baking powder
¾	teaspoon salt
1	cup nuts

Oven temperature: 350°

Preheat oven. Bring the honey to a boil. Add ½ teaspoon soda. Pour over oats in a mixing bowl, stir, and let stand 10 minutes. Beat the butter until creamy, gradually adding sugar, and continue beating until fluffy. Blend in the eggs and add the oat mixture and bananas, blending well. Sift together the flour, ½ teaspoon soda, baking powder and salt. Add this to creamed mixture, then mix in the nuts. Pour into two small greased loaf pans (7½″ × 3½″ × 2¼″). Bake 30 to 35 minutes.

Icing

2	3-ounce packages cream cheese, softened
2½	cups confectioners' sugar

Mix well with an electric beater and spread on the cake with a spatula.

For the picnic you may wrap this loaf-size cake in foil or plastic wrap. Be sure it is packed in an appropriate place in your pack or basket so as not to lose its shape. If you have a plastic container that it will fit into, use this, or you may want to pack the cake right in the loaf pan, wrapped in foil.

GINGERBREAD

Yield: 1 medium (7½″ × 3½″ × 2¼″) loaf pan or
two small (6″ × 3″ × 2″) loaf pans

  1 *tablespoon vinegar*
  ¾ *cup milk*
  2 *cups sifted all-purpose flour*
  2 *teaspoons baking powder*
  ¼ *teaspoon baking soda*
  ½ *teaspoon salt*
1½–2 *teaspoons ground ginger*
    OR
  1 *teaspoon grated fresh ginger*

  1 *teaspoon ground cinnamon*
  ¼ *teaspoon ground cloves*
  ⅓ *cup butter*
  ½ *cup sugar*
  1 *egg*
  ¾ *cup molasses*

Oven temperature: 350°

Preheat oven. Add vinegar to the milk to curdle it and set aside. Sift together twice the flour, baking powder, soda, salt and spices. Cream the butter and sugar together well. Add the egg and continue beating until fluffy. Now add the molasses, and mix together well. Add the dry ingredients slowly, alternating with the curdled milk, stirring after each addition. Turn into greased and floured pans and bake for 45 to 50 minutes.

Take the gingerbread in the pan it is baked in and slice and serve at the picnic.

GRAND MARNIER CAKE

Serves 10

One of the lightest and most delicious cakes we've ever tasted, this cake is easy to make and travels extremely well because it's unfrosted.

  1 *cup butter*
  1 *cup sugar*
  3 *eggs, separated*
  1 *tablespoon Grand Marnier*

   2 *cups all-purpose flour*
   1 *teaspoon baking powder*
   1 *teaspoon baking soda*
1¼ *cups sour cream*
    grated rind of one orange
   1 *cup chopped walnuts*
 ½ *cup sugar*
   1 *cup orange juice*
 ⅓ *cup Grand Marnier*
    slivered almonds

    Oven temperature: 350°

Preheat the oven. Grease well 1 regular-size bundt pan or 2 smaller pans.

Cream the butter and sugar together until smooth and pale. Beat in the egg yolks one at a time and add one tablespoon of Grand Marnier. Sift the dry ingredients together and add to the batter, alternating with the sour cream and beating with each addition until smooth. Stir in the orange rind and walnuts, then fold in the stiffly beaten egg whites and pour into the prepared pans.

Bake for 50 minutes, or until done (when a toothpick comes out of the center clean). Let the cake cool before removing it from the pan.

Prepare a combination of sugar, orange juice and Grand Marnier, and place in a small plastic container. Wrap some slivered almonds in plastic wrap. At the site, pour the topping over the cake. Sprinkle with almonds. To carry in a backpack, we sometimes bake this cake in 2 small round charlotte molds or loaf pans about 4 to 6 inches in diameter. Wrap the cake, pan and all, in foil before putting in your pack.

NANCY'S CAKE

    Serves 6–8

Everyone asks for the recipe for this spice cake made with oatmeal. It's really very simple to make, but tastes as good as many more complicated cakes.

   1 *cup boiling water*
   1 *cup oatmeal*
 ½ *stick butter, softened*
   2 *cups firmly packed brown sugar*
   2 *eggs*
   1 *cup all-purpose flour*

1   *teaspoon cinnamon*
1   *teaspoon cloves*
1   *teaspoon baking soda*
½   *cup raisins*
1   *cup chopped nuts*
⅓   *cup confectioners' sugar*

Oven temperature: 350°

Preheat oven. Grease and flour a round pan—either a casserole or soufflé dish 6–7 inches in diameter and 4–5 inches deep or a charlotte mold. (It's also a good cake to bake in 2 small loaf pans, one for the picnic, one for tea.) Pour boiling water over the oatmeal and set it aside until cool, about 15 minutes.

Meawhile, cream together the butter and brown sugar in a large mixing bowl and beat in the eggs, one at a time. Then blend in the flour, spices and baking soda. Beat in the oatmeal and fold in the raisins and nuts. Pour the batter into the buttered casserole and bake 45–50 minutes. Check for doneness with a toothpick. Insert, and if it comes out clean, the cake is done. When the cake has cooled 10 minutes, take it out of its baking pan. Let it cool longer, and dust with confectioners' sugar before serving.

This cake can be wrapped in foil or put back into the pan it was baked in, covered with foil and placed in the pack.

PRIZE APPLE-NUT CAKE

Serves 10

4–5   *tart cooking apples*
1   *cup sugar*
1   *cup all-purpose flour*
1   *teaspoon baking soda*
1   *teaspoon cinnamon*
½   *teaspoon salt*
1   *egg*
¼   *cup vegetable oil*
½   *cup chopped walnuts*
1   *teaspoon vanilla extract*
    confectioners' sugar OR *lemon icing (see page 258)*

Oven temperature: 350°

Preheat oven. Grease 2 medium loaf pans (about 7½″ × 3½″) or 3 smaller ones (6″ × 3″).

Peel, core and chop the apples or peel and core them and put them through a fine blade of a food chopper. Mix them with the sugar in a bowl and let the mixture stand ½ to 1 hour. Sift the flour, soda, cinnamon and salt together into a bowl. In a medium-sized mixing bowl, beat the egg well with a fork while stirring in the oil. Add the dry ingredients alternately with the apples to the egg and oil, mixing well after each addition. Stir in the nuts and vanilla. Turn the mixture into the greased loaf pans, and bake 1 hour or until a toothpick comes out clean. Cool in the pan 10 minutes and then take the cake out and cool thoroughly on a rack.

Sprinkle with powdered sugar or frost with lemon icing. Wrap the cake in foil to pack.

PRUNE SPICE CAKE WITH LEMON ICING

Serves 6–8
Yield: 1 small round cake

½ cup firmly packed brown sugar
3 tablespoons honey
6 tablespoons butter, softened
2 eggs
3 tablespoons sour cream OR *buttermilk*
1½ cups sifted all-purpose flour
1 teaspoon baking powder
 pinch of salt
¼ teaspoon soda
½ teaspoon cinnamon
1 cup drained, pitted and chopped
 cooked prunes
½ cup chopped walnuts
 confectioners' sugar

Oven temperature: 375°

Preheat oven and butter and flour a 4-cup round charlotte mold or a medium-sized loaf pan.

Cream together in a mixing bowl the sugar, honey and butter. Blend the eggs one at a time, and then the sour cream or buttermilk. Sift the flour with the baking powder, salt, soda and cinnamon. Mix the dry ingredients into the creamed mixture. Stir in the prunes and walnuts. Turn the mixture into the prepared pan. Bake 30 minutes; test for doneness by inserting a toothpick in the middle of the cake.

Cool the cake in the pan. Loosen it by running a knife around the edge, and unmold it. Put it back into the pan to wrap it to travel. Take some confectioners' sugar to sprinkle on top after you invert the cake onto a paper or plastic plate, or frost with:

Lemon Icing

      1 egg yolk
    ½ cup confectioners' sugar
      2 tablespoons lemon juice
      1 teaspoon lemon rind
      4 tablespoons butter, softened

Beat all the ingredients in a small bowl with an electric beater until smooth. Chill and spread on cake at serving time.

STRAWBERRY MERINGUE TORTE

Serves 10

This is a lovely, delectable cake to make in summer when strawberries are at their peak.

    ¼ cup sweet butter
    ½ cup sugar
    ½ teaspoon vanilla extract
      2 eggs, separated
      1 cup sifted cake flour
  1¼ teaspoons baking powder
    ¼ teaspoon salt
    ½ cup milk
    ½ cup sugar
    ¼ cup slivered almonds
      2 cups fresh ripe strawberries, washed, hulled and halved
      1 cup cream, whipped and sweetened

Oven temperature: 350°

Preheat oven. In a medium-sized bowl cream the shortening with the sugar and vanilla. Beat in the egg yolks. Sift the dry ingredients together and add alternately with the milk to the creamed mixture, beating after each addition. Pour into 2 paper-lined 8-inch round pans.

Beat egg whites until frothy; add the sugar slowly and continue beating until stiff peaks form. Spread evenly over cake batter. Sprinkle each cake with almonds and bake for ½ hour or until done. Cool in pans 20 minutes; remove and cool thoroughly. Spread strawberries on the first layer (meringue side up), then place the second cake over it and spread with the remaining strawberries. Slice and serve the cake with whipped cream and extra sweetened berries.

You may prefer to take the cakes in the pans in which they were cooked. If so, take the strawberries and whipped cream in separate containers in a cooler, and put the cake together at the picnic. Or put it together before the picnic, and cover with a plastic cake cover.

Chocolate Cakes

CHOCOLATE PICNIC CAKE

Yield: 2 round cakes

⅞ cup cocoa
2 cups firmly packed brown sugar
1¾ cups milk
¾ cup butter
4 eggs, separated
2⅓ cups sifted cake flour
1 teaspoon soda
½ teaspoon salt
2½ teaspoons baking powder
1 teaspoon vanilla extract

Oven temperature: 350°

Preheat oven. Grease and flour 2 8-inch round cake pans. Bring the chocolate, 1 cup of the brown sugar and ¾ cup milk to a boil in a saucepan over medium heat and set aside to cool.

In a mixing bowl, cream the butter with the second cup of brown sugar, and add to the cooled chocolate mixture. Add the egg yolks one at a time, beating well after each addition. Sift the dry ingredients together and add them to the batter alternately with the remaining 1 cup milk, beginning and ending with the flour. Beat the egg whites until stiff and fold them into the batter. Stir in the vanilla. Pour the batter into the cake pans and bake 20 to 25 minutes. Test with a toothpick for doneness. Cool on racks.

Chocolate Filling

1 8-ounce package cream cheese
8 tablespoons (1 stick) butter
1 pound confectioners' sugar
  hot espresso coffee

Mix the cheese, butter and sugar thoroughly and thin the mixture with a little hot coffee. Spread between the two cake layers.

Chocolate Picnic Frosting

2 egg whites
2 cups confectioners' sugar
¾ cup soft butter

2 *1-ounce squares unsweetened chocolate, melted*
½ *teaspoon vanilla extract*

Beat the egg whites until stiff. Add one cup of confectioners' sugar and beat in the softened butter. Then beat in another cup of confectioners' sugar. Fold in the chocolate and vanilla and spread the frosting over the cake with a spatula, dipping the spatula in warm water from time to time.

Take this cake to a picnic in a box. Cover it with a cake cover until ready to serve.

CRUNCHY WALNUT FUDGE LOAF

1 small loaf cake serves 4–6
1 *cup semisweet chocolate bits*
2 *eggs, separated*
pinch of salt
½ *cup sugar*
½ *teaspoon vanilla extract*
½ *teaspoon vinegar*
¾ *cup chopped walnuts*
⅛ *teaspoon salt*
1 *cup sifted all-purpose flour*
1½ *teaspoons baking powder*
¼ *cup safflower* OR *vegetable oil*

Oven temperature: 325°

Preheat oven. Grease a small loaf pan or 8-inch round pan and a large cookie sheet.

Crunchy Walnut Topping

Melt the chocolate bits in a double boiler over medium heat. Beat the egg whites separately in a bowl with a pinch of salt, until foamy. Add the sugar gradually and continue beating until stiff peaks form. Stir in the vanilla and vinegar. With an electric mixer, beat in the melted chocolate and the chopped walnuts.

Spread one-fourth of the mixture on a large cookie sheet. Bake for about 8–10 minutes. When it is done, scrape the crunchy topping into a bowl, using a metal spatula and crumbling it. Set aside. Raise oven temperature to 350°.

Fudge Mixture

In a medium mixing bowl mix the remaining three-fourths of the walnut
mixture with one cup sifted flour, the baking powder, the oil and the egg
yolks. Blend the ingredients well and put into a small buttered loaf pan
approximately 7″ × 3½″ × 2″. Sprinkle the crunchy walnut topping on
top of the batter. Bake at 350° for 15 minutes. Let cool and pack in the
pan the cake was baked in, covering the top securely with foil held in place
with tape or a rubber band.

GÂTEAU AU CHOCOLAT

Serves 10–12

 1 *cup unsalted butter, softened*
10 *ounces semisweet chocolate squares, cut up,*
     OR *10 ounces semisweet bits*
 6 *tablespoons milk*
 6 *eggs, separated*
 1 *cup sugar (scant)*
 1 *cup cake flour*

Oven temperature: 350°

Preheat oven and grease and flour two 8-inch round pans.
   Put the butter in a large mixing bowl. Melt the chocolate with the milk
in the top of a double boiler. Remove from heat and add to the butter. Now
mix in the 6 egg yolks and beat well with a wooden spoon or mixer. Add
the sugar and flour, mixing in thoroughly and beating a few minutes more.
   Beat the egg whites until light and stiff. Fold a little of the beaten egg
white into the batter to lighten it. Then fold the batter back into the whites.
Turn the batter into the prepared pans and bake about 25 minutes. Test for
doneness with a toothpick. Cool in pans 10 minutes and turn out on rack to
finish cooling.
   Ice the entire cake with Rich Chocolate Cream:

Rich Chocolate Cream

 6 *ounces sweet chocolate*
 ¼ *cup water*

¼ *cup sugar*
4 *egg yolks*
6 *tablespoons butter, softened*

Melt the chocolate with the water and the sugar in the top of a double boiler, stirring till smooth. Turn off the heat and add the egg yolks, one at a time, beating well after each addition. Let cool to lukewarm and add the butter a little at a time, beating after each addition. Let the frosting cool a bit to a good spreading consistency. Spread the bottom layer with the frosting; place the top layer on the cake and frost it. Transport the cake to the picnic in a box or plastic cake container.

LE MARQUIS AU CHOCOLAT

Serves 8–10

This chocolate butter sponge cake with buttercream frosting and chocolate glaze is a festive picnic cake. Although rich, it is very light. It is not recommended for a climbing backpacking trip, of course, but it's a very special chocolate cake for a picnic taken in baskets or coolers by car. When you arrive at your site, put it somewhere in view of the picnickers and cover it with a clear plastic cake cover.

Oven temperature: 350°

Biscuit au Chocolat

Preheat oven. Lightly butter and flour an 8-inch round cake pan.

5 *ounces semisweet chocolate*
1 *heaping tablespoon instant coffee, dissolved in 2 tablespoons boiling water*
3 *large eggs*
½ *cup plus 1 tablespoon sugar*
3½ *tablespoons butter, softened*
 pinch of salt
⅛ *teaspoon cream of tartar*
⅔ *cup sifted cake flour, put back into sifter*

In a medium saucepan, melt the chocolate in the coffee and cool to tepid. Separate the eggs, placing yolks in a large bowl and whites in another. Beat the egg yolks with the sugar until thick and lemon-colored. Beat the butter gradually into the chocolate mixture until smooth, then beat it all into the yolks and sugar. Beat egg whites with a dash of salt and cream of tartar, until soft peaks are formed. Sprinkle in the 1 tablespoon of sugar and beat until stiff.

With a rubber spatula, stir one-fourth of the egg whites into the chocolate–egg yolk mixture; when partially blended, sift in one-fourth of the cake flour. Fold in another quarter of the egg whites rapidly and delicately with the spatula; when partially blended, sift in another fourth of flour, and continue thus, alternating with flour and egg whites, folding rapidly until all is incorporated.

Turn into prepared cake pan; tilt pan to run batter up to top all around. Set immediately in the middle of preheated oven and bake for about 30 minutes. When knife comes out clean, the cake is done. Remove from oven and let cool 5 minutes; unmold on a rack. Refrigerate to cool. (It may be frozen ahead at this point in an airtight bag.)

Crème au Beurre à l'Anglaise

> 4 *egg yolks*
> ⅔ *cup granulated sugar*
> ½ *cup hot milk*
> ½ *pound (2 sticks) unsalted butter, softened*
> Choice of the following flavorings:
> 3 *tablespoons of rum, kirsch, orange liqueur,* OR *strong coffee*
> OR
> 1 *teaspoon vanilla extract*
> OR
> ⅓ *cup (2 ounces) semisweet chocolate bits, melted*

Place egg yolk in a mixing bowl, gradually beat in the sugar, and continue beating until mixture is thick and lemon-colored. Then gradually beat in the milk. Turn mixture into a clean saucepan and stir with a wooden spoon over moderately low heat until it slowly thickens enough to coat the spoon lightly. (Be careful not to overheat or egg yolks will curdle, but mixture must thicken.) Set pan in cold water and stir until tepid. Rinse out mixing bowl and strain custard back into it. Then, using a wire whip or electric mixer, gradually beat in the softened butter by tablespoonfuls. If it begins to curdle, stir over a pan of hot water until it becomes smooth. Chill until thick and malleable.

Filling and Icing the Cake

This cake should be cooled before icing. When cake is thoroughly cold, brush crumbs off surface. Lay the cake upside down and slice it in half horizontally. Spread ¼ inch of the buttercream on the bottom half. Spread icing on top and sides of cake, smoothing with a spatula dipped in water. Chill until frosting is firm. Then glaze the cake.

Transport carefully in a box, cooler or a plate with a plastic cake cover.

Chocolate Glaze

1 *cup (6 ounces) semisweet chocolate bits*
¼ *cup espresso coffee*

Melt chocolate bits with the coffee and let cool to tepid. Place chilled frosted cake on a rack over a tray, and pour all the chocolate over the top, letting it fall down over the sides, which if nicely smoothed and slightly slanting, should take the chocolate coating perfectly. When glaze is set, transfer cake to a serving plate. Cake should be kept cool until serving.

SOUR CREAM CHOCOLATE LOAF WITH PENUCHE ICING

Serves 6–8

½ *cup butter*
1½ *cups sugar*
2 *eggs, separated*
½ *cup cocoa, mixed with enough very hot water*
to make 1 cup
2 *cups plus 2 tablespoons all-purpose flour*
½ *teaspoon salt*
1 *cup sour cream or buttermilk*
1 *tablespoon vanilla extract*

Oven temperature: 350°

Preheat oven. Grease and flour a regular-sized loaf pan (9¼″ × 5¼″ × 3″), or use 2 medium loaf pans (7½″ × 3½″ × 2¼″) if you'll be backpacking.

Cream the butter and sugar together with an electric beater in a large-sized mixing bowl. Beat the egg yolks well and add to the butter mixture, beating well. Now add the cocoa mixture.

Sift the flour with the salt and baking soda. Add the sifted dry ingredients alternately with the sour cream or buttermilk to the creamed chocolate mixture, beating with each addition. Add the vanilla.

Beat the reserved egg whites in a separate bowl until stiff. Fold them into the other ingredients and turn the batter into the prepared pan.

Bake 1 hour at low altitudes, and 1 hour and 20 minutes at higher ones, or until the cake is slightly shrinking from the edge of the pan and a toothpick inserted in the center comes out clean. Cool in the pan and wrap the cake, pan and all, in foil to carry. Unmold the cake at the site and frost with icing you have carried separately in a plastic container.

Penuche Icing

> 1 cup firmly packed brown sugar
> 1/2 cup cream OR evaporated milk
> 1 tablespoon butter
> 1/2 teaspoon vanilla extract

Cook the sugar and cream in a small saucepan over medium heat, stirring constantly until the sugar is dissolved completely. Stop stirring and let the mixture boil until it will form a soft ball when a bit of it is dropped into a cup of cold water. Turn off the heat, stir in the butter and vanilla, and beat the frosting until it is thick and creamy. Add a little more cream if the icing seems too stiff, since the cake should be frosted thinly.

If you prefer, you can ice the top of the cake in the pan before you wrap it, and eliminate the final frosting at the picnic. Just slice and serve the loaf right from the pan.

TORTE CLARICE

Yield: 1 8-inch round torte

1¾ cups flour
1½ cups firmly packed brown sugar
1 tablespoon grated orange rind
½ teaspoon salt
¼ pound (1 stick) sweet butter

  1 *6-ounce package semisweet chocolate bits*
  2 *eggs*
 ½ *teaspoon baking powder*
  1 *teaspoon vanilla extract*
1½ *cups chopped walnuts*

Oven temperature: 375°

Preheat oven. Combine 1½ cups of the flour, ½ cup of the brown sugar, the orange rind and ¼ teaspoon of the salt in a large bowl. Cut in the butter with a pastry cutter (or fork) until the mixture is crumbly. Press evenly over the bottom of an ungreased 8-inch round spring-form cake pan to make the bottom layer.

Bake for 10 minutes or until firm. Remove from the oven but leave the heat on. Sprinkle chocolate pieces over the layer in the pan and then let stand two minutes; spread evenly with a knife over the pastry to make the second layer.

Beat the eggs until thick in a medium-sized bowl. Stir in the remaining ¼ cup flour, 1 cup brown sugar, ¼ teaspoon salt, baking powder, vanilla and walnuts. Spread over the chocolate layer in the pan.

Bake twenty minutes longer or until the top is firm and golden. Cool completely in the pan, and store in a cool place, as the torte improves with age. Slice into wedges to serve. Wrap the wedge-shaped pieces separately in plastic wrap and put in a plastic bag or container to take in a pack. Or you can take the torte to a picnic in the pan it was baked in, wrapped securely in a pack or a basket.

Cookies and Bars

APPLESAUCE COOKIES

Yield: 3 dozen

2 cups sifted all-purpose flour
½ teaspoon salt
1 teaspoon baking soda
½ tablespoon cinnamon
½ tablespoon nutmeg
½ tablespoon cloves
2 tablespoons cocoa
1 cup chopped nuts
1 cup raisins
½ cup butter OR vegetable shortening
1 cup sugar
1 cup applesauce
1 egg, lightly beaten

Oven temperature: 350°

Preheat oven and grease a large cookie sheet. Resift the flour with the salt, soda, spices and cocoa. Add nuts and raisins. Cream the shortening with the sugar and beat until it is light and fluffy. Stir the applesauce and egg into the shortening and sugar mixture. Add the flour mixture to this, a half cup at a time, mixing well after each addition. Drop mixture on cookie sheet by tablespoonfuls and bake for 8–10 minutes.

Let cool and pack them in a hard-sided container so they won't break.

BANBURY TARTS

Yield: 2–3 dozen

Preheat oven to 450°. Grease 2 large cookie sheets.

Pastry

2½ cups all-purpose flour
½ teaspoon salt
4 tablespoons sweet butter
½ cup vegetable shortening
4–5 tablespoons ice water

Sift the flour with the salt. Cut the butter in pieces and add it and the vegetable shortening to the flour, mixing it in lightly using a pastry blender or two knives. When the mixture is a mealy consistency, add ice water, 1 tablespoon at a time, mixing until the dough holds together. Form the dough into a ball, wrap it in wax paper and chill it while you make the following filling:

Filling

> 1 *cup finely chopped walnuts*
> ¾ *cup chopped seedless golden raisins*
> ¼ *cup finely chopped dates*
> *grated rind and juice of 1 lemon*
> ¾ *cup honey*
> ¼ *cup firmly packed brown sugar*
> 1 *tablespoon butter, melted*
> 1 *egg*
> 1 *teaspoon vanilla extract*
> 2 *tablespoons cracker crumbs*

Mix the nuts, raisins, dates, lemon rind and juice, honey, brown sugar, and butter together thoroughly in a medium-sized mixing bowl. Beat the egg lightly and add it and the vanilla to the mixture. Add the cracker crumbs.

Roll out the pastry to ⅛ inch thick and cut it carefully into 3-inch squares with a sharp knife. Put a heaping teaspoon of filling on each square.

Dip your fingers in cold water and moisten the edges of each square. Fold the square over to form a triangle and crimp the edges with a fork dipped in flour, making sure the edges are well pressed together and sealed so the filling won't leak out while baking.

Lay the tarts on the cookie sheets. Prick them with a fork and put in the refrigerator 15 minutes to chill.

After they are chilled, paint the tarts with milk and bake about 20 minutes until lightly browned.

For easy transport, pack in a container after they have cooled.

BROWN-SUGAR BROWNIES

Serves 10

¼ *cup butter*
1 *cup firmly packed dark-brown sugar*
1 *egg*
1 *teaspoon vanilla extract*

½ *cup all-purpose flour*
1 *teaspoon baking powder*
½ *teaspoon salt*
¾ *cup chopped walnuts*

Oven temperature: 350°

Preheat the oven Using an electric mixer or portable beater, cream the butter and sugar until creamy. Beat in the egg and the vanilla. Sift together the flour, baking powder and salt. Fold into the sugar mixture. Stir in nuts.

Spread the batter in a greased 9-by-9-by-2-inch pan and bake about 25 minutes. Cool, cut into squares and pack in a hard-sided container to take in a pack or basket. You can wrap them individually in plastic wrap to keep them fresher and as an additional protective measure.

CHOCOLATE WALNUT PUFFS

Yield: 2 dozen

These delicate, mouth-watering cookies should be carefully arranged in an airtight container for transporting.

1 *cup (6-ounce package) semisweet chocolate bits*
2 *egg whites*
   pinch of salt
½ *cup sugar*
½ *teaspoon vanilla extract*
½ *teaspoon vinegar*
¾ *cup chopped walnuts*

Oven temperature: 350°

Melt chocolate bits in a pan over low heat. Beat the egg whites in a bowl with a pinch of salt until foamy. Gradually add the sugar and contine beating until stiff peaks form. Now beat in the vanilla and vinegar. Fold in melted chocolate bits and chopped walnuts. Drop by teaspoonfuls on greased cookie sheet. Bake for about 10 minutes. Let cool on a wire ra ˙.

GINGER SNAPS

Yield: 3 dozen

⅔ *cup vegetable oil*
1 *cup sugar*
1 *egg*
4 *tablespoons molasses*
2 *cups unsifted all-purpose flour*
2 *teaspoons baking soda*
1 *tablespoon ginger (powdered* OR *freshly grated)*
1½ *teaspoons cinnamon*
½ *teaspoon salt*

Oven temperature: 375°

Preheat oven. In a bowl combine the oil, sugar and egg. Mixing well, add the molasses and stir again. Add the dry ingredients: flour, soda, ginger, cinnamon and salt. You should now have a moist dough. Mold it into small (about 1 inch in diameter) balls and then roll them around on a plate of sugar. Flatten them slightly and arrange 2 inches apart on an ungreased cookie sheet. Bake for 10 minutes. Do not overcook.

Pack the ginger snaps in a plastic container for a backpack or a plastic bag for a picnic basket.

GORP

Serves 10

½ *cup golden raisins*
½ *cup chopped nuts*
¼ *cup shredded coconut*
¼ *cup sunflower seeds*
½ *cup cut-up dried apricots*
¼ *cup cut-up dried apples*

Combine the ingredients and put in a plastic bag. Gorp makes a delicious high-energy trail snack.

GORP BARS

Serves 2 dozen

This is a high-energy trail snack or dessert.

2 *12-ounce packages semisweet chocolate bits*
½ *cup honey*
½ *cup yellow raisins*
½ *cup chopped dried peaches or apricots*
½ *cup chopped dried dates or figs*
½ *cup chopped dried apples*
½ *cup shredded coconut*
1 *cup chopped walnuts*
½ *cup wheat germ*
½ *cup uncooked oatmeal*
½ *cup Bircher Muesli or other similar cereal*

Melt chips in top of double boiler, adding honey. Pour over the other dry ingredients in large bowl. Mix well. Pour mixture into greased pans and cool. Cut into bar-size chunks. Wrap tightly in plastic and store in refrigerator. Put into another plastic bag or plastic container to put in pack.

HONEY DATE-NUT BARS

Serves 16

3 *eggs*
1 *cup honey*
 grated rind of 1 lemon (about 2 teaspoons)
¼ *teaspoon salt*
1 *cup all-purpose or whole wheat pastry flour*
1 *teaspoon baking powder*
1 *package (8 ounces) dates, chopped*
1 *cup chopped pecans or walnuts*
 confectioners' sugar

Oven temperature: 325°

Preheat oven. In mixing bowl, beat eggs until light and foamy. Add next 3 ingredients and mix well. Mix flour and baking powder and add with dates and nuts to first mixture. Mix well.

Grease 13-by-9-by-2-inch baking pan and line bottom with waxed paper. Spread batter in pan and bake about 40 minutes.

Let stand a few minutes, then loosen around edges with small knife. Turn out on board and pull off paper; cool. Wrap in foil, seal and let ripen in cool place several days.

Cut lengthwise in ½-inch strips, then crosswise 4 times to form bars about 2 inches by ½ inch. Sprinkle with confectioners' sugar just before packing. Wrap the bars individually in plastic wrap and pack them in a plastic container.

LEMON BARS

Serves 12–14

These delectable bars have a tart lemon flavor. Picnickers are never able to resist having several.

- ¼ *pound (1 stick) butter*
- ¼ *pound (1 stick) margarine*
- 2 *cups all-purpose flour*
- ½ *cup confectioners' sugar*
- 4 *eggs*
- 4 *tablespoons flour*
- 2 *cups sugar*
- ½ *teaspoon salt*
- 1 *teaspoon baking powder*
- 6 *tablespoons freshly squeezed lemon juice*

Oven temperature: 350°

Preheat oven. Cream the first 4 ingredients together. Press the mixture into a baking sheet with sides about 1 inch deep. The pan should be approximately 15½ by 10½ inches. Press the dough gently about ¾ inch up the sides of the sheet. Bake it for 20 minutes.

While the dough is baking, mix the eggs, flour, sugar, salt and baking powder together in a bowl. Mix in the lemon juice. Take the baked shell from the oven and pour this mixture over it, spreading evenly. Return to the oven, still at 350°, to bake for 20 minutes, or until brown.

Let the cake cool and sprinkle it with confectioners' sugar. Cut it into bars. Pack the bars in a hard-sided plastic container to travel so that they won't be broken in transit.

MOUNTAIN BARS

Serves 14–16

- 2 *cups crushed vanilla wafers*
- 1½ *cups finely chopped pecans*
- ½ *pound finely chopped dates, walnuts* OR *almonds*
- 1 *cup finely chopped dried apricots* OR *peaches*

1 *cup seedless yellow raisins*
2 *tablespoons real maple syrup* OR *molasses*
6–8 *tablespoons honey*
½ *teaspoon vanilla* OR *maple flavoring*
    (OR *almond if almonds were used*)
2 *tablespoons wheat germ*
    confectioners' sugar

Combine the first five ingredients in a large bowl. Combine the next four ingredients and then add to the first mixture. Knead to mix—a tablespoon of water or orange juice helps if the mixture is difficult to knead. Press and shape into small log shapes about 2 inches by 5 inches. Roll in confectioners' sugar and wrap in plastic. Store in the refrigerator and put in a plastic bag or container for the trip.

PEANUT BUTTER CONFECTIONS

Yield: 3 dozen

½ *cup peanut butter*
½ *cup currants*
½ *cup honey*
½ *cup shredded coconut*
2 *tablespoons lemon juice*
1 *tablespoon nutritional yeast*
¼ *cup wheat germ*
½ *cup carob powder* OR *instant chocolate*
½ *cup powdered milk*

Mix all ingredients and shape into balls. Roll in chocolate powder or coconut. Store in tight container and pack in plastic bag or container for trail snacks or dessert.

POPPY-SEED COOKIES

Yield: 3 dozen

2 *cups flour*
1½ *teaspoons baking powder*
½ *teaspoon salt*
½ *cup butter*
1 *cup sugar*

1 *teaspoon vanilla extract*
2 *eggs*
1 *cup sour cream*
⅓ *cup poppy seeds*
½ *cup sherry*

Oven temperature: 350°

Preheat oven. Sift the flour, baking powder and salt together in a bowl. Cream the butter and sugar well, then add the vanilla, eggs, sour cream, poppy seeds, and sherry. Blend all the ingredients thoroughly and bake on a greased cookie sheet for 8 to 10 minutes.

Whole-wheat pastry flour, brown sugar and cottage cheese or yogurt (instead of sour cream) may be used for a different kind of cookie.

WALNUT SHORTBREAD COOKIES

Yield: 3 dozen

1 *cup sweet butter* OR *margarine*
½ *cup sugar*
2 *teaspoons vanilla extract*
2 *cups sifted all-purpose flour*
½ *teaspoon salt*
1½ *cups finely chopped nuts (pecans, walnuts, filberts, etc.)*
confectioners' sugar

Oven temperature: 325°

Preheat oven. Cream the butter, sugar and vanilla until fluffy. Sift the flour with salt and add to the creamed mixture, blending well. Add nuts. Work in with hands, if necessary. Shape into 1-inch balls and place on an ungreased cookie sheet about 2 inches apart. Bake about 20 minutes. Cool, then roll in confectioners' sugar.

Pack in a hard plastic container for easy transport.

WASPS' NESTS

Yield: 3–4 dozen

1 *cup sugar*
½ *cup water*
1 *pound unblanched almonds, slivered*

6 *egg whites*
⅛ *teaspoon salt*
1 *teaspoon vanilla extract*
1 *pound confectioners' sugar*
4 *ounces unsweetened chocolate, melted*

Oven temperature: 350°

Preheat oven. Grease 2 large cookie sheets.

Cook granulated sugar and water until syrup spins a thread (234° on a candy thermometer). Add nuts slowly and continue stirring until all syrup is absorbed. Beat egg whites until frothy; add salt and vanilla, and continue beating until whites are very stiff. Gradually beat in confectioners' sugar. Fold in nut mixture and chocolate. Drop by teaspoonfuls onto well-greased cookie sheets. Bake 20 to 25 minutes.

This recipe makes a large batch of cookies, but they can be frozen. Pack the ones you are taking for a picnic in a hard-sided plastic container so they won't break en route.

Fruits

COUPE DE FRUITS

Serves 8–10

- ¼ cup honey
- 1 large crisp red apple, cored and diced
- ½ fresh pineapple, peeled and cut into bite-sized pieces
- 1 pear, cored and diced
- 2 bananas, sliced
- 2 oranges, peeled and cut into bite-sized pieces
- ½ cup pitted cherries
- ½ cup strawberries, washed, hulled and sliced
- ⅓ cup walnuts, chopped
    several sprigs fresh mint
- 1 orange, peeled and sliced

Wine Dressing

juice of 1 lemon

- ½ cup sugar

  OR

- ⅓ cup honey

- 1 cup red wine

Toss the fruits and nuts, saving the sliced orange and mint sprigs for garnish. Refrigerate for a few hours and put into a plastic container to carry. Combine lemon juice, sugar or honey and wine. Chill in a plastic container. When you are ready to lay out the picnic table, spoon the fruits into large plastic goblets and pour the chilled red wine dressing over each serving. Decorate with the sliced orange and mint sprigs.

Variations: For an unusual flavor especially good with spicy food, serve the salad with one of the following:

Cardamom Orange Dressing

juice of 2 oranges
  OR
- ¾ cup orange juice

3　*tablespoons brandy*
3　*tablespoons honey*
3　*crushed cardamom seeds*

Yogurt Honey Dressing

¾　*cup plain yogurt*
¼　*cup honey*

ORANGES NAPOLEON

Serves 8–10

6　*seedless ripe oranges*
½　*cup sugar*
1　*vanilla bean*
2　*ounces Grand Marnier*

Using a potato peeler, peel the oranges. Julienne the peels lengthwise as finely as you can; they should be no larger than toothpicks.

Cover the peels with water and bring to a boil in a saucepan.

Drain and re-cover with cold water. Add the sugar and the vanilla bean and simmer the slices until they become translucent and the liquid is syrupy.

Using a long, thin, sharp knife, skin the oranges, including the white part and the membrane of the orange itself. Very neatly and carefully slice the oranges crosswise ¼ inch thick. Quarter each slice so that you have bite-sized pieces. Remove the vanilla bean from the syrup and pour it with the julienne strips of orange peel over the orange pieces. Refrigerate. When serving, place in big clear-plastic cups, as this is a very refreshing dessert and lovely to look at. (It is served in restaurants in big glass goblets.) You can prepare it 24 hours in advance.

ORANGES AND RASPBERRY SAUCE

Serves 8–10

This combination is especially good with carrot cake or gingerbread. We have often served it in winter when we could chill it in the snow during the picnic.

6　*seedless oranges, peeled and sliced*
1　*10-ounce package frozen raspberries, thawed*

¼ *cup raspberry preserves*
¼ *cup kirsch* OR *Grand Marnier*

Arrange orange slices in serving bowl; cover and chill 3 hours or longer. Place raspberries, preserves and liqueur in electric blender and purée at high speed. Strain raspberry sauce into a bowl and chill before ready to use. Mix orange slices and raspberry sauce together and place in a plastic container with a leakproof lid.

PEACHES STUFFED WITH SWEET ALMOND CREAM CHEESE

Serves 6

3 *large peaches*
½ *pound cream cheese*
3 *good macaroons, crumbled in a blender*
1 *teaspoon ground almonds (grind in blender)*
   peach pulp from seed cavities
   fresh mint leaves

Choose large ripe peaches, and scrub the outside skin. Cut each peach in half, take out the seed, and enlarge the seed cavity with a spoon. Reserve the peach pulp taken out.

Mix the rest of the ingredients in a small bowl. Pack the peaches and filling separately. To serve, place a teaspoonful of filling on each peach center. Garnish and decorate the plate of filled peach halves with fresh mint leaves. These can usually be picked on the trail or at the picnic site.

PEARS STUFFED WITH GORGONZOLA

Serves 6

Whenever you can get beautiful large ripe pears, put together this delicious combination as the grand finale to a picnic. It is best made with a rich creamy green-veined Italian Gorgonzola. You can also use a good-quality Roquefort or blue cheese.

3 *pears, not soft, but just to the point of ripeness*
½ *pound Italian Gorgonzola cheese, at room temperature*

Halve the pears and take out the center with a melon-ball scooper or a teaspoon. With a small sharp knife, remove the vein and woody part that runs to the stem. Leave stem on. Fill the cavity with cheese, pressing it down with your fingers and packing it in a mound. Wrap each pear half in plastic wrap, and then pack in a hard-sided plastic container to protect the fruit from bruising during the trip. Arrange stems to the outside edge on a paper plate. Allow one half for each person, and expect a truly wonderful taste experience.

This dessert deserves a wine, and almost any wine would be complementary. A slightly sweet German white wine, or a light Sauterne, would be nice.

STUFFED FIG CONFECTIONS

Yield: one dozen

These are delectable!

1 *dozen large dried figs*

½ *ounce semisweet chocolate bits*
   OR
½ *a 1-ounce square semisweet chocolate*

½ *cup whole blanched almonds*

Oven temperature: 350°

First cut the stems off the figs with scissors.

Grate the chocolate or put it in a blender briefly. Toast the almonds in a medium oven until brown (about 10 minutes). Cool, then pulverize them in a blender, reserving 12 to top the figs. Mix the nuts and chocolate together with a small wooden spoon to form a thick paste.

Stuff the figs with this mixture by making a hollow with your index finger. Push the chocolate nut mixture in carefully so that the fruit is well-packed but maintains its original shape. Pinch the opening closed so that the stuffing will be a surprise. Bake for 10 minutes. Press an almond into the top of each fig.

These can be taken in a plastic bag or packed in a plastic container. They are best served at room temperature.

Tarts

INDIVIDUAL TARTS, FRESH FRUIT ON BAKED ALMOND CREAM

Yield: 10 3-inch tarts

The dough recipe we use here for sweet short dough, or pâte sablée, is good for any dessert tart. It will make enough for two 8- or 9-inch pastry shells.*

Make the dough first.

Pâte Sablée†

   ½ *pound (2 sticks) plus 2 tablespoons butter*
   3⅓ *cups all-purpose flour*
       pinch salt
   2 *tablespoons sugar*
   1 *whole egg,*
          beaten with 3 teaspoons cold water

Cut the butter into little pieces and put into a large bowl into which you have put the flour mixed with salt. Using a pastry blender or fork, mix to a mealy texture like oatmeal. Make a well in the center. Pour in the egg-water mixture, and mix with a fork until you can form a ball.

Flour your hands and remove a small handful at a time. Put it on a floured board, and push the dough down and away from you on the board until no lumps remain. (This process is really easy and takes almost no time.) Wrap the ball of dough in waxed paper and refrigerate at least a half an hour but remove it from the refrigerator at least one hour before rolling out in a floured board. Like *pâte brisée,* this dough will keep well for 3 or 4 days, and it can also be frozen.

Divide dough into 10 equal parts and chill about half an hour.

Almond Cream Filling Base

   4 *egg yolks*
   ⅔ *cup sugar*

---

* To prebake a tart shell, cook it at 375° for 10–12 minutes. Prick the bottom and sides of the dough with a fork before baking.
† For a variation, substitute 1 cup whole-wheat flour for 1 cup of white. This would be particularly good for an apple tart. You can also add ¼ cup finely chopped pecans to the pastry for an interesting taste.

    1 *stick sweet butter, softened*
    4 *ounces pulverized almonds**

        Oven temperature: 400°

With an electric beater, beat egg yolks in a medium-sized mixing bowl until the mixture is a pale yellow. Cream the butter with the sugar. Blend the egg yolks into the creamed butter and sugar mixture and mix in almonds.

On a floured board, roll out the pastry and line ten tart molds with it. Fill the tart shells with almond cream. Bake the tarts for 8–10 minutes until golden brown. Let cool 10 minutes.

Use fresh berries or any fresh fruit arranged on top of the almond cream tarts. Glaze over the fruit with apricot or red currant glaze made by putting heated apricot jam or red currant jelly through a sieve with a wooden spoon. Pour this glaze over the fresh fruit and chill it to set.

Small fresh strawberries arranged in circles on the tarts and glazed with red currant glaze makes very pretty and tasty tarts.

For backpacking we take the fresh berries or other fruit in a separate container with a bit of lemon juice and honey on them and the glaze in another container. The tarts are wrapped individually in plastic wrap and carried in a hard-sided container. When we arrive at the picnic site we assemble the tarts and set them on display during the meal.

---

* Put about ¾ cup whole almonds in a blender. Turn blender on briefly, only till the nuts turn to powder, but be careful, or they will become pasty.

FRESH FRUIT GÂTEAUX

We've never known quite what to call these delectable cake-pie concoctions, though in Austria they're called fruit kuchens. The pastry is cakelike, but when it's pressed into a pie tin with fruit cooked on top, it looks more like a tart. By any name, they are an ideal picnic dessert—very quick and easy to prepare. Here are two versions for you to try:

Apple Gâteaux

Batter:

    1¼ *cup all-purpose flour*
    1 *teaspoon baking soda*
    5 *tablespoons firmly packed brown sugar**
        pinch of salt
    1 *stick butter, softened*

---

* You can substitute honey for brown sugar by adding ¼ cup more flour.

1 *egg yolk*
1 *teaspoon vanilla*
1 *teaspoon canned almond paste (optional)*

Fruit:

2 *cups peeled and sliced tart apples*
    OR *any other fresh fruit like berries*
    OR *apricots*
1 *tablespoon lemon juice*
1 *teaspoon grated lemon rind*
1 *tablespoon dry vermouth*
2 *tablespoons firmly packed brown sugar* OR *honey*
2 *tablespoons butter*

Oven temperature: 375°

Preheat oven. Make the batter first. Put all the dry ingredients into a bowl and mix in the butter, egg, vanilla and almond paste, stirring and mixing quickly but thoroughly with a fork. Press the dough with your fingers into 2 small (3″ × 6″ × 2″) loaf pans, or 3 small (4″) or 1 regular (8″) tart pans. Press the dough up the sides of the pans.

In a small bowl, toss the fruit with the lemon juice, the rind and vermouth. Drain. Press the fruit into the dough decoratively, making a design from overlapping wedges. Sprinkle with the brown sugar or honey and dot with butter. Bake for 35–45 minutes, or until the crust is nicely puffed up and golden brown. Let the cakes cool in the pans in which they were baked, and wrap them, still in the pans, in foil to pack. In a separate container take a glaze of clear jelly or apricot jam which you have put through a strainer if you wish. Dribble it over the tart to serve.

Plum Gâteau, Baked Upside Down

This version is great fun to unmold at the picnic, since it's so very pretty to look at.

Batter:

1¼ *cups all-purpose flour*
 ⅓ *cup firmly packed brown sugar*
     OR *honey*
 1 *teaspoon baking powder*
     pinch salt
 3 *egg yolks, beaten*
 1 *tablespoon melted butter*
 ¼ *cup milk*

Fruit:

> 2 *cups ripe purple plums, washed and halved but not peeled,*
>   *OR fresh berries OR apple or peach slices*
> 1 *tablespoon lemon juice*
> 1 *teaspoon grated lemon rind (optional)*
> ¼ *cup clear crabapple jelly glaze*
> ¼ *cup firmly packed brown sugar OR honey*
> 3 *tablespoons butter, in small pieces*
> 3 *tablespoons sliced almonds*

Oven temperature: 400°

Preheat oven. Make the batter first by putting the flour, brown sugar or honey, baking powder and salt into a medium-sized mixing bowl, and adding the egg yolks, butter and milk. Mix thoroughly.

Toss the fruit in a bowl with the lemon juice and rind.

Make the crabapple jelly glaze. Warm the jelly first and thin it with a little fruit juice or water, and then press it through a sieve. (If you're using other than plums, you might want to make your glaze from currant or apricot jam.)

Pour the glaze into a buttered 3- or 4-cup round mold or an 8-inch round tart pan, spreading it with the back of a tablespoon. Dot with sugar and butter. Drain the fruit and arrange it decoratively on the glaze, cut side up so that the round part of the plum lies in the glaze. Pour the batter over all. Bake 35–45 minutes. Cover the batter with foil if it browns too quickly.

Let the tart cool in the pan in which it's baked; wrap in foil and again in a leakproof plastic bag tied tightly.

Unmold the tart onto a paper plate. Put the almonds in the center in a little mound.

If you make this tart with a sliced fruit, such as apples, pears, peaches or apricot halves, take care to arrange the fruit nicely, overlapping in circles. Peel all fruits except plums or apricots.

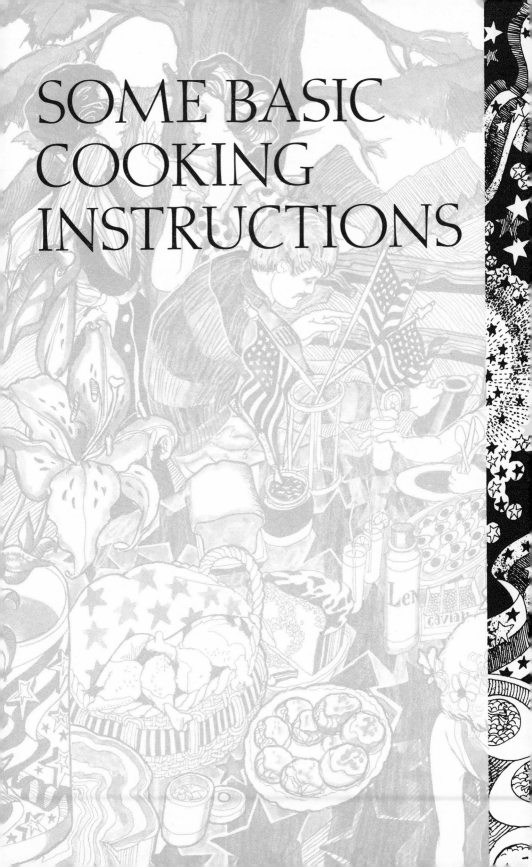

SOME BASIC
COOKING
INSTRUCTIONS

TO COOK CHICKEN

You can simmer a whole or part of a chicken according to the instructions on page 122. For a quicker method, when you need only 1 cup or less of cooked chicken, use the following method.

1 *whole chicken breast*
¼ *wedge fresh lemon*
  salt and pepper
1 *tablespoon butter*
1 *tablespoon dry white wine*
¼ *cup water*

Rub the chicken breast with lemon, salt and pepper. Melt the butter in the wine and water in a small heavy saucepan with a tight-fitting lid. Bring this liquid to a boil. Turn down heat and put the chicken breast in skin side up. Cover and barely simmer until just tender, about 15 minutes. Cool in the cooking liquid. When cool remove skin and bones. It's now ready to use.

TO HARD-BOIL EGGS

4 *eggs*
  water to cover

Put the eggs gently into a large saucepan and cover with water. Bring them to a boil and boil 12 to 14 minutes, depending on altitude. Add one minute for every additional two eggs. Take eggs out of the boiling water and immerse in cold water immediately. After a few minutes tap each shell to crack it and leave the eggs in the cold water until cooled completely. Then peel and use or refrigrate until needed.

TO BOIL POTATOES

Wash the amount of potatoes you need. Put them in a pot with enough salted boiling water to cover the potatoes by 1 inch. Boil them uncovered until a knife point pierces them easily, about 20 minutes. Remove the potatoes from the pot, drain them and let them cool until you can handle them easily to peel and cut them up into the desired cubes or slices.

TO COOK RICE

It is important to cook rice so that it is dry and fluffy for a rice salad. The grains must never stick together or your salad won't have the right texture. One cup of raw rice will yield 2½–3 cups of cooked.

To cook 1 cup of rice (brown or white), add it slowly to a large pot of about 6 cups of boiling water. Stir once and boil uncovered about 20 minutes. Test for doneness by biting a grain. It should be tender, but firm. Drain the cooked rice in a colander and rinse it with cold water, lifting it with a fork to fluff it up as you rinse.

TO BOIL SHRIMP

Cook one pound fresh shrimp in the shell in this court-bouillon:

> 2 *cups water*
> 1 *cup dry white wine (dry vermouth works well)*
> (OR *reverse proportions of water and wine*)
> 1 *small onion, peeled and chunked*
> 1 *small carrot, pared and chunked*
> 1 *small celery stalk with leaves, washed and chunked*
> 2 *parsley sprigs*
> 4 *peppercorns*
> ½ *bay leaf*
> *pinch of thyme*

For each additional pound of shrimp add 1½ cups of water to the court bouillon.

Put all the above ingredients in a kettle with a tight-fitting lid. Bring to a boil, turn down heat and simmer 15–30 minutes. Bring to a boil again and add the shrimp. Cover and boil 5 minutes only; turn off heat and let the shrimp cool in the liquid. When cool enough, peel them. They are now ready to use in many picnic recipes. Save the liquid to use for stock.

Index

About the Authors

JOAN HEMINGWAY studied cooking at Paris's Cordon Bleu. She is the co-author of *Rosebud,* a thriller novel that was made into a movie last year. Recently married, she has moved from the Hemingway family home in Sun Valley, Idaho, to New York City.

CONNIE MARICICH, a graduate of Berkeley, owns a boutique in Sun Valley, Idaho. An experienced cook and wild-foods enthusiast, she is the mother of two children.